DATE DUE

Roscoe Pound

THE LAWYER
FROM
ANTIQUITY TO MODERN TIMES

With particular reference to
The Development of Bar Associations
in the United States

by

ROSCOE POUND
Dean Emeritus of the Harvard Law School

*A study prepared for and published by the
Survey of the Legal Profession*

Under the Auspices of American Bar Association

St. Paul   1953   Minnesota

Pound Bar Assoc

This book was published for The Survey of the Legal Profession by West Publishing Co. whose generous assistance and sincere cooperation the Survey Council's Committee on Publications has authorized me gratefully to acknowledge.

REGINALD HEBER SMITH,
Director

*

SURVEY OF THE LEGAL PROFESSION
Under the Auspices of the American Bar Association

REGINALD HEBER SMITH, Director

OFFICERS

Chairman, ORIE L. PHILLIPS
Secretary, ALBERT J. HARNO
Treasurer, WALTER M. BASTIAN
Ex-Officio, ROBERT G. STOREY

COUNCIL

HOWARD L. BARKDULL
JAMES E. BRENNER
HERBERT W. CLARK
CHARLES P. CURTIS
JOHN W. DAVIS
JOHN S. DICKEY
CHARLES E. DUNBAR, JR.
ALBERT J. HARNO
PAUL G. HOFFMAN *

DEVEREUX C. JOSEPHS
WM. CLARKE MASON
PHILBRICK McCOY
HAROLD G. MOULTON
ORIE L. PHILLIPS
CARROL M. SHANKS
REGINALD HEBER SMITH
ROBERT G. STOREY
ARTHUR T. VANDERBILT

*A member of the council until his appointment as ECA Director

*

Survey of the Legal Profession
Its Scope, Methods and Objectives

The Survey of the Legal Profession is a broad study of the functioning of lawyers in a free society.

Under a government of laws the lives, the fortunes, and the freedom of the people are wholly dependent upon the enforcement of their constitutional rights by an independent judiciary and by an independent bar.

The legal profession is a public profession. Lawyers are public servants. They are the stewards of all the legal rights and obligations of all the citizens. It is incumbent on stewards, if they are to be faithful to their trust, to render an accounting from time to time.

This Survey is an honest effort to make a complete audit and report for submission to the American people.

1. History

When World War II was drawing to its close and the thoughts of men were turning again to the future, the American Bar Association's Section of Legal Education and Admissions to the Bar proposed a study of those subjects for the purpose of improving professional standards.

It soon became apparent that a worth-while study of the proper objectives of legal education involved the much wider problem of finding out what lawyers actually do in present-day society and whether they are adequately meeting the needs of the public.

This broader plan was approved by the House of Delegates in 1944. Under this authority, the project was carefully developed until it was in the blue-print stage.

By 1947 financial support for the undertaking had been secured. The Carnegie Corporation of New York made a grant of $100,000. The American Bar Association appropriated $50,000, payable over a five-year term, and authorized its President to select a group of lawyers and laymen who would constitute an independent Council having complete charge of the undertaking.

2. Independence

Early in 1947 President Carl B. Rix had recruited the original personnel of the Council, and the group at once went to work to organize the survey.

From the moment of its inception, the Council has been independent, autonomous, and self-perpetuating with its own constitution, its own officers, and its own treasury.

[VIII]

This cardinal fact cannot be emphasized too much or stated too often. It has been expressed most clearly by Judge William L. Ransom, Editor-in-Chief of the American Bar Association Journal in its issue of May, 1947 (33 ABAJ 423):

> "The Survey will be conducted as an independent project in the interests of the profession and the public by the Director and the staff which he selects, and will go forward with the advice of the Council.
>
> "The relationship of our Association is that it perceived the need for finding out the facts about our profession, arranged for the financing of the Survey jointly by the Carnegie Corporation and the Association, sponsored the selection of the Council from among lawyers and non-lawyers with outstanding qualifications, and committed the project to the independent judgment of this distinguished body and the Director chosen by it. With these steps of organization completed in April, the Survey and its results are completely in the hands of the Director and Council."

3. Objectivity

As to whether a profession can be surveyed impartially by one of its own members, there are two schools of thought.

On the one hand it is maintained that a lawyer (for example), however honest he may be, cannot study his fellow lawyers with objective impartiality because he has "blind spots" of which he is wholly unconscious.

He is so close to the trees that he cannot see the forest. On the other hand it is claimed that a learned profession, such as that of law, can be grasped only by devoting a lifetime to it, that the true nature of the client-lawyer relationship can be understood only by having lived in that confidential relationship.

Concerning research in the field of medicine, Professor Lawrence J. Henderson has commended the method of Hippocrates and said:

> "The first element of that method is hard, persistent, intelligent, responsible, unremitting labor in the sick room, not in the library: the all-around adaptation of the doctor to his task, an adaptation that is far from being merely intellectual. The second element of that method is accurate observation of things and events, selection, guided by judgment born of familiarity and experience, of the salient and the recurrent phenomena, and their classification and methodical exploitation. The third element of that method is the judicious construction of a theory —not a philosophical theory, nor a grand effort of the imagination, nor a quasi-religious dogma, but a modest pedestrian affair, or perhaps I had better say, a useful walking-stick to help on the way—and the use thereof."

It is demonstrably true that today the sharpest critics of the legal profession and the administration of justice are judges, lawyers, and teachers of law. It is historically true that the great legal reforms of the

[X]

twentieth century have been devised, fought for, and established by lawyers. Often they have been opposed by too many members of the profession; often they have won the day only by securing public support; but the fact remains that the constructive leadership came from within the legal profession itself.

In any event, and for better or worse, when the Council met to organize, all its members—laymen and lawyers alike—voted to elect as first Director of the Survey, The Honorable Arthur T. Vanderbilt of Newark, a highly successful general practitioner with wide experience in litigation who was also Dean of New York University School of Law.

4. Organization

As an independent entity the Council chose its own officers and elected the following: chairman, Judge Orie L. Phillips of Denver, Chief Judge of the United States Court of Appeals for the Tenth Circuit; secretary, Dean Albert J. Harno, of the University of Illinois College of Law; and treasurer, Judge Walter M. Bastian of Washington, D. C., Judge of the United States District Court for the District of Columbia.

In a sincere effort to secure objectivity, the Council created an Advisory Committee of Laymen which has met regularly, been given access to all material, been furnished with all reports, and which has the right at any time to speak its own mind. This Advisory Committee has itself supervised the preparation of the Survey report entitled "Complaints Against Lawyers."

To round out the account of personnel, it is necessary to report three events which took place later. In the fall of 1947 Dean Vanderbilt became Chief Justice of New Jersey and felt obliged to resign as Director. To succeed him the Council elected Reginald Heber Smith of Boston.

When it became apparent that all members of the Council could not be expected to read all Survey reports, that burdensome duty was entrusted to a Committee on Publications consisting of Wm. Clarke Mason of Philadelphia, former Chancellor of the Philadelphia Bar Association; Charles P. Curtis of Boston, author as well as practicing lawyer; and Devereux C. Josephs of New York, President of the New York Life Insurance Company.

In 1951 it was decided that it would be highly advantageous to have a layman make an appraisal and report on the work of the Survey. For that responsible task the Council selected George Waverley Briggs, Vice-President and Trust Officer of the First National Bank in Dallas, who had long shown a deep interest in the field of law reform.

Under Dean Vanderbilt's direction the basic organizational structure of the Survey was designed. The whole field was divided into six major divisions as follows:

I. Professional Services by Lawyers and the Availability of Lawyers' Services
II. Public Service by Lawyers
III. Judicial Service and Its Adequacy
IV. Professional Competence and Integrity
    A. Legal Education
    B. Admission to the Bar
    C. Professional Ethics, Discipline, Disbarment
V. Economics of the Legal Profession
VI. The Organized Bar

Under Mr. Smith's direction the first task was to assemble the large number of persons needed to do the spade work in so vast a field. Over four hundred men and women have been recruited for that purpose.

They constitute the "Survey team" and the credit for what has been accomplished belongs to them.

More than ninety per cent of them have been volunteers serving without compensation.

[XIII]

To keep the record straight, it may be appropriate to add here that the members of the Council, the officers, and the two Directors have all served without compensation. All men have stayed at their posts throughout the seven years which the Survey has required. When Chief Justice Vanderbilt resigned as Director, he remained on the Council. The one exception was the obviously necessary resignation of Mr. Paul G. Hoffman from the Council when he became Director of E.C.A.

5. Censorship

Just as objectivity was the Council's first great problem, so ultimate control of and responsibility for all the Survey work, reports, and findings became its second. This is the age-old problem of censorship.

Inasmuch as there were no strings on the grants of money by the Carnegie Corporation and the American Bar Association, they had no power of censorship. The issue, if it ever arose, would be between the Council and the Director.

At its organization meeting, Mr. Hoffman explained to the Council the principles involved and illustrated them out of his experience as chairman of the Committee on Economic Development. On the one hand no self-respecting person will give years of his

[XIV]

life to an undertaking if, at the end, his report is to be suppressed or thrown away. On the other hand, self-respecting persons cannot afford to serve on a Council if, at the end, they are to be held publicly responsible for proposals which they believe to be evil.

The only tolerable solution was written into the Survey's constitution and provides:

> "The Director of the Survey shall have academic freedom to determine the scope of the various divisions of the Survey, the selection of the staff to conduct the work of the Survey and the order of conducting the same. The Director shall make report to the Council from time to time of the conduct and progress of the Survey and, as and when the divisions of the Survey shall in the judgment of the Director be concluded to the point of forming a basis for publication, shall make report to the Council before actual publication thereof shall be made. Matters concerning publications may, by the Council, be referred to its Committee on Publications.

> "The Council shall consider with the Director all matters with respect to the Survey intended for publication and, in the event that there may be disagreement between the Director and a majority of the Council with regard to conclusions based upon recorded facts, the Council shall record its conclusions and they shall be published simultaneously with the report of the Director."

[XV]

This academic freedom accorded to the Director has in practice also been extended to the writers of Survey reports after their selection by the Director and approval by the Council.

6. Reports

A good many people have in their minds a stereotyped picture of how a survey is conducted. A group of workers busily amass a mountain of data. Then the man in charge writes it all out and the result is a tome of forbidding proportions. It may cause a momentary agitation of public opinion but it is likely to end up gathering dust on a library shelf.

In the hope of escaping such a fate, the Council decided upon the seriatim publication of reports as rapidly as they were ready and had the approval of the Committee on Publications.

The Survey's first report appeared as the leading article in the April 1949 issue of the American Bar Association Journal. It was "Law Practice in Russia: The Organized Bar in the U.S.S.R." by Professor John N. Hazard of Columbia University School of Law. Although it dealt with a territory where emotions are quickly aroused, this report set a standard for accuracy and impartiality. It quickly became recognized as the authoritative treatise on the subject.

By the steady publication of report after report the Survey became a dynamic undertaking, and it began to exercise more and more influence.

A good illustration of how this comes about is afforded by the Survey's report on "The Lawyer Reference Plan" by Charles O. Porter, now of Eugene, Oregon, which was published in booklet form in November, 1949.

The report was released at a press conference in New York. As it deals with the legal problems of middle-income or average Americans, it had a wide appeal. The daily newspapers carried the story and then it was picked up by periodicals with wide circulation such as Nation's Business, This Week Magazine, Atlantic Monthly, and Reader's Digest.

The president of the American Bar Association, Harold J. Gallagher, made a coast-to-coast radio broadcast on the subject. As he went about the country speaking to state and local bar associations, he emphasized the importance of the plan.

In 1949 there were fewer than 30 Lawyer Reference Services; now there are more than 80. The American Bar Association has created a Standing Committee on Lawyer Reference Service. This, together with

Legal Aid, constitutes one of the six primary objectives of the American Bar Association in its long-range program.

The Survey's overall plan called for somewhat more than 150 separate reports. By September 1949, 10 reports had been brought to completion; by September 1950, 66 had been completed; by September 1951, the number of completed reports had risen to 118; and by September 1952, the score was just over 150.

7. Publication

To avoid publishing costs that would have been far in excess of the Survey's financial resources, two procedures were adopted which have turned out to be successful.

As to longer reports which must be published in book or booklet form, the Survey has appealed to law book publishers for their cooperation. In practical terms this has meant that the publishers have produced the book at their own expense and then sold 1,000 copies to Survey at a price far below cost. The distribution of these copies will be explained a few paragraphs later.

The shorter reports constituted excellent articles for law reviews, bar journals, and other periodicals. The articles were published without cost to the Survey; but the Survey bought between 500 and 1,000 reprints at cost of each report-article.

It was plainly essential that every member of the Survey team should be kept informed as promptly as possible of what other members were accomplishing.

Thus the nucleus of the Survey mailing list was the Survey team itself and this constituted a remarkable cross-section of lawyers throughout the nation. To this were added the law schools, the larger libraries, bar association officials, and a list of persons who asked to be placed on the mailing list.

While no exact count has been kept, it is conservative to say that the copies of books distributed plus the copies of article reprints would number more than 100,000 items.

The Survey's supply is virtually exhausted; but as the demand for copies is now steadily increasing, it is hoped that some plan may be evolved whereby the scattered reports may be put together in two or three volumes.

The longer reports which are in book form can be purchased from the publishers.

8. Conclusions

The Survey is now completed for all practical purposes except for two final reports.

One is being written by the Director. It is entitled "The Legal Profession in the United States." It is addressed to the American people. It will contain the Survey's final conclusions and recommendations.

The other will be written by Mr. George Waverley Briggs. It will appraise the whole Survey undertaking from the point of view of an informed layman and will discuss the merits or demerits of the Survey's recommendations.

REGINALD HEBER SMITH

February, 1953

Introduction

Roscoe Pound, Dean Emeritus of Harvard University Law School, the author of this book is well known to every member of the profession. His contributions to the law and to the legal profession are multitudinous and his influence upon the law and the many lawyers who have sat in his classes, listened to his lectures or read his books will provide a lasting monument to his wisdom and devotion to the ideals of his profession.

It was truly a memorable day when the author turned his thoughts toward the law which he has served with such distinction, first, as a practicing lawyer at Lincoln, Nebraska, then as a Commissioner of the Supreme Court of Nebraska, as Dean of the University of Nebraska College of Law, as a member of the faculties at Northwestern University School of Law and the University of Chicago Law School and then as a member of the faculty of Harvard University Law School where he served as Dean of the Law School for 20 years. He is presently a Visiting Professor at the University of California School of Law, Los Angeles.

Honorary and scholastic degrees conferred upon the author have been numerous and much has been written about this impressive figure of the modern legal world. In 1940 the Gold Medal of the American Bar

Association for Conspicuous Service in the cause of American Jurisprudence was presented to the author.

In the preparation of this timely study for the Survey of the Legal Profession he has added to the long list of notable services to the profession. It is strongly urged that every member of the profession and student of the law read and familiarize himself with this history of the legal profession and bar organization in the United States.

Robert G. Storey

President, American Bar Association.

February, 1953.

Preface

There is more than one purpose of a preface. If I may explain one synonym by another, this preface has the purpose of a prologue to a history of bar organization in the United States.

When lawyers speak of law, the word law has two meanings. One is what is called in Continental Europe the legal order: The regime of adjusting relations and ordering conduct by the systematic application of the force of a politically organized society. The other is what is commonly meant by law in the law books, namely, the body of authoritative models or patterns of decision which, because they are applied by the courts in decision of controversies, serve as guides of conduct to the conscientious citizen, as threats to the wrongdoer, as grounds of determination to the magistrate, and as bases of prediction to the counsellor. Law in this sense is experience developed by reason and reason tested by experience. From antiquity it has been found that law in the first sense can only be maintained by law in the second sense and that law in the second sense requires lawyers. But although from Roman times the two propositions have been demonstrated over and again by experience, it has never been easy for the lay public to accept them completely. Certain general and certain other local causes of popular dissatisfaction with the administration of justice operate perennially and the dissatisfaction they bring about is transferred from law to lawyers.

There are four general causes of dissatisfaction with any system of law which have been manifest more or less in all times in all places. These are: Inevitable greater or less degree of mechanical operation of rules and so of laws; the inevitable difference in rate of progress between law and public opinion; a general popular assumption that the administration of justice is an easy task to which anyone is competent; and, not least, inborn human impatience of restraint. These operate differently in different times and places. At present, as in all periods of social and economic transition, the first and second are felt strongly. In pioneer frontier America the third and fourth had serious effects upon law and lawyers. In addition a number of causes must be recognized which are peculiar to our Anglo-American legal system, such as the individualist spirit of the common law which agrees ill with collectivist tendencies of today; the common law contentious procedure which tends to turn litigation into a game; political jealousy due to the strain put upon our legal system by our doctrine of the supremacy of law; and the indifference to legal philosophy and general ideas, characteristic of

American law resulting in petty tinkering with details where comprehensive reform is needed.

For a time also organization of courts to the needs of pioneer, rural, agricultural America, outgrown in the transition to urban industrial America, and legal procedure similarly inadapted to the times, had like effects. Thus at one time and another in our legal history the perennial popular dissatisfaction with the law in action has reacted upon lawyers and has left its mark upon the profession.

Throughout the history of civilization there have been abortive attempts to set up or to maintain a polity without law. Every Utopia that has been pictured has been designed to dispense with lawyers. This has been manifest particularly in the ideal schemes imagined after Revolutions. The organized legal profession was abolished following the French Revolution and again after the Russian Revolution. In each case the attempt proved vain. Marx believed that the real function of law was to hold one class in subjection to another and hence, as social classes disappeared with the abolition of private property, the law would "wither away". Nevertheless the Soviet law books today make up a library of no mean proportions and *collegia* of lawyers are an established institution.

[XXV]

Colonial America had visions of a New World society without law, as distinguished from laws, and without lawyers. New England sought an administration of justice by the clergy according to "the word of God". The Quakers sought to set up a regime of amicable adjustment of relations by friendly neighbors. Yet Boston and Philadelphia had by the time of the Revolution a notable body of educated, well trained lawyers practicing in the courts.

Law and hence lawyers are the enemies of autocracy. In consequence American states, as constitutional democracies, are characteristically legal polities in which the constitution is the "supreme law of the land". An American state constitution is not merely a frame of government. It is also a body of law to be interpreted and applied by the courts as the highest law of the land. Under our polity many political questions are as well legal and many legal questions are also political. Thus our constitutional polity is so legal as to be dependent upon lawyers for interpretation, application and maintenance against official absolutism and legislative encroachment.

More than any other people, the American people, more than any other society in history, American politically organized society, a democratic society constitutionally and federally organized, relies upon law and so upon lawyers. Yet after developing a strong profession by the time of the American Revolution and setting up a legal constitutional government in each state at the Revolution and a legal federal constitutional government at the outset of our formative era, the people at two points in our legal history all but destroyed the profession, while permitting the calling.

Instead of a profession, an organized body of men pursuing a learned art in the spirit of a public service, the era of emergent democracy, in its leveling zeal, and the succeeding era of hegemony of the frontier, in its faith in the ability of any man to do anything and its zeal for unrestrained individual freedom, sought to substitute for the profession pursuing a learned art, an uneducated, untrained trade pursuing a money-making calling in the spirit of a business.

Today the rise of other callings claiming to be professions, which should result in raising them to the level of a spirit of public service, not in lowering the level of the spirit of the recognized professions, the rise of the service state and tendency of the government to take over every form of public service and substitute bureaus for professions, seem to threaten another era of deprofessionalizing at a time when we had definitely reprofessionalized.

Organization of the profession as such was the way out at the end of the colonial era and at the end of the frontier era. I submit that completion and perfection of professional organization is what may save us from another era of decadence and resulting injury to law and to constitutional democracy.

Law School, University of California,
   Los Angeles, February, 1953.

Roscoe Pound

Table of Contents

TABLE OF CONTENTS

TABLE OF CONTENTS

Bibliography

Hill, Bar Associations, 5 Rep. Georgia Bar Assn., 51 (1888).

Warren, History of the American Bar (1911).

Wickersham, Bar Associations, Their History and Their Functions, 11 Misc. Bar Assn. Rep., Assn. of the Bar of the City of New York, 12 (1914).

Small, Check List of Proceedings of Bar and Allied Assns. (1923).

Reed, Training for the Public Profession of the Law, Bulletin No. 15, Carnegie Foundation for the Advancement of Teaching (1921).

Wickser, Bar Associations, 15 Cornell Law Quarterly, 390 (1930).

Pound, The Legal Profession in America, 19 Notre Dame Lawyer (1944).

Brand, Bar Organization and Judicial Administration, 34 Journal Am. Judicature Soc. 38 (1950).

†

I.

What Is a Bar Association?

*

I.

What Is a Bar Association?

1. Scope of This Book. This is defined by the Director in The Final Progress Report of the Survey of the Legal Profession and accompanying table.[1] As the voluntary, selective bar association, such as we have known it in this part of the world, is a characteristically American institution, except for indication of the historical origin and model, I shall not go into, much less discuss in detail, the organized bar and organization of the agents for litigation (attorneys, solicitors), in England, nor the organization of lawyers in Continental Europe. Organization of lawyers in other lands has been covered by a number of papers already published and listed in the Report above referred to. Also organizations and associations, other than bar associations, potentially organizing not the general body of practicing lawyers, national or local, but practitioners in special fields only, have been treated of in a number of published papers set forth in that Report. Moreover papers published or to be published treat fully the history and activities of the

---

1. Smith, The Survey of the Legal Profession: Final Progress Report, 37 ABA Journ. 645 (1951).

American Bar Association and of a number of state and local associations. All of these are referred to in the Report. One special type of organization, however, the bar library organization, which has often grown into a true bar association, will, on that ground, call for special consideration.

2. **What is a Profession—the Elements of a Profession.** We may start with the proposition that a bar association is an association of persons practicing the profession of law formed and maintained to promote the administration of justice according to law and to promote and uphold the purposes and spirit of that profession. This requires us to ask what we mean by a profession, what elements go to make up a profession, and what are the purposes and what is the spirit of a profession in distinction from other callings, and, in particular, from a trade. Unhappily the term "professional" has obtained a bad connotation in general understanding from the absorbing public interest in sport. There the distinction between the amateur and the professional has led to thinking of "professional" and "profession" as referring to a money-making calling. Undoubtedly the exigencies of the economic order require most persons to gain a livelihood and the gaining of a livelihood must be a purpose to which they are constrained to direct their activities. But while in all walks of life men

[4]

must bear this in mind, in business and trade it is the primary purpose. In a profession, on the other hand, it is an incidental purpose, pursuit of which is held down by traditions of a chief purpose to which the organized activities of those pursuing the calling are to be directed primarily, and by which the individual activities of the practitioner are to be restrained and guided.

By a profession, such as the ministry, medicine, law, teaching, we mean much more than a calling which has a certain traditional dignity and certain other callings which in recent times have achieved or claim a like dignity. There is much more in a profession than a traditionally dignified calling. The term refers to a group of men pursuing a learned art as a common calling in the spirit of a public service—no less a public service because it may incidentally be a means of livelihood. Pursuit of the learned art in the spirit of a public service is the primary purpose. Gaining a livelihood is incidental, whereas in a business or trade it is the entire purpose. Thus, if an engineer discovers a new process or invents a new mechanical device he may obtain a patent and retain for himself a profitable monopoly. If, on the other hand, a physician discovers a new specific for a disease or a surgeon invents a new surgical procedure they each publish their discovery or invention to the profession and thus to the world. If a lawyer has learned some-

[5]

thing useful to the profession and so to the administration of justice through research or experience he publishes it in a legal periodical or expounds it in a paper before a bar association or in a lecture to law students. It is not his property. He may publish it in a copyrighted book and so have rights to the literary form in which it is expounded. But the process or method or developed principle he has worked out belongs to the world.

Historically there are three ideas involved in a profession: organization, learning, i. e., pursuit of a learned art, and a spirit of public service. These are essential. A further idea, that of gaining a livelihood is involved in all callings. It is the main if not the only purpose in the purely money-making callings. In a profession it is incidental.

Today we have come to recognize, what had almost been forgotten in the middle of the last century, that organization is a necessary element. Indeed today almost every calling is organized in some sort of trade association. Also, it is true that except as twenty-five states have gone back to the common law idea of an organized body of lawyers, in almost half, including some of our most important states, there is no all-inclusive and responsible organization. The number of states which have incorporated their bars continually increases. But

[6]

in almost half of the states there is no bar in the sense of the bar of England or the Faculty of Advocates in Scotland, or the Colleges or Societies of Advocates in Continental Europe. It is less true than when I said it in 1928 but still too true that in many of our jurisdictions, except as local bar associations temper the situation, there are simply so many hundred or so many thousand lawyers, each more or less a law unto himself and too often accountable only to God and to his conscience, if he has one.[2]

It must not be supposed, however, that an organized profession of lawyers or of physicians is the same sort of thing as a retail grocers' association or that there is no essential difference between an organized bar and plumbers' or lumber dealers' associations. The conditions of an unorganized body of lawyers, with no differentiation between advocates and agents for litigation, which obtained in the United States in the last century, gave to bar associations in the decadence of professional organizations something of the look of trade associations or else of dinner clubs. But this condition, as it existed in the last third of the century, was the lingering effect of a general movement to deprofessionalize the

2. A Task for the University Law School, Address of Dean Roscoe Pound and Exercises at the Dedication of Richardson Hall, Brooklyn Law School (1928).

[7]

traditionally professional callings and put all callings in one category of money-making activities, which was characteristic of frontier modes of thought in the formative era of American institutions. Fortunately, after formal organization for the most part lapsed or disappeared, the legal profession had inherited a tradition of solidarity and traditional incidents of professional organization which survived and were of real value for our administration of justice. But the ideal of the profession involves an inclusive and responsible organization toward which we have been moving back steadily since the revival of bar associations in the last third of the nineteenth century and more rapidly since the first quarter of the present century.

Both in idea and as a matter of history a profession is a learned profession; a body of learned men pursuing a learned art. The frontier idea which was expressed in the Constitution of Indiana in 1851—"Every person of good moral character, being a voter, shall be entitled to admission to practice law in all courts of justice"—is characteristic of the era of deprofessionalizing the professions. The only requirements for practice of law were to be good moral character and being a voter. The practitioner need not be educated and need not be trained in the learned art he was to practice. As will be set forth later, in the later colonial period and the earlier

[8]

part of the formative era of American law between the Revolution and the Civil War, the bar rules governing admission had relatively high standards as to general education and study of law much like those to which we have come back in the present century. Experience has taught the practical importance of the professional idea of those who are to assist the courts and litigants in the courts, and persons hoping to keep out of controversies in the courts, in the administration of justice. Learning is one of the things which sets off a profession from a calling or vocation or occupation. Professions are learned not only from the nature of the art professed but historically have a cultural, an ideal, side which furthers the exercise of that art. Problems of human relations in society, problems of disease, problems of the upright life guided by religion are to be dealt with by the resources of cultivated intelligence by lawyer, physician, and clergyman. To carry on their tasks most effectively they must be more than resourceful craftsmen. They must be learned men.

In the third idea, however, we have the point of chief importance. It is of the essence of a profession that it is practiced in a spirit of public service. "A trade", says Professor Palmer, "aims primarily at personal gain; a profession at the exercise of powers beneficial to mankind." If, as in the era of wide free opportunity, we

[9]

think of free competitive self assertion as the highest good, lawyer and grocer and farmer may seem to be freely competing with their fellows in their calling in order each to acquire as much of the world's goods as he may within the limits allowed him by law. But the member of a profession does not regard himself as in competition with his professional brethren. He is not bartering his services as is the artisan nor exchanging the products of his skill and learning as the farmer sells wheat or corn. There should be no such thing as a lawyers' or physicians' strike. The best service of the professional man is often rendered for no equivalent or for a trifling equivalent and it is his pride to do what he does in a way worthy of his profession even if done with no expectation of reward. This spirit of public service in which the profession of law is and ought to be exercised is a prerequisite of sound administration of justice according to law. The other two elements of a profession, namely, organization and pursuit of a learned art have their justification in that they secure and maintain that spirit.

3. **What is a Bar Association?** In this connection we have to do immediately with the first of the three elements of a profession. The bar association as an organization of those practicing the profession is an essential element of professional life. It is only through or-

ganization that the spirit of public service can be developed and maintained and crucial types of public service can be rendered effectively. It is the bar association, not the individual lawyer that can maintain high educational standards insuring a learned profession, that can maintain high standards of character as a prerequisite of admission to practice, that can formulate and maintain high standards of ethical conduct in relations both with clients and with courts. The public has a deep interest in having a well organized bar part of the machinery of administering justice in a complex social and economic order.

Law as a profession goes back in the English-speaking world to the great formative era of our institutions in the later Middle Ages. Medieval society, like the society of Antiquity was close to a kin organized society and used the latter for a model. Accordingly medieval organizations tended to assume the form and to take on some of the attributes of a kin organization. Not long after the time the common-law courts at Westminster got the form which they kept with little change till the last quarter of the nineteenth century we find the lawyers who practiced in those courts living in houses (Inns) with a common table, with common educational exercises, with control over training for and admission to the bar, and control of discipline, subject only to the visitatorial jurisdiction of the judges of the superior courts. The serjeants, the upper rank of the advocates, addressed each other as "Brother" and, as down to well into the nineteenth century only serjeants were made judges, the judges so addressed each other and the serjeants who appeared before them. A tradition of the judges so addressing lawyers in the forum and of the lawyers so addressing each other still obtains in some parts of the country. American lawyers in the period before the Revolution studied in the Inns of Court in London, and they and the lawyers who studied under them were brought up in the idea of the bar as an organization of professional brethren, not soliciting employment nor in competition with each other, but on cordial terms with each other in the common exercise of a learned art.[3] Also these English trained leaders of the profession in the period before the Revolution brought back with them the English institution of the Circuit Mess and its Grand Court, which, as Lord Campbell tells us, exercised a "sound surveillance" over the professional conduct of its members.[4] Accordingly we see in the formative era of American law local bars framing rules as to the general education, training in law, character, and admission of law students, formulating standards of profes-

---

3. Dr. Johnson, when asked whether lawyers should solicit clients said: "I should not solicit employment as a lawyer—not because I should think it wrong, but because I should disdain it." 7 Campbell, Lives of the Lord Chancellors, 72.

4. 7 Campbell, Lives of the Lord Chancellors, 5 ed., 379 (1868).

[12]

sional conduct, holding "bar dinners", and exercising the "useful surveillance" of which Lord Campbell speaks.[5]

Institutions are shaped by their beginnings. The bar in England kept the aspect of a fraternity which grew out of the system of training which brought lawyers together in their Inn (medieval word for house) at the common table with the common life and closeness of association of a kin group. The colonial lawyers brought from their training in England the outstanding characteristic of the English bar, which has remained a marked characteristic of American lawyers, namely the fraternal spirit which after forensic contests lays aside all antagonism and enables them to strive mightily against each other as advocates without arousing jealousies or developing enmities.

Thus we made a good beginning of professional organization in America in meetings of the whole bar with rules of general application to all its members. But, with the rise of a feeling that professions were undemocratic and un-American, legislation took training and admission to practice out of the hands of the bar. Local bar meetings and local bar rules were succeeded by voluntary, selective associations of lawyers, which, however, keep up the traditions of the bar as they had come over from England. From the end of the second third of the nine-

5. Details will be set forth under VI and VII *post.*

teenth century these voluntary selective associations stood for organization of the legal profession. But they gradually decayed or became dormant almost everywhere [6] until a revival set in to some extent in the last third of the century, becoming stronger with the organization of the American Bar Association in 1878. It led to strong active bar associations in each state and in almost every locality,[7] culminating in the restored inclusive organization known as the integrated bar in the third decade of the present century, now prevailing in over half of the states.[8]

By a bar association, then, we mean an organization of lawyers to promote and maintain the practice of law as a profession, that is, as a learned art pursued in the spirit of a public service—in the spirit of a service of furthering the administration of justice through and according to law. This is brought out in the declared purposes of bar associations in their several constitutions, put in many varying ways, but almost universally coming substantially to the proposition just stated.[9] The purposes generally declared are: (1) To advance the science of jurisprudence, (2) to promote the administration of justice in the jurisdiction in which the association exists, (3) to uphold

6. See *post* VIII.
7. See *post* IX.
8. See *post* X.
9. These purposes, as set forth in the constitutions of bar associations existing in 1887 are considered in detail in Hill, Bar Associations, 5 Rep. Georgia Bar Assn., 51, 55–60.

[14]

the honor of the profession of the law, and (4) to establish cordial intercourse among the members of the bar of the jurisdiction. These are set forth in the Constitution of the American Bar Association (1878) adding to the second a further purpose "to promote uniformity of legislation throughout the Union." This formula has been followed by most of the state associations since 1878.

It is instructive to compare older formulas during the era of decadence and in the earlier years of the era of revival before 1878.

Some typical examples are: *The Fraternity of the Suffolk Bar* (Boston, 1836) organized on the dissolution of the old Suffolk Bar because of legislation taking admission out of control of the Bar Rules.[10] "The object of this fraternity is to cultivate a spirit of friendship, kindness and good will toward each other, to preserve the purity of the legal profession, to discountenance all abuse of legal process and all such practices as might bring odium or disgrace upon the administration of the law." [11]

Essex Bar Association (Massachusetts, 1850) organized at a meeting of the bar upon lapse of an association formed in 1831, which had revived one formed in

10.   Mass.Rev.Stat. 1836, Chap. 88, §§ 19–60.

11.   MS in the possession of Frank W. Grinnell, Esq., of the Boston Bar.

1806—an inclusive bar—which had lapsed. The preamble of the constitution adopted in 1856 reads: "To promote fraternal feeling and ensure conformity to a high standard of professional duty, to establish a uniform method of practice, and to discountenance and prevent the abuse of legal process either by members of the bar or by unsuitable and unqualified persons." [12]

Association of the Bar (Massachusetts, 1849). Report of a Committee appointed at a large meeting of the Bar from all parts of the State holden at Boston, January 4, 1849.[13] The preamble reads:

"The undersigned members of the Bar in the Commonwealth of Massachusetts, actuated by a sense of the dignity and honor that should pertain to a profession established for the administration of justice—upon whose fidelity to its high obligations the security, welfare, and moral elevation of society must in great measure depend; and believing that an organized system of communion of its members throughout the state, will be productive of equal gratification and advantage and promot-

12. Rules and Regulations of the Bar of the County of Essex Agreed Upon at the March Term, 1806, Salem, 1806, in the Essex County Law Library; MS. A Record of the Proceedings of the Essex Bar Preliminary to the Organization of the Essex Bar Association, 1856, in the Essex County Law Library. I have used a photostat copy.
13. Printed pamphlet in the Massachusetts State Library. I have used a photostat copy.

ing more frequent and extensive social and friendly intercourse, and in the increase of mutual respect and confidence, and may be alike beneficial to the public and themselves, as conducive to the maintenance of high standards of professional duty and character, and as distinguishing those who recognize and desire to sustain the true position of members of the Bar, and exonerating them from all communion in reputation with those who disgrace it—hereby declare and assent to the following Articles of Association." Article One sets forth as a purpose "elevation of the standard of professional duty, education, and character".

Cumberland Bar Association (Maine, 1864) organized upon lapse, about 1835 with no record of dissolution, of an organized bar which published printed rules in 1829 and was apparently in existence in 1790.[14] The preamble reads: "Whereas it has been an ancient custom for members of the legal profession, in view of their obligations to the community whose peace they are bound to

14. W. W. Clayton, History of Cumberland County, Maine, (Philadelphia, Everts and Peck, 1880) Chap. 16; Rules and Regulations of the Bar in the County of Cumberland. Drafted March 13, 1829, Portland, Fraser Bros., 1829; Rules and Regulations of the Cumberland Bar Association, Portland, 1864. (Pamphlet in the Maine State Library). I have used photostat copies of the last two.

preserve, and to their clients whose rights and whose interests are entrusted not only to their learning and ability but to their prudence and discretion, and also to themselves as members of a long honored profession, to unite as a fraternity under such rules and regulations as shall tend to promote their own honor and usefulness and the best interests of their fellow citizens."

Pittsburgh Law Association (1870) which in 1880 became the Allegheny County Bar Association. The object is said to be " . . . the elevation of the character, superintendence of the general interests, and cultivation of fraternal feeling among the members of the profession of law in said county." [15]

Bar Association of the State of New Hampshire (1873) inactive 1875–1878; in 1899 two local associations formed the present association under the charter of 1873. The object is said to be "maintaining the honor and dignity of the profession of the law and cultivating social relations among its members, and increasing its usefulness in promoting the administration of justice." [16]

Iowa State Bar Association (1874). The object is said to be: "To promote mutual acquaintance and har-

15. An Act to Incorporate the Pittsburgh Law Association and Giving Certain Privileges to the Same, approved February 28, 1870.

16. Proceedings of the Bar Association of the State of New Hampshire, Old Series, vol. 1.

mony among members of the Iowa Bar; to maintain a high standard of integrity, honor, and court courtesy among them; to encourage a thorough and liberal legal education; to give expression to the deliberate and well considered opinion of the legal profession upon all matters in which its members are expected to speak as a body; and to assist in the improvement of the laws and the better administration of justice to all classes of society without distinction." [17]

New York State Bar Association (1876). The stated object is: "To cultivate the science of jurisprudence, to promote reform in the law, to facilitate the administration of justice, to elevate the spirit of integrity, honor, and courtesy in the legal profession, and to cherish the spirit of brotherhood among the members thereof." [18]

Queen's County Bar Association (New York, 1878): "To maintain the honor and dignity of the profession of the law, to increase its usefulness by promoting the due administration of justice, and to cultivate social intercourse among its members." [19]

17. Original communicated in letter of Wiley C. Mayne, Esq., of Sioux City.

18. Constitution as printed in 1 Reports of New York State Bar Association (1876).

19. As communicated by the President, S. S. Tripp, Esq., Jamaica, N. Y.

Thus the tradition of a profession, pursued in a spirit of public service by a body of learned men, not as competitors but as professional brethren, brought to America by the lawyers in the Colonial Era who studied in the Inns of Court, and transmitted from preceptor to student under the apprentice system of legal education, came down from eighteenth century English lawyers to the colonial lawyers who read law under them, from the students who read under the colonial leaders to the pupils of the latter, from the inclusive bar meetings of the forepart of our formative era to the exclusive, selective association of the revival after 1870. Consciousness of the meaning of a profession, feelings of the need of organization in a professional association as an element of the calling, and continuity of purpose to maintain the profession according to its high traditions stand out in the statements of the objects of association from the inclusive local bars of the beginnings to the American Bar Association which has set the pattern since 1878. Hence we might well start with the colonial bars of the eighteenth century. But there was a long history of development of a profession behind them.

II.
Origins: The Lawyer in Antiquity

.

II.

Origins: The Lawyer in Antiquity

1. Types of Professional Activity. "Historical continuity," says Mr. Justice Holmes, "is not a duty, it is a necessity." We are not bound as a duty to keep institutions to their historical form. But they are given shape by their history. It is not the least factor in making trained lawyers effective in the mechanism of administering justice that the lawyer is brought up in consciousness of a profession with a long and honorable history, high ideals, and great tradition; that he reads in his students' texts the memorable words of D'Aguesseau: "An order as old as the magistracy, as noble as virtue, as necessary as justice." [1]

There are three branches of professional activity. The lawyer may be agent for litigation or may be advocate, or may be counselor or adviser to which is often added the function of law-teaching and law-writing.

Probably the oldest is the adviser's function, the function of advising as to how to conduct legal trans-

---

1. As to D'Aguesseau, see Charles Butler, Memoir of H. F. D'Aguesseau (1830).

actions and how to bring and defend legal proceedings. Out of this there develops the function of law-teaching and the jurisconsult's or law writer's function. Hardly less old is the function of the agent for litigation. A later development is the advocate's function. In addition certain specialized functions develop, such as those of special pleaders formerly in England, of conveyancers in England, and of title searchers in America, which have or have had importance at one time or another. Such functions are sometimes highly specialized and performed by differentiated practitioners, or may be combined in various ways, or may be undifferentiated in a common body of lawyers, as in the United States. The aggregate of those who perform these functions or some of them under license from some public authority may be called the profession of law.

It will be worthwhile to remind ourselves why it is that law, lawyers, and a profession of lawyers have come to be developed in all civilized societies and have maintained themselves so persistently that in Soviet Russia it has been found necessary more and more to restore them as an institution.[2] The task of law is to adjust relations and order conduct so as to give the most effect to the whole scheme of expectations of man in civilized society

2. See 1 Gsovski, Soviet Civil Law, 854–855 (1948), and my review, 50 Mich.Law Rev. 55, 109–111 (1951).

with a minimum of friction and waste. Unless this task is performed, a politically organized society tends to be disrupted or to be dissolved. Controversies must be decided and the general security requires that they be decided according to law, that is, by applying an authoritative technique to authoritative norms or patterns of decision provided for like cases. This can be done well only by judges experienced in the technique and trained in the norms of decision after argument by lawyers who know the technique and have had experience in applying it. Nor are the questions of fact upon which tribunals must pass as a rule so simple or so easy to solve that the untrained man may pass upon them with assurance without assistance of argument by trained advocates. Usually what seems a plain proposition of fact and, when determined, is put as a simple result, follows from a complicated series of disputed facts, frequently disputed in good faith at almost every step in the series. The average controversy is likely to have two sides, each believed in, in good faith by honest men. In order to decide such controversies satisfactorily the case of each party must be presented thoroughly and skilfully, so that things are put in their proper setting and the tribunal may review the whole case intelligently and come to a conclusion with assurance that nothing has been overlooked, nothing misapprehended, and nothing wrongly valued. The litigant cannot do this adequately for himself. It can only be done by well trained specialists.

[25]

Furthermore proper presentation of a case by a skilled advocate saves the time of the courts and so public time and expense. It helps the court by sifting out the relevant facts in advance, putting them in logical order, working out their possible legal consequences, and narrowing the questions which the court must decide to the really crucial points. Good advocacy reduces the work which falls upon judges to decision upon the vital points in carefully selected, appraised, and presented materials. Experience has shown abundantly the waste involved in inexpert presentation of cases by laymen or by inexperienced or inept practitioners.

Along with training and experience, in order to be a help to the courts and an aid to the administration of justice, advocacy demands the professional spirit. In order to further justice, in order to insure that the machinery of justice is not perverted, those who operate the machinery must not merely know how to operate it, they must have a deep sense of things that are done and things that are not done. They need the guiding restraint of the professional spirit to prevent misuse of the machinery, to prevent waste of public time in useless wrangling, to promote proper forensic treatment of witnesses so that witnesses will not be unwilling to come forward to testify. They need it to inspire confidence on the part of courts in being able to rely upon what counsel represent to them

[26]

instead of having to waste time in looking up everything because unable to assume the face of things as presented by the advocates.

No less important in the busy and complicated world of today is the function of the agent for litigation (attorney, solicitor, proctor). Simply from an economic standpoint there is a very great saving of public time and public money in having cases prepared thoroughly and intelligently in advance of trial. The trial brief, prepared carefully beforehand for the advocate, insures that the crucial points will be distinguished from irrelevant details, that time will not be wasted during the trial on matters which a careful preliminary investigation would have settled, and that the energies of judge and advocate will be directed to the real issues in the controversy.

As to the function of advising upon the law, the sound lawyer is a needed guide for those engaged in enterprises and entering upon undertakings, and those settling trusts or making wills or administering estates or trusts, as well as those seeking reparation of injuries or relief from wrongs in a complex economic order calling for increasing legislation and administrative regulation. The adviser has a function of prevention of or forestalling controversy, preventing needless resort to the courts, and keeping enterprises and undertakings to the straight paths

[27]

prescribed by law. Every man his own lawyer is even more wasteful than every man his own advocate.

2. Lawyers in Ancient Greece.[3] In classical Greek thinking law in the lawyer's sense is not clearly differentiated from other agencies of social control. Even today, after law as the legal order, the regime of adjusting relations and ordering conduct by systematic application of the force of a politically organized society, and law, as the body of authoritative models or patterns of decision and authoritative techniques of applying them, by which that regime is maintained, has become the paramount agency of social control, it by no means does the whole. The internal discipline of the household, the internal discipline of religious organizations, of fraternal organizations, of trade, professional and business organizations, and of social clubs, as well as neighborhood, community, and general public opinion, still play a large part in constraining men to avoid anti-social activities and leading or pushing them into the paths indicated for the maintenance and furtherance of civilization. In classical Greece these things are not well differentiated from law. The Greek word which we translate as "law" is used to mean ethical custom, religious rites, law in general, a rule of law, and social control as a whole.

---

3. Bonner, Law and Lawyers in Ancient Athens, The Genesis of the Legal Profession, Chap. 10 (1927). As to Greek law see 2 Vinogradoff, Historical Jurisprudence, Jurisprudence of the Greek City (1922).

Although the Greek city was a politically organized society, it was very close to and in some respects in transition from a kin-organized society. Much of its ethical custom and codified customary law spoke from an older tribal society. It was tending to but had not attained a stage of legal development which may be called the stage of strict law. In that stage social control through norms authoritatively established by politically organized society has been set off definitely from religion and ethical custom and is governed by ideas of certainty and uniformity in that ordering and of rule and form as the means thereto. Classical Greek law had not reached this stage. In consequence classical Greece did not develop lawyers, for law and lawyers grow up together. Yet here, as in nearly every connection in the social sciences, the germs of our institutions are to be found in Greece.

In a kin-organized society and in a religious-organized society, the received forms of transactions, the received modes of appealing to the king or magistrate for redress, and the received norms of decision are a tradition of a priestly caste or, later, of an oligarchy by which alone they are known and handed down. Hence when one wished to know how to carry on a transaction so as to give it legal efficacy or how to bring a legal proceeding, or how to carry on a litigation, or how to predict a decision, or, if called on to decide a controversy, how to decide, he

[29]

consulted one of those who knew the received tradition. At Rome these repositories of the received tradition grew into jurisconsults. In Greece also we see the germ of the jurisconsult's function in what were called interpreters.

According to the Greek dictionary-writers of antiquity, these interpreters were resorted to for authoritative pronouncements on the traditional law. But of the three categories of interpreters they described, only one had to do with authoritative materials of judicial decision. Where causes were decided by large bodies of citizens analogous to popular assemblies, no interpreter could expect to predict what the course of decision would prove to be and the advice of the interpreter was not so much counsel as to the law as a general explanation of the probably expedient course of action. At Athens in cases of homicide, arson, and some like crimes, jurisdiction was in the Council of the Areopagus, made up of the acting and former magistrates, and that tribunal was governed by traditional custom. In this limited field there was scope for the jurisconsult's function. Beyond this the interpreter ceased to be of importance.

Another type which must be noted is the scribe. But the scribes can hardly be thought of as lawyers although some part of the lawyer's functions have been differentiated from their manifold tasks. The scribe is an oriental institution while the lawyer comes rather from the west.

[30]

On the other hand we may trace a continuous development of the advocate of today from those who represented or assisted others in litigation in Greek tribunals. In the beginnings of law the kin group rather than the individual is the legal unit. Hence in politically organized societies still close to an older kin organization dependents are represented before tribunals by the head of the kin group. If one is not a dependent, he must represent himself. There is no advocacy. The kin group speaks through its head on behalf of dependents because their cause is its cause. The kinless man, the emancipated man, the man who is not a dependent, speaks for himself.

Yet there were exceptions to and relaxations of this rule. A city could only speak through a representative. Also in public prosecutions and impeachments a representative of the public was called for in the nature of the case. Likewise an accused might call in someone (probably originally a kinsman or the head of the kin group) to stand beside him and assist him, and to a less extent this sort of assistance was allowed to an accuser. The beginnings of law do not distinguish crime and tort. The remedy is in the nature of composition for an injury or a penalty of reparation and the normal proceeding to enforce a penalty is private. Also in certain rare cases the tribunal might authorize a parent, a friend, or a member of the same tribe to complete or supplement the explanation of his case made by the party in person. One who thus represented a city or the public or assisted accused or accuser or supplemented another's exposition of his case was called a *synegoros*. He was in some degree an advocate. The same name, *synegoros,* was given to one who was chosen to speak on behalf of the state with respect to proposed legislation.

A more significant person, however, is the speech-writer (*logographos*). In order to understand his function we must remember that in the Athenian polity there was little of what we now call separation of powers. Political and judicial functions were little differentiated. The citizen was both legislator and judge. The people judging and the people deliberating and legislating were not well distinguished. The ordinary tribunal was a large body of citizens under oath to decide a particular cause and addressed not as jurors (dikasts) but as citizens. Those dikasteries, as they were called, might contain as few as two hundred and one or four hundred and one, or as many as fifteen hundred and one citizens. It was a difficult task for the ordinary man, even at Athens where citizens were accustomed to public speaking in the political assemblies, to present one's own case before so large a tribunal. The timid, the inexperienced, the ignorant were at a great disadvantage before such a court as compared with trial before a single judge who by questioning can patiently and skilfully bring out what is to be said on both sides. In the Greek trial each party made a speech in the course of which he adduced evidence, brought forward witnesses, and cross examined his adversary in connection with his several points as he went along with his narrative. The speech was undifferentiated, or little differentiated, narrative, proofs, and argument. In a case of any complexity, it called for a degree of skill beyond the everyday citizen. Hence the average litigant employed a speech-writer or logograph who, for a fee, drew up a speech and turned it over to his client. The client learned it by heart and delivered it before the tribunal.

Manifestly the speech-writer was not an advocate. Yet the Roman orator, from whom the advocate of to-day is derived, historically, took the Greek orator for his model. Indeed the successful speech-writer had to be something very like a lawyer. He had to be well versed in Athenian law and procedure. He might have to argue that the popular tribunal should steadfastly apply the law. In the next case he might have to urge the tribunal to rise above the rule of law and decide on sympathy or emotion or lay ideas of justice. In either event he had to know the law which was to be applied or to be dispensed with. Also he had to know the psychology of Athenian juries and be sensitive to their passions and prejudices. Above all he had to know how to adapt the speech which he wrote to the age, the condition, and the character of his clients and make it seem to flow naturally from the mouth of the speaker. All this is closely akin to the task of the advocate.

There was no clear differentiation of the function of the agent for litigation from that of the advocate. The word syndic (which came to mean agent) and *synegoros* (which denoted something very like an advocate) were often used as synonyms. Etymologically "syndic" means one who intervenes in a legal proceeding. A city-state, a foundation, an association, and the like, could not appear in court in person. They could only be represented by agents. It is significant that the name given to such an agent was the same as was given to the representative of a city-state before the Amphictyonic Council,[4] but also the same as that often given to *synegoroi,* and to the assistant to the demarch or presiding official of an Attic deme or township in a prosecution or when the deme was proceeded against before the popular tribunals.

In ancient Greece we have the beginnings of lawyers rather than lawyers as we know them in developed legal systems.

4. The name commonly given to the council of the Delphic Amphictyony, originally a league of 12 neighboring tribes centering in a shrine, which became a religious and political association of city states. It sought to enforce certain rules as to the relations of states. Its judgments, or more properly resolutions, had only moral authority. See Freeman, History of Federal Government in Greece and Italy (1895).

3. **Law and Lawyers at Rome.**[5] (a) *The development of representation at Rome.* In the Roman law
of the later republic and especially in the classical Roman
law of the early empire, we find law in the sense of the
legal order—of a regime of social control adjusting relations and ordering conduct by the systematic and orderly
application of the force of a politically organized society
—well set off from other agencies of social control, and
law in the sense of an authoritative body of materials for
the guidance of judicial action well differentiated from
ethical custom, religion, and public opinion. Also there is
a well developed legal procedure, with a system of actions
leading to defined remedies and grounded in defined legal
duties, established by definite legal precepts, by which the
judges considered themselves bound. In other words we
find law in the lawyer's sense.

Actions and defenses in the later republic and earlier
empire were governed by the edict of the praetor or judicial magistrate. On taking office the praetor announced
in his edict the relief he would be prepared to grant and
the defenses he would allow on application of anyone as-
serting that the state of facts contemplated had arisen.
As each new praetor took office he issued his own edict.
But the greater part of it was transmitted from his
predecessors, only a few paragraphs, diminishing in num-

5. Schulz, Roman Legal Science, 15–22, 111–122, 266–277 (1946).

ber as time went on, being his own contribution. Under the emperor Hadrian (A.D. 117–138) the edict was revised and given legislative authority.

An intending litigant had to go before the judicial magistrate and point out the particular provision of the edict upon which he relied as the basis of his action. Also a defendant who desired to assert a defense other than that the plaintiff's case was not made out must point out to the judicial magistrate the particular clause of the edict on which he relied. One not thoroughly versed in the law would need advice or, better, would need someone to make the application to the judicial magistrate on his behalf.

But there was another difficulty which called no less or even more for representation of litigants before the magistrate in the preliminaries of legal proceedings. As the Roman state outgrew the confines of the city of Rome, the persons on whose behalf applications were to be made to the praetor at Rome and those who had to ask that the formula (a written appointment of and instructions to a trier, setting forth the plaintiff's claim which he must prove and any affirmative defense which his adversary must prove, and the judgment to be rendered according to what was proved) include a statement of their defense, might live at a distance and so it might be very inconvenient for them to be at Rome to make personal applications and requests. Also as the law of the city of Rome came to be the law of the world, litigation according to the Roman law was carried on in the provinces. In the provinces the governor had the jurisdiction and authority of the Roman praetor. But the provinces were often of wide extent and there was the same difficulty and inconvenience in personal attendance and personal application. This need for representation in legal procedure led to a practice of appointing agents or attorneys.

There were two modes of appointing a representative for litigation, the formal and the informal. The agent appointed by the older or formal mode was called a *cognitor*. He had to be appointed by the party using a set form of words in the presence of his adversary. The person named as *cognitor* might be either present or absent, but if absent it was required that he consent and undertake the attorneyship.

An agent for litigation appointed by the later and informal mode was called a *procurator*. He might be appointed by any words amounting to instructions to sue or defend, as the case might be, and without the presence or even the knowledge of the adverse party. Indeed it was enough that the *procurator* undertook the agency in good faith and undertook that his principal would ratify what he did. He could begin an action without producing his instructions, and it became a usual practice not to produce the instructions until the trial before the *judex* (trier appointed by the praetor). Thus far the procedure was much as by an attorney at common law, or by a solicitor in the Court of Chancery, or by a proctor in the ecclesiastical courts.

Roman Law, however, did not have modern ideas of agency. What the agent did was not thought of as done by his principal. As the law saw it, what the agent did he did himself. But he was bound contractually that the benefit of what he did should inure to his principal, and the principal was bound contractually to indemnify the agent for loss and expense incurred in his carrying out the agency in good faith. Applying these notions to procedure and bearing in mind the idea of the beginnings of law that parties other than dependents must carry on their legal proceedings in person, it is evident that the plaintiff's *cognitor* or *procurator* must be taken to be carrying on his own case and the defendant's cognitor or procurator likewise be carrying on his own case. Hence, to put it as the Romans did, if Lucius Titius (the Roman John Stiles) is *cognitor* or *procurator* for Aulus Agerius (i. e., Peter Plaintiff) who is suing Numerius Negidius (i. e., Dan Defendant), the formula delivered to the *judex* would read: "If it is proved that Numerius Negidius ought to pay to Aulus Agerius ten thousand sesterces, O *iudex* condemn Numerius Negidius to pay to Lucius Titius

[38]

ten thousand sesterces." In like manner if Negidius was defending by a *cognitor,* say Publius Maevius, the formula would say that if it was proved that Negidius owed Agerius ten thousand sesterces, the *judex* was to condemn Maevius to pay Titius that amount. Thus the judgment might be in favor of one attorney and against another, in the case of one principal against the other. But there was a contractual duty on the one side to account for the benefit of the judgment and on the other to indemnify against it. Accordingly an action might be brought by the attorney or by the party, as the case might require, to charge the real defendant with the judgment or to give the real plaintiff the benefit of it. Later the simpler device obtained of a transfer of the judgment to and against the real parties by operation of law. When this step had been taken, the agents for litigation had become truly attorneys.

In the maturity of the Roman law the formal mode of appointment of *cognitores* had become obsolete. Also much of the old law as to the objections which a defendant might interpose as to the competency of a *procurator* had been done away with. The praetor's edict had forbidden persons under the age of seventeen, the deaf, the blind, women, and persons of bad character making applications in litigation on behalf of others. Soldiers also were not competent to act, even on behalf of a parent or wife, and could only represent themselves so far as they could do so without breach of discipline. Thus it is evident that while there was no profession of attorneys or agents for litigation, and except for the cases prohibited by the edict, anyone might be appointed for the case in hand, yet certain persons had begun to act regularly in this way.

We know from Latin writers of the Empire that there were habitual practitioners in the courts who were of a very low type, despite the provisions as to character in the praetor's edict. Perhaps one need not say that to allow the defendant to challenge the character of the plaintiff's lawyer, by way of a dilatory plea, and thus put off a trial of the merits, was to provide a cure worse than the disease. It gave no effective check upon the low and unscrupulous type of practitioner that is apt to develop from the need of representation in litigation and the opportunities which that need offers for preying on the ignorant and extorting from the timid. So long as a body of agents for litigation is unorganized, subjected to little or no scrutiny before entering upon that calling, and without the check of discipline by responsible authority, serious abuses have always followed.

Much remained to be done before the Roman *procurator* became the attorney or solicitor of today. Yet when we compare the *procurator* with the beginnings of agency in litigation in Greece, we must recognize that great progress has been made. The old idea that the litigant must conduct his case in person had disappeared as to the technical legal proceedings leading to the trial. A class of, on the whole, skilled and experienced agents for litigation had developed, and the crude idea of the agent as assuming the litigation had been superseded by a recognition of the agent for what he was, a representative, and of the principals as the real litigants. There had even been some development of judicial checks upon the personnel of the calling. The praetors had at least tried to confine the calling to men of good character in a position to give their time to cases without interfering with their other tasks. Thus when we leave the Roman law in its final form for the ancient world, we are well upon the road to one important branch, to one of the important functions, of the legal profession of today.

(b) *The development of advocacy at Rome.* In order to understand the role of the advocate at Rome, we must look more closely at Roman legal procedure.[6]

First of criminal procedure.[7] In some cases, after preliminary inquiry and condemnation before a magis-

---

6. The best exposition of Roman legal procedure in English is Wenger, Institutes of the Roman Law of Civil Procedure, translated by Fisk (1940).

7. As to Roman criminal procedure: Greenidge, The Legal Procedure of Cicero's Time (1901); Strachan-Davidson, Problems of the Roman Criminal Law (1912).

trate, there was appeal to and trial before an assembly of the people. This trial before the people necessarily came to an end when a world state succeeded to a city state under the empire. In other cases the prosecution was tried before what we may well call a jury of from thirty-two to seventy-five *judices*. This trial before a jury decayed under the empire and an inquisitional procedure before magistrates developed in its place. In others a penalty was sued for before one or more, sometimes a considerable number, of *judices*. Thus Roman criminal procedure afforded much the same scope for an orator as trials before the popular tribunals at Athens.

As to civil procedure, it was divided into two stages—a stage *in jure* before the magistrate, and a stage *in judicio* before the trier or triers. In the stage before the praetor or judicial magistrate the purpose was to frame the issues to be tried and appoint a *judex* or a number of *judices* to try them. There might be a hearing at this point as to whether the action desired should be allowed to the plaintiff. If it was allowed, the praetor settled the formula or set of instructions to the *judex,* containing what in our law we should call the pleadings of the parties and directions as to what judgment to render in case certain issues were found or not found.

When the formula was complete the parties joined in what is called the procedural contract. That is, they undertook to abide the result of the submission to the *judex* and the judgment was binding on them by virtue of that contract. Under the later empire the *judex* was no longer a private person chosen as arbitrator. He was an official. The plaintiff submitted a written statement of his case and the defendant in like manner a written statement of his defense. There was no formal procedural contract. Also the court could refer some particular point to the oath of a party, leaving other issues to be tried, so that a cause might not be tried as a whole but only on issues remaining unsettled.

At the trial there might be speeches with introduction of evidence in the course of the speech, as in the Greek practice, or speeches followed by evidence, or a speech for the plaintiff, a speech for the defendant, then evidence on each side, then speeches by way of summing up; or there might be evidence followed by speeches on each side. There was no limit to the number of orators who might speak, but, though six are known to have spoken on each side in one case, usually there were not more than four on a side. Also one might speak on his own behalf and have his argument reinforced by the speeches of from one to four orators. When more than one they were supposed to divide the points. But Cicero tells us that they frequently forgot this and made separate set speeches without having heard the argument they were to answer.

[43]

Thus they tired the court by going over the ground already covered by those who had preceded them.

Originally the proceeding *in judicio* took place in the forum, an open space used at first as the market place but later used chiefly for judicial proceedings, so that we have spoken of a court and of a place where orators are heard as a forum ever since. Still later basilicas were built around the forum and were used for the trial of civil cases while state trials continued to be held in the forum. Literally the word basilica means a royal hall, i. e., a hall in which the king sits to do justice. As the matters coming before tribunals became more complicated and as permanent judges began to sit in them, the old open air trial became obsolete and the trials were held in a basilica.

Roman practice permitted a litigant to be represented at the trial by an advocate. But he was not called advocate originally. Cicero tells us that an advocate was one who assisted with advice on points of law or by his presence as a person of influence gave weight to one side of a case. One who engaged in public speaking, either in the popular assemblies or in the courts, was called an orator. He was, like Cicero, both statesman and advocate. When he appeared in court to argue he was called a *patronus causarum* or simply *patronus,* and the person he represented was called a client. These terms take us back to the origin of Roman advocacy in the relation of

[44]

the head of a patrician household to his dependents in the polity of the old city. In that polity those who were not members of patrician households attached themselves to some household as dependents, and slaves who had been set free were still in a relation to the master who had freed them and was said to be their patron. These dependents were called clients. They were entitled to be protected by the patron. In particular the patron was bound to appear in court for his clients, originally as representing the kin group of which they were taken to be members and explain the law to them, since knowledge of the old customary law of the city was a monopoly of the heads of patrician households. Thus this duty of the patron toward his client was the basis both of the advocate's function and of the jurisconsult's function as they developed at Rome.

In the beginning the patron, as to his dependents, was both jurisconsult and advocate—both legal adviser and trial lawyer. Indeed in the classical period, although a differentiation had gone on, the same person might be both. Also with increasing complexity of social and economic development it became increasingly necessary to resort to jurisconsults and to be represented by an advocate. Thus a patron who had numerous clients in the older sense, when he had formed a habit of answering questions and arguing cases, might find that others, not technically his clients, were resorting to him to obtain the

[45]

benefit of his knowledge, experience and skill. As he undertook to advise and represent them, they became his clients to that extent and the term client came to have the new meaning which it has today.

Public speaking was the high road to a political career. The great men of the city sat in the courtyards of their houses to give advice and the ambitious young men prepared themselves for a forensic career by attending and taking notes of the advice given and by listening to the forensic exertions of noted orators. When the Roman youth laid aside the dress of a boy and put on that of a man he went to the forum with a company of friends and was introduced by some distinguished citizen as a practitioner in the courts. By Cicero's time the function of jurisconsult and that of advocate had begun to be differentiated. It was well differentiated in the classical period of Roman law from Augustus (emperor B.C. 27 to A.D. 14) to Alexander Severus (A.D. 222–235).

In Cicero's time there were abuses of advocacy such as might be expected from the composition of the trial courts in republican Rome. One of the advantages of a permanent judiciary trained in law is that it is not, or at most little, and rarely to be swayed from decision upon the law and the evidence by appeals to prejudice and emotion. In a common-law trial the tendency to be moved by such appeals is mitigated by the charge of the trial judge.

[46]

In a Roman proceeding *in judicio* there was nothing but the formula to hold in a *judex* who was moved to run away with the law. Accordingly we see in some of Cicero's speeches for the defense quite irrelevant rhetorical devices for working upon the feelings of the tribunal, and he tells of more than one case where such advocacy prevailed at the expense of the law. Indeed the advocate's dramatic efforts were often supplemented by those of the parties and their friends. An accused came before the tribunal dressed carefully for his part, sometimes accompanied by a swarm of friends dressed in mourning in token of their sympathy. But these sorrowing friends might be brought in also to intimidate the tribunal. Hence it was found necessary to forbid any appearing in that role beyond relatives within a near degree.

Another abuse was extreme license of oral examination. There was no law of evidence in our sense of that term, as, indeed, there is not today in the Roman-law world. Anyone who had anything to say about the case could say his say for what it was worth. There were rules as to the capacity of witnesses and as to quantum of proof, and witnesses who had taken part in certain formal transactions (e. g., a formal conveyance of property) were bound to appear and testify. Also the orators regularly argued that the uncorroborated evidence of one witness ought not to suffice for conviction in a criminal

[47]

case and vouched the character, social position or wealth of witnesses in support of their credibility. But there were no rules of admission or exclusion and the orator could examine any number of prominent persons on their hearsay opinions favorable to his client and set forth to the *judices* the high standing of these personages giving weight to this substitute for evidence. In criminal cases it was a matter of course to bring these *laudatores* or witnesses to character, and Cicero tells that to have fewer than ten of them was thought hardly respectable. One need not say that for political reasons this sort of evidence was given lightly and perfunctorily, and yet might draw jury tribunals away from the real case. It was prohibited in B.C. 52 by legislation but the older practice was restored a few years later.

Cross examination was highly developed. The Roman advocates knew and the Roman books on advocacy taught the principles and cautions which are common place to the writers on advocacy of today.

High-water mark of Roman advocacy was attained in the last period of the republic and the beginning of the empire. The great advocates of the generation before Cicero (B.C. 106–43) and his older contemporaries are known to us from Cicero's dialogue *de oratore*.[8] That

---

8. Cicero's *Brutus*, a history of Roman eloquence, and his *Orator* a description of the perfect orator, complete the account in his *de oratore*.

dialogue, Cicero's orations, many of them delivered before the tribunals, and Quintilian's treatise, *de institutione oratoria,* are our chief authorities.[9] The treatise of Quintilian (c. 35–95 A.D.) has been classical ever since and is still worth reading by those who make a serious study of the subject.

Later under the empire, although the development of the law went forward, advocacy began to degenerate. In part the system of permanent judges and obsolescence of the popular tribunals made for greater importance of the jurisconsult and less of the advocate. In part the development of law from the time of Cicero to the third century made for certainty and uniformity in the administration of justice in which the role of sheer advocacy in bringing about forensic results was continually less. The historian Tacitus (c. 55–120 A.D.) tells us of the beginnings of this decadence. In place of the rigorous training and apprenticeship of the advocates of the late republic, he says that those who intended to become advocates formed no habits of study, took no pains to prepare themselves, and pretended to despise knowledge of law as something unnecessary for their calling. He says that they cultivated dec-

---

The orator of whom Cicero writes is chiefly a forensic orator, i. e., advocate.

9. On Roman advocates see Forsyth, Hortensius, an Historical Essay on the Office and Duty of an Advocate, 2 ed. 1875, Chaps. 4, 5.

lamation and ornaments of style and so delivered speeches after school models, filled with rhetorical commonplaces.

But this was not the worst. Pliny the Younger (61 or 62–c. 113 A.D.) tells us that a bad practice had grown up of hiring a *claque* to applaud forensic speeches. This advocate's *claque* may have been a development of the crowd of supporters, the mourning friends and character witnesses of an earlier time. At any rate according to Ammianus Marcellinus, a Roman historian of the fourth century A.D., the advocates both at Rome and in the provinces had fallen very low. No doubt his extravagant picture of them is in part a caricature. Yet there is sometimes more truth in a caricature than in a photograph.

In the fifth and sixth centuries great improvements took place which gave advocacy something very like its modern organization. Indeed the modern continental organization is simply a development of the Roman in this its final form. The advocates ceased to be merely orators. They were no longer trained merely in rhetoric. They had studied in one or another of the law schools which had grown up in the chief cities of the empire and attained the leading position once held by the jurisconsults. A certain number of advocates was fixed for each of the courts in the leading cities. Those attached to a court formed a sort of corporation. The law recognized fees and fixed the

[50]

scale. Professional discipline was provided for. Thus the main lines which exist today had become established.

In the fifth century and first quarter of the sixth legislation went forward steadily toward a well organized bar for each of the great courts. A statute of 468 prohibited the practice of advocacy by those not admitted to practice. One of 440 limited the praetorian advocates to 150, and in 450 it was enacted that the number should not be raised beyond 150 by recognizing assistants. A statute of 469 provided that there should be 50 at Alexandria. In 474, 64 were recognized to practice before the praetorian prefect at Constantinople and 15 were said to hold first rank after the advocates of the fisc, i. e., legal representatives of the government. In 486, 150 were provided for in the prefecture of Illyria and in 508, 30 in Syria. In the meantime a statute of 452 had provided for two advocates of the fisc who were to be lawyers of the highest reputation. This office seems to go back to the reign of Hadrian (A.D. 117–138). In the sixth century the number of advocates before the praetorian prefect at Constantinople was reduced to 80. But a certain number of supernumeraries was allowed.

Remuneration of advocates has a significant history. In the beginning the patron advised his client and supported his client's case or defended him because these were duties the patron owed to one dependent upon him. In consequence when regular advocacy arose the assistance rendered to suitors in the forum was gratuitous. Of necessity, however, as there came to be a profession of advocates, requiring time and study and preparation if one were to undertake another's case, and as the client was no longer a dependent of a patron but one who sought to employ the skill and training and experience of an orator who stood in no relation to him, a practice sprang up of paying a gratuity to the advocate. It was natural also that those who had trained themselves for forensic exertion should, in a changed social order, employ their skill and training and experience as a means of making money. But the old idea was so strong that this was felt to be an abuse and a statute known as the *lex Cincia* (204 B.C.) forbade anyone from accepting money or gift on account of pleading a case.

It must be remembered that under the republic the calling of orator opened the way to the highest political preferment. Those who followed it were in the public eye, and in any time and place where office is held by tenure of popular election, publicity is the politician's chief asset. Moreover at this time the orators were usually members of wealthy families. They were men of rank and distinction with a strong sense of duty and trained in the older ideas which made advocacy a duty to be performed without reward. They could well afford to despise remun-

eration for a service done from quite different motives
than expectation of gain. Later the ideas and motives
which made advocacy a gratuitously performed duty
ceased to exist. Political office no longer depended on
popular election. Advocates were no longer as a matter
of course heads of wealthy houses, scornful of gain. Men
came to practice advocacy as a money-making calling—
certainly as a means of livelihood. Yet the *lex Cincia*
stood as law. Indeed Augustus reinforced it by procuring
a resolution of the Senate prohibiting advocates from taking fees under penalty of a fourfold forfeiture.

One need not say that such legislation could not be
enforced. Tacitus tells us of a debate in the Senate in
the reign of Claudius (A.D. 41–54) in which strong arguments were made for remuneration of advocates. The old
patrician houses had passed or were passing. Those who
were to come forward to do the work of the state would
have largely to do so by way of the forum. Hence a strong
legal profession was required for other reasons than as an
aid to the due administration of justice. But to insure
such a profession there must be a possibility of pursuing
it in a society of individual competitive acquisition. Claudius was moved by such considerations and fixed the
maximum fee at ten thousand sesterces, or one hundred
aurei (about $475), and made advocates liable to prosecu-
tion if they accepted more. The statue of St. Yves, the

patron saint of the lawyers, a great advocate of thirteenth century France, shows him carrying in his left hand a bag marked 10,000, that is, the ten thousand sesterces fixed by the Roman law as the maximum which he could take as a gift-fee. Thus the medieval artist sought to bring home to the observer that our patron saint was so great an advocate that everyone always gave him the maximum fee by way of gift, and yet so honest and law abiding that his bag would hold no more.

In the decadence of advocacy many abuses grew up as to fees, such as accepting a gift by way of fee in advance and then refusing to go on with the case, taking gifts by way of fee from both sides, and taking bribes not to exert the advocate's best efforts. In consequence in the reign of Trajan (A.D. 98–117) a resolution of the Senate required an oath by both parties before trial that they had not given or promised any sum of money to their advocates. Thus the fee, not exceeding the legal amount, was to be paid after trial. This regulation also proved ineffective. In Justinian's codification in the sixth century we find legislation from the third century on, which shows that fees were habitually paid in advance and deals with the abuse of receiving them and not conducting the case.

This history of the remuneration of advocates at Rome has had a profound effect on remuneration of advocates in the modern world. In the Middle Ages, when modern institutions were formative, the Roman law was

supposed by the learned to be a universal law binding
upon all Christendom. Later in the seventeenth and
eighteenth centuries it was held to be embodied reason.
Moreover, Quintilian's treatise, discussing the whole subject of remuneration of advocates very sensibly, yet on
the whole took the traditional position that advocacy was
a service gratuitously rendered for its own sake, for which
the advocate might honorably accept a fair honorarium,
voluntarily bestowed on him as a gift, but for which no
bargain as to compensation and nothing in the way of hire
was permissible. The influence of the great treatise of
antiquity was decisive, if anything more than the rule of
the Roman law had been needed.

(c) *The development of legal advisers at Rome—the
jurisconsults.*[10] There were three purposes for which a
lawyer might be needed at Rome. First, one might need
an agent or representative in the proceedings *in jure;*
second, he might need a trial lawyer in the proceedings *in
judicio*; third he might need an adviser as to wills and conveyances, and formal transactions, and as to his legal
rights and duties. For the first he appointed a *procurator.*
For the second he retained an orator or advocate. For the
third, he consulted a jurisconsult. The Roman jur.iscon-
sults played a leading part in the development not only
of Roman law but of all law. Their great work was done

10. Buckland, Text-Book of Roman Law, 2 ed., Chap. I, §§ IX–XIII (1932).
    As to the beginnings, see Schulz, Roman Legal Science, 6–14 (1946).

as law writers and law teachers. The writings of the jurisconsults of the classical era from Augustus to the end of the first quarter of the third century, as put in statutory form in the Digest of the emperor Justinian (533), have been a quarry for jurists and law givers ever since.

After the Twelve Tables (450 B.C.) the form of the Roman law was threefold: (1) The written law, The Twelve Tables; (2) an undefined mass of uncodified tradition; and (3) a growing mass of "interpretation". Also there came to be a certain amount of legislation upon legal matters and of interpretation of that legislation. Along with the still uncodified tradition the interpretation was handed down traditionally in the pontifical college and connects with the earlier time when social control was quite undifferentiated and law was merged in religion. Interpretation, i. e., the traditional development and application of the texts of the written law, handed down traditionally in the pontifical college, became the foundation of the legal science of a later period.[11] Except for occasional legislation it was the way in which the law

11. There were four of these groups of priests of which the college of *pontifices* was the most important. *Collegium* is a Roman-law term, meaning an association with legal personality. The best account of them is in 1 Mommsen, The History of Rome, bk. 1, Chap. 12, English trans. Everyman's Library, 1911. The *pontifices* were not "holy men" but men of high social standing whose economic position enabled them to undertake public duties without remuneration.

grew, although largely unconsciously, since men were slow to admit that they could change the ancient customs deliberately and avowedly. But in the course of the third century B.C. a secular science of law gradually developed beside the pontifical tradition. The great man, who knew the law, sat in the court of his house and advised his dependents, drew legal documents for them, and if need be conducted their causes for them. In time those who knew the law gave advice to all comers. Also they gave opinions on the law to *judices,* who were not learned in the law and might require advice in applying the formula. These opinions, called *responsa,* became increasingly important in making and shaping the law, so that Cicero enumerates *jurisperitorum auctoritas,* the authority of those learned in the law, among the forms of Roman law in his time. This development of jurist-made law culminates in giving the *responsa* formal legal standing. Augustus began the practice of licensing jurisconsults who might then give opinions with the authority of the emperor in his capacity of supreme judicial magistrate. Later Hadrian made the opinions of the jurisconsults binding upon the judge, but the details are in dispute.

Throughout the classical era juristic writing was the chief form of the law. In the republican period it appears as commentaries on the *jus civile,* the law of the city or strict law, i. e., the Twelve Tables and the traditional law of the city as traditionally interpreted. Later came commentaries on the edict and presently collections of *responsa*. Still later came commentaries on the writings of the great jurists of the past and treatises on particular subjects or particular branches of the law. In addition there were institutional treatises for students and practical handbooks. The whole is a body of legal writing quite without parallel until recent times, and standing in relation to the law as the literature of Greece has stood in relation to letters.

Along with writing, teaching became a major function of the jurisconsult. Indeed after the third century, when legislation superseded juristic writing as the growing-point of the law, the law teacher took the place of the practitioner-writer. From that time in the civil law the jurisconsult is a law teacher.

Looking back over the development of law and the administration of justice at Rome and in the Roman world, it will be seen that the three main functions of the lawyer, the agent's function, the advocate's function, and the jurisconsult's function were well developed. Here as elsewhere in the legal order, the Romans laid well the foundations on which the Middle Ages and the modern world have built.

III.

The Organization of Lawyers in the Ecclesiastical Courts
and in
Tribunals of the Civil Law

.

III.

The Organization of Lawyers in the Ecclesiastical Courts and in Tribunals of the Civil Law

1. Representation in Litigation in the Earlier Middle Ages.[1] We have seen that in Roman law the three functions of agency or representation in litigation, advocacy, and advice—the functions of procurator or attorney, advocate, and jurisconsult—had become differentiated and had each attained a high degree of development. Also we have seen how by the time of Justinian the jurisconsult had become a law teacher, so that for the future in Continental Europe the advocate's function and the jurisconsult's function of advising were merged and the term jurisconsult was applied only to teachers and writers.

Germanic law brought back into Western Europe the ideas of primitive law as to representation in litigation. Parties were required to appear in person and conduct their cases in person except in case of dependents. It is laid down in the Frankish law that "No one in France

---

1. Brissaud, History of French Private Law (transl. by Howell) 544.

may appear by attorney except the king." [2]   But the ecclesiastical courts, following the Roman practice, allowed representation in litigation. In the earlier Middle Ages the courts of the church are more significant in Western Europe than the civil courts, and we must look to the former for the earlier history of the modern profession.

2. The Ecclesiastical Tribunals. In the Middle Ages a law of the church had been developing for a long time. As far back as the third century there had been a rapid growth of internal control in Christian religious societies. A system of what was to become law gave large powers of judging and of discipline to the overseer (bishop) of each congregation.

Christianity became a lawful religion in 313, and soon after the only lawful religion. In 385 the Bishop of Rome issued a decretal, the forerunner of an era of papal legislation. The church had a disciplinary jurisdiction over the clergy. It soon acquired a large jurisdiction over lay Christians, since in the anarchy of the breakdown of the empire men turned to the bishop to arbitrate temporal controversies. About 500 a collection was made of canons or regulations of the councils of the church and of decretals of the popes from 384 to 498. This is regarded as the foundation of the Corpus of the Canon Law, which

2. Brissaud, History of French Public Law (transl. by Garner) 464.

stood alongside Justinian's codification of Roman law, the Corpus of the Civil Law, as an authoritative law book for Christendom down to the Reformation. In the ninth century a collection including what purported to be decretals of the earliest of the popes was universally accepted also. Thus the popes appeared to have been declaring the law or legislating for the universal church from the beginning. In the twelfth century these collections of decretals were included in the Decretum of Gratian, which is the first part of the *Corpus Juris Canonici.*

In the West the Roman Empire fell in 476. Roman law in Western Europe was decaying from the fifth century to the revived study of law in the Italian Universities in the twelfth century. Germanic law, brought in by the invaders who overthrew the Empire, had no means of growth because it was not a taught law and had no *corpus juris* and no organs of legislation. In the earlier Middle Ages only the law of the church was growing. Each bishop had his court. Each ecclesiastical province had its court of appeal before the archbishop or metropolitan. Also appeals lay to Rome, as in Roman practice they had lain to the emperor, and the pope became supreme legislator and judge in ecclesiastical causes as the emperor had been in temporal causes. Matrimonial causes, testamentary causes, matters of good faith, defamation, where money reparation was not sought but rather correction of the defamer for his soul's good, and cases of correction, as distinguished from criminal prosecution, came to be in the jurisdiction of the ecclesiastical courts. After the twelfth century the study of Roman law in the universities and spread of the law, as taught in the universities, to the lay courts on the Continent, gradually gave the preponderance to the Civil law, or law of the state. But we have a survival from this time in the academic degress in legal education today. Bachelor, Master, and Doctor of Laws (notice not of law) and the continental degree of Doctor of Either Law (J.U.D.), in each of these cases referring in terms to two systems, bear witness to the two coordinate systems of law which obtained in the Middle Ages.

In the *Corpus Juris Canonici* there are two titles *de procuratoribus* (on proctors), one in the Decretals of Gregory IX (published about 1230), the other in the Sext, i. e., the Sixth Book of Decretals (published by Boniface VIII after 1298). In the first there is one regulation of Gregory the Great (596). There are two from the latter half of the twelfth century. The rest belong to the fore part of the thirteenth century. In the title in the Sext they date from 1299.[3]

In the Eastern Empire in the fifth century it was considered that practice of law by clergymen in the courts

3. Decretals of Gregory IX, book I, tit. 38; Sext, book I, tit. 19.

was an abuse, since it distracted from the due discharge of their sacred functions by the ministers of the church. So Justinian, in the end, strictly forbade any one in holy orders from pleading in the courts, no matter what was the nature of the case. It was prohibited even where he was personally interested and although his church or monastery might be a party.[4] In the West this legislation did not obtain. The medieval clergy had a monopoly of learning and there was a saying, often quoted from William of Malmesbury, an English historian of the twelfth century, *nullus clericus nisi causidicus*.[5] It was long afterwards that the Church forbade practice of law by the clergy in the lay courts.

Litigants in the ecclesiastical courts could appear either in person or by a proctor, unless the court considered the assistance of a proctor or of an advocate necessary under the circumstances of the case. As in Roman law, a party could choose his own proctor. But that proctor could not substitute another in his place unless the power had been given him expressly. Also the same person was allowed to act both as proctor and as advocate, even in the same case and for the same client. That is, a qualified advocate might act also as a proctor. But the

4. Nov. 123, cap. 6.
5. 1 Pollock and Maitland, History of English Law, 85.

requirements for an advocate were much higher than those
for a proctor and a proctor could not act as an advocate.
To be a proctor one had to be of age and of good character. If he was a monk he had to have a license from
his superior. He had to file in the court a special mandate (i. e., power of attorney). If the client could not
write it must be signed for him by his parish priest or
by a notary or by two witnesses. As a consequence in
civil-law countries today, it is highly important to have
express powers of attorney, since the authority of an attorney is not presumed as is the case in the common law.
Proctors were forbidden to "buy the litigation". They
were to be agents, not parties to the cause. Without a
special mandate, they could not dismiss an action, com-
promise, or settle it, or do anything beyond due prosecution of the claim or making of the defense before the
tribunals. They could take appeals without special authority unless forbidden by the client. The client could
terminate their authority by notice. But if this was done
after *litis contestatio* (originally the procedural contract—
the termination of the stage corresponding to the proceedings *in jure* in Roman law) there must also be notice to
the judge and to the adverse party. There were provisions for discipline and for exclusion from practice of
proctors who took or contracted for a share in the sub-

ject of litigation or excessive fees, or betrayed their duty to their clients.[6]

In the ecclesiastical courts in England the proctor had to be appointed by the party himself either before the judge or by a formal act in court or else by a proxy or power of attorney under seal. The proxy had to be exhibited in court and entered in the registry. Special proxies for representation of a client on one day or for one occasion were forbidden as they had led to delays and abuses. It was required that they be for a number of days to be continued if need be. Also proctors were forbidden to entertain a case for two court days without the advice of an advocate. In the later practice of these courts, proctors were commissioned by the Archbishop of Canterbury after completion of an apprenticeship.[7] The profession came to be divided into two branches, advocates and proctors, in the ecclesiastical courts in England with as sharp a line as that between the corresponding branches of the common-law courts.[8]

Advocates were required to be doctors of law or otherwise qualified in the canon law. They were admitted by the bishop, either to practice generally or for a particu-

6. See *ante*, note 3. In their modern form the regulations of the canon law as to proctors and advocates may be found in Codex Iuris Canonici, canons 1655–1666.
7. 3 Burn, Ecclesiastical Law (9 ed.) 375 ff.
8. 2 Holdsworth, History of English Law, 311–312.

lar case. They were required to have a mandate either from the party they were to represent or from the judge, similar to the mandate required for a proctor. They were not permitted to purchase the litigation nor to contract for a share in the subject of the suit, nor to take fees from the other side, nor to take excessive fees. For doing such things they were subject to fine and to suspension or expulsion. The advocate, as at Rome, had no legal claim to a fee. He received a gift-fee.[9]

Originally the advocate was required to have studied five years. In the English ecclesiastical courts this was modified by requiring three years of study of the civil and the canon law, and it came to be the practice in all countries to admit as advocate anyone who had taken the degree of Doctor of Laws.[10] In the English ecclesiastical courts a libel (that is, the first pleading in a case in the ecclesiastical or in the admiralty jurisdiction) was required to be subscribed by an advocate, who thus added the responsibility of a learned lawyer to the mere agency of the proctor. Also a proctor was required to obtain the advice of an advocate before any but the preliminary investigation of the case.[11]

9. 1 Burn, Ecclesiastical Law (9 ed.) 2–5.
10. Ibid. This is still true in the courts of the Catholic Church today. Codex Iuris Canonici, canon 1657, § 2.
11. 1 Burn, Ecclesiastical Law (9 ed.) 3–4, 3 id. 378.

In 1511 the head of the Court of Arches (the court of the Archbishop of Canterbury) formed the "Association of Doctors of Law and of Advocates of the Church of Christ at Canterbury" to do for the lawyers in the ecclesiastical courts and admiralty courts what the Inns of Court did for the common-law lawyer. In 1565 this association took a long lease of the premises in Knightrider Street in London, south of St. Pauls, which came to be known as Doctors' Commons. In 1767 the Doctors' Commons was incorporated and purchased the property. This corporation was dissolved in 1858, after the jurisdiction of the ecclesiastical courts over probate, divorce and matrimonial causes was abolished. The advocates then became barristers and the proctors became attorneys or, as they are now called, solicitors.[12]

As it was down to 1858, in order to be admitted as an advocate one had to be a Doctor of Laws of Oxford or Cambridge, must have been admitted by the Dean of the Arches (the head of the ecclesiastical court of the Province of Canterbury) and must have attended the court for a year. Control and discipline of the practitioners were in the Archbishop of Canterbury. How lax this was in the first half of the nineteenth century Dickens tells us in David Copperfield.

12. 4 Holdsworth, History of English Law, 235–237.

3. The Civil Tribunals on the Continent. As has been said the Germanic law, like primitive law generally, did not admit representation in litigation. Normally the litigant had to conduct his case in person. The nearest approach to the attorney's function was the forspeaker. Where two kin-groups were negotiating as to the composition to buy off a feud, where a kinsman of one had injured a kinsman of another, negotiations on behalf of each were initiated by forspeakers—an obvious device to prevent the negotiations from ending in war rather than in peace. Attorneyship did not develop from this crude device but from the ecclesiastical courts which in turn followed the Roman practice. The forspeaker became advocate.[13]

In France,[14] which we may conveniently take for the course of development on the Continent, the parties appeared in person in the civil tribunals as late as the year 1200. The rule of the Frankish law that only the king could appear by attorney was not formally abrogated as to the civil courts till the sixteenth century. But the

13. "Forspeakers" as advocates in "temporal causes" were required to take an oath by statute in Scotland in 1429. 1 Green. Encyclopaedia of the Law of Scotland, 142. Forspeaker is English for the Latin "narrator" and its French equivalent "conteur." 1 Pollock and Maitland, History of English Law (2 ed.) 215, n. 1.

14. A convenient short account of the development of the legal profession in France may be found in Forsyth, Hortensius, An Historical Essay on the Office and Duties of an Advocate (2 ed. 1875) chap. 7.

example of the ecclesiastical courts, where litigants had the advantage of representation, made it hard to maintain such a rule, and in practice from the middle of the thirteenth century, employment of attorneys became frequent in the French courts. Legal procedure had become a difficult art, and there came to be organized at each court corporations of men who made a business of receiving mandates *ad litem,* i. e., powers of attorney to conduct causes. In the seventeenth century, appointment of a duly qualified attorney was made compulsory. These attorneys had less rank and less repute than the advocates. Down to the French Revolution they were called *procureurs,* i. e., procurators or proctors (Latin, *procuratores*). After the Revolution they were called *avoués* (solicitors) and one might appear in person or by attorney. Down to the Revolution the office was purchasable.[15]

Advocates, too, disappeared with the downfall of the Roman judicial organization. But the Germanic law allowed forspeakers in certain cases to conduct causes before the tribunals. In the twelfth century these forspeakers became prominent in the church courts. Later they got a monopoly of advocacy in the parliaments (i. e., the French superior courts of the old regime) and in the civil tribunals. In the fourteenth century they formed a

15. Brissaud, History of French Public Law (transl. by Garner) 464–465.

brotherhood. The chief of the brotherhood carried a *baton*. Hence the head of the bar in France to this day is called *batonier*. In the sixteenth century the advocates came to be called an order. The order was abolished at the French Revolution, but was restored in 1810.[16]

As has been said in another connection, the function of the classical Roman jurisconsult passed to the teachers in the universities in the later Middle Ages, if not, indeed, in the eastern Roman Empire of the fifth century.

So there were in the church courts proctors and advocates. In admiralty courts, as it was in England till 1875, there were proctors and advocates. In the United States the agent for litigation in admiralty is still frequently called a proctor. In the French courts there are *procureurs* (proctors) or in modern phrase *avoués* (solicitors) and *avocats* (advocates). In Scotland, which received the Roman law in the sixteenth century, we find writers to the signet, or today solicitors or law agents (i. e., proctors) and advocates. The advocates are organized in a corporate body, the Faculty of Advocates.[17] The law agents are not required to be members of any organization, but are well organized in a number of associations.[18]

16. Id. 461–464.
17. 1 Green, Encyclopaedia of the Law of Scotland, 142–152 (advocates); 7 id. 307–326 (law agents).
18. 7 id. 325–326.

It will have been observed that in the earlier development of the profession in the modern world the practice of law was chiefly in the hands of the clergy. For a long time the clergy were the only educated element in society and so had a monopoly of the things that called for learning. The judges and counsel were clergymen not only in the courts of the church but in those of the state as well. But a development of lawyers went along with the development of law. In the twelfth century the lawyers became prominent in the courts. In the thirteenth they became dominant. Presently the church forbade the clergy practicing in the courts generally and the lay lawyer got the monopoly he has held ever since. One became a lawyer by being admitted to a place in the brotherhood.

•

IV

The Organization of Lawyers in Medieval England

•

IV.

The Organization of Lawyers in Medieval England[1]

1. The Rise of the Legal Profession. Advocacy was not needed in the era of the old mechanical trials of Anglo-Saxon law. Germanic law divided all litigation into an issue term and a trial term. At the issue term the parties stated their contentions. This was done in a very formal way. By applying highly formal rules to their statements it was determined whether there was anything to try and if so what, reducing the case to a simple, narrow issue. The issue having been settled, the mode of trial was directed, the burden of the issue assigned, and the case proceeded to the trial term. The trial was not an investigation of the facts. It was an arbitrary mechanical device expected to reveal the judgment of God or predicated on fear of ill consequences from a false oath, or presupposing the unchallengeable verity of certain records and undoubted authority of charters.[2] The one who had

---

1. A good general account may be found in Plucknett, Concise History of the Common Law (4 ed.) chap. 12.

2. 2 Pollock and Maitland, History of English Law (2 ed.) 598–604.

the burden of the issue at the trial term had no need of legal assistance. But a litigant could need a lawyer's help, if allowed, at the issue term in order to persuade the tribunal to frame the issue, direct the mode of proof, and assign the burden of the issue as favorably to him as might be. There could, however, be no development of a legal profession until a system of courts had grown up and a body of law, as distinguished from laws, had begun to be developed by judicial decision, requiring knowledge and skill and experience in presenting the claims of litigants and aiding the courts in applying the law to those claims.

By the time of Edward I the common-law courts had become well established. The formative period of the courts is from Henry III to Edward I. The legal profession is definitely formative in the reign of Edward I. Its formative period is from Edward I to Henry VI. Under Edward I the books show a body of lawyers practicing in the courts. There are two types, attorneys and pleaders, called also *narratores, counteurs,* or *serjeants-counteurs.* The distinction is the familiar one we have seen in Roman law. If one appeared by attorney the attorney represented him. If he had the assistance of a pleader, he was present by himself or by his attorney, but the pleader supported the case by his learning, ingenuity, and zeal.[3] It is the difference between the agent for litigation and the advocate, which goes back to antiquity.

Representation in litigation was regarded in the beginnings of English law, as in the beginnings in all systems, as something exceptional. As in all systems it developed slowly. As originally at Rome, the appointment of an attorney was thought of as unusual and only to be allowed on special grounds and with the solemn formality of a power of attorney. On the other hand, as in Roman law, the appointment of a pleader required no form. It was only gradually that the attorney was allowed to take the place of his client or represent him for all purposes. Thus, at first he could not make admissions, binding upon his client.[4] But by the end of the thirteenth century the distinction between the pleaders, who became later the serjeants, and the attorneys was well drawn. Until the fifteenth century, however, the same person might act as "apprentice" i. e., a junior being trained by a serjeant, and as attorney.[5]

As late as Blackstone's day it was "a settled rule at common law that no counsel shall be allowed a prisoner upon his trial upon the general issue in any capital crime,

3. 6 Holdsworth, History of English Law, 432.

4. Glanvill, bk. 11.

5. 2 Holdsworth, History of English Law, 313–318, 505.

unless some point of law shall arise proper to be debated." But a statute of William III allowed counsel in prosecutions for treason. Otherwise, however, parties were allowed the services of a pleader as far back as the laws of Henry I.[6] As was pointed out above, the pleadings at first were oral and jury trial was for a long time a mechanical trial, the jury giving their verdict upon a narrow issue on the basis of their knowledge or of neighborhood repute.[7] Thus there was no scope or need for advocacy at the trial. On the other hand, skill and learning were eminently required in the process of pleading by which the issue to be tried was arrived at. The influence of the church courts, and so of the Roman tradition, as against the idea of the Germanic law, made it possible speedily to develop the type of counsel which was needed.

In the thirteenth century many professed both the civil and the common law and many practiced both in the common-law courts and in the ecclesiastical courts. Many of the practitioners were in orders. But in that century the church began to discourage the clergy from practicing law and the Fifth Lateran Council (1512–1517) forbade their acting as counsel in the secular courts. In 1237 the

---

6. 1 Pollock and Maitland, History of English Law (2 ed.) 211.

7. As to how the jury was informed of facts upon which it rendered a verdict, see Thayer, Preliminary Treatise on Evidence, 90 ff.

advocates in the ecclesiastical courts were subjected to regulations, and those regulations seem to have furnished the model for regulation of the pleaders in the King's courts.[8] All through the thirteenth century we find references to pleaders. The Year Books of the time show a small group of them doing all the work of framing the pleadings in a colloquy with the judges. Also the opinions of these pleaders are cited or reported in the earlier Year Books on a par with those of the judges. We are reminded of the Roman *jurisperitorum auctoritas* and the weight of doctrine, i. e., opinions of jurists, in the civil law. Indeed, the older English admiralty reports reported opinions of doctors of the civil law along with decisions of the courts.[9]

We first hear of the coif, the characteristic headdress of the serjeant at law, in a chronicle under the date 1259 and about this time we begin to read of serjeants and apprentices.[10] These apprentices, who were being trained by the serjeants, became the barristers of today.

8. 1 Pollock and Maitland, History of English Law (2 ed.) 215.

9. Another example may be seen in the Maryland Reports. There were no reports until 1809. In the first volume of Harris & McHenry's Reports, covering the period from 1700 to 1774 there are a number of opinions of Daniel Dulany, Jr., e. g. an important one on pp. 247–258. It has been said of these that the reputation of this great lawyer was such that until the publication of reports his manuscript opinions were accepted as authoritative. Tyler, Memoir of Roger Brooke Taney, 133 (1872). See The Charming Nancy, Opinion of G. Hay (1761), Marsden's Admiralty Cases, 398; The Patrixent, Opinion of Wm. Wynne (1781) ibid.

10. 2 Holdsworth, 314.

Fortescue, in the reign of Henry VI, shows us a complete development of the profession at the end of the Middle Ages.[11] It has been formed and organized and the lines of the organization he sets forth have endured. As he describes it there are three categories: (1) The judges and serjeants; (2) the apprentices, organized in the four Inns of Court and the Inns of Chancery, comprising (a) the benchers or readers (i. e., lecturers), and (b) the inner barristers or students, eventually to divide again into utter barristers or juniors and inner barristers or students; and (3) the attorneys.

2. The Judges and Serjeants.[12] Fortescue tells of a close gild from which the judges were taken. The members were appointed by the Crown on nomination by the judges. It is not known exactly when the serjeants attained the position they held at the end of the fifteenth century. In the reign of Edward II it was not yet necessary to be a serjeant in order to be eligible for the bench. But it became settled in the fourteenth century that the justices were to be lay lawyers and serjeants. Fortescue compares the serjeants to the doctors of the civil law, who

---

11. Sir John Fortescue, c. 1385–1479, Chief Justice of the King's Bench 1442–1461, given the title of Chancellor by Henry VI in exile, 1461. His De Laudibus Legum Angliae (written between 1468 and 1471) is the best authority for the legal profession in English at the end of the fifteenth century. The best edition, text and translation, is by Chrimes (1942).

12. Fortescue, De Laudibus Legum Angliae, caps. 50, 51.

alone could be advocates in the ecclesiastical courts and the court of admiralty. The Chief Justice of the Common Pleas gave the Chancellor a list of seven or eight of the best lawyers who had been practicing at least sixteen years and the Chancellor then by writ commanded them to take on the degree and state of a serjeant. They took an oath to serve the King's people and not to delay justice for profit, so that the degree of serjeant was a public office. They were often made itinerant justices and were regarded as already members of the Court of Common Pleas. They had a distinctive dress, especially the white silk coif which they did not put off even in the presence of the King. They were created by letters patent and were paid a fixed salary by the Crown, doing some of the work of representing the Crown done later by the Attorney General and Solicitor General. On becoming serjeants they took a solemn leave of the Inn in which they had been called to the bar and became members of Serjeant's Inn. They were inducted by an elaborate ceremony.

Serjeants had a monopoly of practice as leaders in the Common Pleas and could also practice in the other courts of common law and before the Chancellor. Fortescue tells us that large fees were paid them. They seem to have dealt directly with their clients instead of with the clients' attorneys, whereas in modern times all degrees

[83]

of counsel came to be retained by and deal only with the attorneys or solicitors. When made judges they retained the coif although they had new robes. As they remained members of the order and of Serjeant's Inn, they addressed the serjeants from the bench as "Brother." It will be recalled how in Pickwick Papers during the trial of Bardell v. Pickwick, Mr. Justice Stareleigh addresses Serjeant Buzfuz from the bench as "Brother Buzfuz."

3. **The Apprentices.**[13] Apprentices, that is the branch of the profession from which the serjeants were chosen, are believed to have become organized in the fourteenth century and were thoroughly organized by Fortescue's time. But they were not organized as a whole body. Instead they were members of some one of a number of societies, one might say colleges, called Inns. The word "inn" here is used in an old sense of "house." There were four Inns of Court and a number, perhaps ten, of Inns of Chancery. Their origin is not known. There are only a few records of them in the fourteenth century. In 1355 there is a reference to "apprentices in their hostels," indicating that they had already been organized in that way at least for some time. The common law was not taught in the English universities of that time. The universities were clerical institutions teaching the Roman and the canon law. With the rise of the lay lawyer

13. 2 Holdsworth, History of English Law, 315-317, 493-496.

it was necessary to set up institutions for training in the law of the land. The Inns of Court were educational institutions for the study and teaching of the common law. Probably a group of law students lived together in a house and this grew into a college, the Roman law term for a corporation. The Inns of Court are corporations by prescription. That is, they have acted and have been recognized as such for centuries without any written charter. In fourteenth-century England the bodies of teachers and students of law living together like the fellows and students in one of the colleges in a university of that time, differentiated into three groups: (a) the older men, the teachers, who became the benchers or readers we meet with in Fortescue's account, (b) their assistants, the advanced students or utter (i. e., outer) barristers who could plead from without the bar in the days of oral pleading, and (c) the students. Call to the bar was, as it still is in England, call to the bar of the Inn. This admitted to practice in the courts as the doctorate of a university admitted to practice as an advocate in the courts of the civil law.

4. **The Attorneys.**[14] As always in the beginnings of law, attorneys, not allowed at first, were for a long time only allowed grudgingly. Originally one could appoint another to appear and act for him as his attorney

14. 6 Holdsworth, History of English Law, 450–453.

only by royal consent. In the King's court it was necessary that the appointment be made in court. If not there had to be a special writ authorizing it. But exceptions grew up between the reigns of Henry III and Elizabeth which in the end left nothing of the rule. Professional attorneys begin under Edward I. As late as the fifteenth century, however, apprentices at law might be professional attorneys and in that century attorneys might be members of the Inns. But the Inns and the judges came to discourage calling them to the bar, and by the seventeenth century they had become a wholly separate branch of the profession. They were not members of the Inns nor had they studied there. Nor were they organized in any other way. They were simply admitted to practice in and borne on the rolls of the common-law courts. The result of this bit of history was that, while the barristers were well organized, had a fine professional tradition, and were subject to effective discipline, from the fifteenth century almost to the middle of the nineteenth century the attorneys at law and solicitors in chancery had no organization, had come to lose much of the professional tradition, and had ceased to be under effective discipline. This was increasingly so in the seventeenth, eighteenth and fore part of the nineteenth centuries. The effects are to be seen in Caleb Quirk of Alibi House, and Oily Gammon in Ten Thousand a Year, and in Sampson Brass, Dodson and Fogg, and Mr. Vholes in the pages of Dickens. But this complete separation of the attorneys from the organized profession is postmedieval.

5. **The Inns of Court and the Training of Lawyers in Medieval England.**[15] There are four of these societies of barristers which in England still have charge of the education and admission of members of the upper branch of the profession. These four Inns of Court go back almost to the beginning of the common law. Fortescue tells us that there were also ten Inns of Chancery [16] of which we know of nine. Attached to Lincoln's Inn, Thavy's Inn and Furvival's Inn; attached to Gray's Inn, Staple Inn and Barnard's Inn; attached to the Inner Temple, Clifford's Inn, Clement's Inn, and Lyon's Inn; attached to the Middle Temple, New Inn and Strand Inn. Just what control the four Inns of Court had over the lesser Inns is not known and seems to have been indefinite. It is known that the greater Inns supplied readers or lecturers to the lesser ones. Sometimes they were landlords of the lesser ones. Sometimes they had visitatorial authority. Visitation was a familiar idea in the Middle Ages. Authority to look into the affairs of a church or a religious foundation or society, in order to prevent or correct abuses was an everyday matter going back to the Roman law of

15. Fortescue, De Laudibus Legum Angliae, caps. 48, 49; 2 Holdsworth, History of English Law, 504–512.

16. 2 Holdsworth, 498–508.

Justinian as to pious uses and gifts to charity and provided for in the canon law from the earliest times. As a matter of course every ecclesiastical corporation had a visitor and in consequence the colleges in the English universities still have them. Indeed, it came to be laid down as a rule of English law that every corporation must have a visitor. The judges were and still are visitors of the Inns of Court.[17] Naturally the Inns of Court were visitors of the Inns of Chancery attached to them. Sometimes they exercised disciplinary power, subject to appeal to the judges. Probably the four great Inns were distinct from the first from the "hospices" which grew into the lesser Inns. It is supposed that the students were later brought together in them in order to preserve discipline when the students in hired houses had proved a source of disturbance. They were in the end reserved for attorneys.

As to the government of the four Inns of Court, it is now, as it was when Fortescue wrote, in the Benchers or Masters of the Bench. At Lincoln's Inn they meet in a council; at Gray's Inn in a pension; at the Temple Inns in parliaments. They are self-perpetuating bodies, each presided over by a member elected annually called the Treasurer or Pensioner. They have powers of education,

---

17. At common law all corporations were subject to visitation to maintain their good government and secure their adherence to the purposes of their institution. 2 Kyd, Corporations (1794) 174.

discipline, and government very like those of the Fellows of a college at Oxford or Cambridge.

As to the grades of membership, first were the Benchers and Readers—those who had publicly lectured in the Inn. As has been said, they were the rulers of the society. The serjeants were chosen from them. Second, there were the utter barristers. These were said to be "such that for their learning and continuance" (i. e., continual attendance and attention to study) "are called by the said readers to plead" (i. e., to frame the pleadings in) "and argue doubtful cases" in the moots. The Benchers were chosen from these; one a year to lecture in the Inn, who was then called a reader, and a certain number for the Inns of Chancery attached to the house. Third, there were the inner barristers. They were the younger members who were not yet ready to argue in the moots. They were not yet called to the bar of the Inn.

As to the periods of study, the year was divided into "learning vacations" (between the terms of court in Lent and Summer); term time (when the courts were sitting); and "dead time" which was an actual vacation. The chief study was in the "learning vacations."

There were three parts of the program of legal education:[18] Lectures, moots, and taking notes in court. For

18. 2 Holdsworth, 506–508. See Fletcher, Introduction, 1 Pension Book of Gray's Inn (Records of the Honourable Society) 1569–1800, i, xxii.

[89]

the learning vacations the Benchers chose a summer reader (i. e., lecturer) from among the senior utter barristers.
He was given half a year's notice in order to enable him
to prepare his lectures. On the first day of vacation, at
eight o'clock in the morning, he lectured publicly in the
hall of the Inn, usually on some statute or on some subject
of the law. He commented and raised doubtful questions
and drew distinctions and put principles behind them,
much as the first type of teachers of Roman law in the
Italian universities had done. Then one of the utter barristers took up one of the questions put by the reader and
sought to prove that the reader's solution was wrong in
point of law. Next the other utter barristers in order of
seniority gave their opinion on the point. Thereupon another question was taken up in the same way. We are told
that the whole exercise took about two hours. This ended
the formal lecture. But after dinner the other hypothetical
cases put by the reader were argued by the utter barristers
and students, and every night after supper the reader
and the benchers discussed questions put by one of the
utter barristers.

Then came the moots or arguments of moot cases.
The benchers acted as judges and two utter barristers as
counsel. These arguments were sometimes so well done
that we find them reported along with the decisions of
the courts, and they were sometimes even cited by the

courts.[19] Then moots were held also in the dead vacations, the utter barristers taking the place of the benchers. Naturally it was important to compel attendance during the vacations, and strict rules were prescribed to this end. In the case of students it was a condition precedent to call to the bar that they had kept a certain number of vacations. It should be noted specially how all the members kept on learning after call to the bar, either by formal study or by teaching.

During term time the students attended the courts at Westminster and took notes. As late as the end of the eighteenth century there was a students' box in the Court of King's Bench, and an obliging judge would hand the record down to the students so that they could understand what was going on.[20] Such was legal education in the Inns of Court in its heyday as Fortescue described it about 1468. But this medieval system of training gradually decayed and by the eighteenth century had become a mere form. Reading of books and what was in substance an apprentice education succeeded it. Also after the sixteenth century the attorneys were apprenticed and had only apprentice training. This had important consequences for the training for the profession in America.

19. See an instance in Marginal Note, in 1688 ed. of Dyer, 111 *b*.

20. 3 Campbell, Lives of the Chief Justices, Life of Lord Kenyon, Library ed. 85.

Legal education in the Inns of Court revived in the present century but in a more academic form. The medieval education in the Inns of Court, however, was for its time an admirable system. In contrast to the Continental training it was not academic. The teachers were not professors in universities teaching from books. They were not jurists writing commentaries as authoritative texts and seeking to organize and systematize the learning which had grown up about them in the universities. They were practicing lawyers, in touch with the law in action, seeking to develop the common law of England as a workable system for meeting concrete problems of adjusting human relations and ordering conduct. This gave a color to the common law which it has retained. Teaching in the Inns of Court was tied to the work of the courts. The common law became characteristically a law of the courts and has been such ever since, whereas the civil law is a law of the universities. This close contact of legal education and the work of the courts had much to do with enabling the judges to develop the common law through judicial decision.

We owe it to this system that the common law was able to withstand the triumphal march of the Roman law in the period of its reception when, as Maitland put it, the three R's, Renaissance, Reformation, and Reception swept

[92]

over western Europe.[21] To it we owe nothing less than the common law.

But what is significant for our present purpose is that the English lawyers at the end of the Middle Ages had become a well developed, well organized profession, maintaining a system of societies or associations promoting a professional tradition, providing adequate training of those who were to enter the profession, and actively furthering the development of the law.

---

21. Maitland, English Law and the Renaissance, 9.

V.

The Organization of the Profession in England from the End of the Middle Ages to the American Revolution

.

V.

The Organization of the Profession in England from the End of the Middle Ages to the American Revolution[1]

Sharp lines grew up in the legal profession which have since obtained in England with little modification. The organization as it was in the eighteenth and nineteenth centuries arose by significant changes at each end of the medieval profession. At the top, the law officers of the Crown, the Attorney General and Solicitor General, came to be the leaders, and the King's Counsel came to contest the leadership of the serjeants. At the bottom, as has been said, the attorney's calling came to be distinct, there came to be an increasingly sharp line between the attorneys and the barristers, and three new types arose, namely, special pleaders, conveyancers, and solicitors; the first two akin to the barristers, the third growing up with the rise of the Court of Chancery, the equivalent in chancery of the attorneys in the courts of law. The attorney rather than the barrister was the model for the organization of the profession in America. Hence it is well to look more

1. 6 Holdsworth, History of English Law, 439-499.

in detail at the development of the attorney in sixteenth and seventeenth-century England and the thoroughgoing separation between attorney and barrister.

1. Attorneys and Solicitors.[2] As the idea that representation by an attorney was an exceptional privilege gave way in the fourteenth century, legislation began to separate the agent for litigation from other agents. Attorney originally meant agent. The agent for litigation became subject to control by the courts and was beginning to be regarded as an officer of the courts. As has been said, for a time he might have the advantage of training in an Inn of Court or Inn of Chancery, and might be an apprentice at law and so plead for his client. Even in the seventeenth century attorneys might be heard from the side bar in the King's Bench and Common Pleas. The older seventeenth-century advocates (e. g., Serjeant Maynard, called to the bar in 1626, made Serjeant in 1654, Serjeant of the Commonwealth in 1658, King's Serjeant at the Restoration, and still a leader of the bar at the English Revolution, 1688) still dealt with clients directly instead of through the medium of attorneys. For a time it looked as if the two branches of the profession might fuse, as they did in the United States and in Canada. The seventeenth century is the century of colonization of America and so the time of the beginning of our re-

2. Ibid. 432–444, 448–457; Cohen, History of the English Bar, 277–306.

ception of English law and English legal institutions.
It is important, therefore, to trace the process of separation and its causes and effects.

While the line of differentiation is an old one, new
reasons arose to emphasize it and give it permanence. The
old difference turned on primitive ideas that one could not
be represented in litigation but that he could be assisted
in the proceedings before the trial tribunal. The new
reason grew partly out of the nature of the work of the
two types of lawyer, but also upon the difference in the
mode of entrance upon the profession, the discipline, the
personnel, and the education of the two branches. I have
spoken of the beginnings of this differentiation in the
Middle Ages. In the seventeenth century it was still further developed, so that the judges, the Inns of Court, and
Parliament began to make distinct regulations for attorneys and for barristers.

As to barristers, the judges had long before delegated
to or perhaps more truly acquiesced in leaving to the Inns
of Court their power of admitting to practice in the courts.
Those whom the Benchers had called to the bar of the Inn
were received by the courts as qualified practitioners. On
the other hand, attorneys were admitted directly by the
court in which they sought to practice. With respect to
discipline, the barrister was directly under the control of
the Inn which had called him to the bar. He could be

[99]

disbarred either by the Benchers of his Inn or by the judges. But the judges seldom acted and Parliament made no attempt to supersede or supplement the control by the Inns of Court.

In contrast, the attorneys were strictly regulated both by Parliament and by the judges. Medieval statutes gave the courts power both to control and to admit them. All through the sixteenth and seventeenth centuries this control became increasingly strict. Orders of court were made as to admission of attorneys, requiring examination, and as to conduct and discipline. The courts were very severe in enforcing these orders. In 1605 a statute regulated the rendering of accounts to clients, provided penalties for fraud and negligence, and sought to eliminate unqualified practitioners.[3]

As to personnel, the expense of education at the Inns of Court led to a marked difference. The barristers were younger sons of the nobility or gentry, or were men of independent means. The attorneys were recruited from clerks. Indeed, the nature of their work was largely clerical and in their mode of appointment as well as the requirements of their calling, their contacts were with the clerical staff of the courts, as the contacts of the barristers were with the judges.

---

3. "An Act to reform the multitudes and misdemeanors of attornies and solicitors at law, and to avoid unnecessary suits and charges at law," 3 James I, chap. 7 (1605).

At first the King's Bench and the Common Pleas had each its own roll of attorneys. The Exchequer had a staff of clerks who acted as attorneys. But more and more the same person came to act as attorney in all the common-law courts. An order of 1564 sought to prevent this. It was not effective, however, and the attorneys came to be competent to practice in each common-law court. Also, because of their being regarded more or less as part of the clerical staff of the court, they were required to be in constant attendance on it and were exempt from suit except in their own court on the roll of which they were carried. The orders of court at that time required that one who sought admission as an attorney must have served five years as a "common solicitor", i. e., an agent not admitted as an attorney, or a clerk to a judge, serjeant, barrister or attorney.[4] The practice came to be to prepare by serving as an attorney's clerk.

In the seventeenth century the term "barrister" came into general use in place of the older "apprentice at law." It is first found in connection with utter (i. e., outer) barristers. Plowden insisted on being called a "learned apprentice of the law" even after he became a serjeant in 1558.

Change from the late medieval tendency to fuse the two branches of the profession was accelerated by the

4. 6 Holdsworth, 436.

system of written pleadings which grew up in the late Middle Ages and wholly superseded the old oral pleadings carried on in court by the pleaders.[5]   In the eighteenth-century practice, from which our American practice is derived, the several pleadings were in writing, were exchanged by the attorneys for the respective parties, and were entered on the record by the clerk.   In the Middle Ages the pleadings were settled orally before the justices by the pleaders and put in formal shape by the prothonotaries or their clerks.   Also if one was not represented by counsel, he explained his claim or defense to the court, and the prothonotaries put his pleading in proper form. In the sixteenth century the practice grew up of putting in paper pleadings settled in the prothonotaries' offices without any oral discussion.   In that century it came to be allowable that the pleadings might be either written or oral except that in the real actions which soon became obsolete, they remained oral in the seventeenth century.

As the art of pleading grew in complexity and technicality it came to be best learned in the offices of the prothonotaries instead of in the oral exercises in the Inns of Court.   Indeed, the clerks of the prothonotaries were for a time employed by the attorneys to draw their pleadings, and these clerks often acted as attorneys.   Thus the art of special pleading tended to drop out of the repertoire of

5.   3 Holdsworth, 615–653.

the advocate. The attorney collected the facts and the proof, and he, or a special pleader whom he employed, put them in due form. The barrister carried the case raised by the pleadings through the courts, arguing the validity of the pleadings, attempting to prove the issue raised by the pleadings, and arguing the questions of law arising upon them.

Moreover, development of jury trial into a real trying of the issue upon evidence adduced instead of a mechanical pronouncement upon personal knowledge or neighborhood repute, made the role of the barrister as trial advocate one of first importance.

These changes tended to differentiate the education of the attorney from that of the barrister.[6] Both required training in the body of authoritative materials of judicial decision and administrative determination. But the attorney needed to learn the use of the common forms of procedure and the practical processes of obtaining legal results. These things were best learned by apprenticeship to a practitioner. The barrister, on the other hand, required to know how to argue points of law effectively and to obtain results in the forum. Barristers learned draftsmanship so as to be able to advise on the pleadings. But their education was in the form of moots and discussions

6. 6 Holdsworth, 435–441.

and noting decisions in court while the education of the attorney had to do with practical preparation of the materials with which the barrister was to work. In the second half of the seventeenth century this division became substantially complete. It had two consequences. One was that the barrister ceased to be directly in touch with the client. If difficulties arose as to the law a barrister might have to be consulted. But the attorney had to discover the difficulty and state it to the barrister for his opinion. So it was the attorney who retained the barrister, not the client. The attorney prepared the written pleadings from the client's instructions, originally with the help of the officials of the court, later with the assistance of counsel in cases of difficulty. The barrister argued or tried the case on the basis of pleadings so prepared—very likely pleadings advised by a different barrister. The change was under way in the reign of Elizabeth. It was substantially complete after the Restoration.

Again a difference arose as to fees. In the Middle Ages there was no difference. But in 1629 it was laid down that an attorney could sue for his fees, although a barrister could not. The honorarium of the latter was held to be not a sum due on contract but a gift or honorarium. This doctrine came in from Roman books in the Court of Chancery where Roman influence was strong.[7]

7. Moor v. Row, 1 Chan.Rep. 38 [1629–30]. The whole subject is elaborately discussed in Kennedy v. Broun, 13 C.B.N.S. 677 (1863).

But it seems to have accorded with the views of the barristers, who considered themselves on a higher professional plane.

Exclusion of attorneys from the Inns of Court,[8] which has been spoken of in another connection, was obviously a part of this change. It, too, became complete in the seventeenth century. Sir William Holdsworth says justly that this "was not beneficial either to the attorneys or to their clients. It deprived the attorneys of the benefit of a professional organization. It deprived the clients of the safeguards given by the responsibility and power of discipline which a professional organization gives."[9] Discipline by the courts proved difficult and ineffective. Hence throughout the century and down to 1704, the judges made orders that attorneys, to be admitted, must be admitted members of an Inn of Court or of Chancery. But the Inns of Court refused to admit them to the bar and the Inns of Chancery were decaying. Hence as the attorneys had only the status of students in the Inns, and the government of those societies was in the Benchers, for practical purposes the attorneys had no professional organization. Accordingly in the eighteenth century some of them formed the "Society of Gentlemen Practitioners

8. Bellott, The Exclusion of Attorneys from the Inns of Court, 26 Law Quarterly Rev. 137.

9. 6 Holdsworth, 442.

in the Courts of Law and Equity," a voluntary society much like a bar association in the United States. But there was no effective organization till the establishment of the Incorporated Law Society in the nineteenth century.[10]

As late as 1850 the Court of Queen's Bench held that there was no binding rule of law against a barrister accepting a brief (i. e., instructions to act as counsel in a case, the brief containing a statement of the issues, the documents, if any, and the names of the witnesses and what it was expected they would testify) directly from a client instead of from an attorney for a client.[11] But this rule that the barrister must take his instructions only from an attorney had been insisted on by the Society of Gentlemen Practitioners and had become settled usage in the eighteenth century. A barrister knew that if he did not conform he would get no briefs from attorneys.[12]

Now as to the solicitors,[13] that is until recent times, the agents for litigation in the Court of Chancery. In the

10. Christian, A Short History of Solicitors, 120–122.
11. Doe d. Bennett v. Hale, 15 Q.B. 171. Sir William Holdsworth, following a like error in Christian, A Short History of Solicitors, 137, speaks of this case as decided in the Common Pleas in 1846. But see Thompson v. Maskery, 79 Law Times, 40. The court refused costs to a plaintiff because the plaintiff's instructing counsel directly was "an invasion of those just privileges of solicitors which ought in the interests of the public to be upheld."
12. Christian, A Short History of Solicitors, 138.
13. Cordery, The Law Relating to Solicitors (8 ed. 1935); Christian, A Short History of Solicitors (1896); 6 Holdsworth, 448–458.

Middle Ages solicitors were not at all members of the
legal profession. What is now the everyday jurisdiction
of a court of equity was then the "extraordinary" jurisdiction of the Chancellor. It was exercised on an "English
bill," (i. e., an informal petition in English to the Chancellor, whereas the writs and pleadings and records in the
courts of law were in Latin till the reign of George II.
"Bill" (in Latin *libellus*) means originally a petition. The
bill in equity began: "Humbly complaining showeth unto
your Lordship." The complainant referred to himself as
"your orator," i. e., one who prays, and prayed for relief
which could not be had in a court of law. Any one could
represent this petitioner. "Solicitor" meant one who conducted business on behalf of some one else, and so came to
mean one who conducted legal business for another without being an attorney or a barrister. The solicitors began
to appear as a professional class in the middle of the
fifteenth century, and it should be noted that the rise of the
Court of Chancery is in this period from the fifteenth to
the seventeenth century. But they had no recognized
status till the sixteenth century, and it was not till the
beginning of the seventeenth century, when the Court of
Chancery was well established in its jurisdiction, that no
distinction came to be made between attorneys and solicitors.

Apart from the rise of the Court of Chancery, a reason for the growth of a group of agents for litigation who were not attorneys at law may be seen in the centralization of justice at Westminster. A litigant living in the country, represented by a local attorney, might need an agent at Westminster to keep him informed of what went on there, and of the progress of the case before it came on to be tried in the locality. A solicitor could do this sufficiently. It did not call for an admitted attorney. Attorneys also employed solicitors for such purposes, and today country attorneys (or solicitors as they are now called) still have "London agents." But chiefly the rise of the solicitor is due to the rise of administrative tribunals under the Tudors and Stuarts—Chancery, the Star Chamber, the Court of Requests, and the like—just as accountants and lay representatives have been gaining in importance as representatives in litigation with the rise of administrative tribunals today. However, the solicitor came to be associated in the main with the Court of Chancery and thus came to have a definite place in the legal system alongside of the attorney. At first the Court of Chancery had its own staff of six clerks and the litigant was required to retain a clerk in Chancery. But a practice grew up of retaining a solicitor who then retained one of the six clerks. This became a form only and a source of delay and expense in equity.

A statute of 1605 [14] treated solicitors as belonging to the same class as attorneys and subjected them to like rules. In 1750 [15] it was provided that solicitors could be admitted as attorneys. By this time the two types of agents for litigation became substantially fused.

These changes had profound effects upon the system of education in the Inns of Court. Four points are noteworthy. First, more and more students began to live outside of their Inn and residence came to mean dining there. Second, it became difficult to maintain order by the self-discipline of the Inn. The students had at times to be taken before the Star Chamber, an extraordinary tribunal of what in some features might be called criminal equity. Those were days when every gentleman carried a rapier and street brawls and sword fights were common. The Inns were called on to admit fewer students, but the pressure to enter for social reasons was great. Third, large numbers joined for social purposes who did not intend to study law. The Inns engaged in many social activities, masques and revels—elaborate entertainments—and ceased to do the real work of professional education. Unhappily our American era of colonization was in this time of decadence of education in the Inns and before the revival which came after our independence. Thus we did

14. 3 James I, chap. 7.
15. 23 Geo. II, chap. 26, § 15.

not inherit the great medieval institution of a well organized legal profession and organized professional education.

Fourth, printing also had a profound effect upon the old system of education in the Inns of Court. It led to the growth of a much larger legal literature and made this literature more accessible. The student could buy books which would tell him what he wished to learn. Thus reading law books became a part of legal education along with moots, listening to lectures, and taking notes in court. The moots and lectures decayed because the printed books seemed to be short cuts to legal learning and students felt they could neglect "readings," moots, and attendance on the courts, and confine themselves to reading law books. They began to get substitutes to argue for them in the moots. The benchers and readers gave up trying to coerce the students into *bona fide* study by the old plan, and the old exercises turned into mere forms. Law business in the courts had increased greatly and the leaders no longer had time to devote to the students and so came to acquiesce in their plan of reading law books in the chambers of a barrister.

During the Commonwealth the whole teaching system of the Inns of Court collapsed and, in spite of vigorous efforts after the Restoration to set it on its feet again, it could not be restored. The fines imposed by the old orders for non-residence, for non-attendance at readings, and for not taking part in moots, turned into a system of compounding for not doing these things by paying a sum of money to the Inn. By the end of the seventeenth century one could compound in this way for all the obligations of a student and be called to the bar after eating the stated number of dinners (taken to show residence) and such study as he had chosen to do by reading the printed books. The readers (lecturers) were deep in heavy practice. They ceased to prepare careful lectures or to give attention to the moots. All public teaching of English law stopped for nearly a century and a half.[16]

2. The Rise of the Law Officers of the Crown.[17]

Those who are now ranked as the leaders of the legal profession in England, the Attorney General and the Solicitor General, are not medieval officials. In the Middle Ages the King had his serjeants [18] and his attorney or attorneys, and after Edward IV, his solicitor.[19] They did much of what is done today by the Attorney General and Solicitor General. Those officers began in the sixteenth century and became in the seventeenth century what they are now. The Attorney General and Solicitor General are the legal advisers of the Crown. Until recently one of

16. 6 Holdsworth, 481–499.
17. Id. 458–469.
18. Manning, Serviens ad Legem, ix, 246; Pulling, Order of the Coif, 38–42.
19. 6 Holdsworth, 462.

[111]

them at least has been in the cabinet. Also they usually sit in the House of Commons, where they attend to the details of answering legal questions for the government. By themselves or their deputies they appear in the courts on behalf of the Crown. As legal advisers of the Crown, they give legal advice to all the departments of government and appear for them in the courts.

From the beginning, the King had attorneys and pleaders *(narratores pro rege)* and serjeants. The first appointment of a King's Solicitor was under Edward IV. He had the same relation to a King's Attorney that a private solicitor had to a private attorney. He was an agent for the attorney's business; not unlike the "investigators" employed by attorneys today. In the Middle Ages the road to the bench was by way of Reader, Bencher, Serjeant, King's Serjeant. But from the middle of the sixteenth century as to the Chancellorship and Chief Justiceship, it became Solicitor General, Attorney General, although those were still regarded as inferior offices which could not be held by a serjeant.[20] The serjeants had been attached to the House of Lords to give legal advice to that

20. At least if a serjeant was appointed to one of these offices he was discharged of his office of serjeant by writ. Dugdale, Origines Juridiciales (2d ed. 1671) cap. 54. See also Plucknett, Concise History of the Common Law, 217, note 1. But in 1814 when Serjeant Shepherd, the King's Ancient Serjeant, was made Solicitor General, the King made an order giving the Attorney General precedence over him. Pulling, Order of the Coif, 192, n. 1.

house. With the rise of the House of Commons to chief importance there was a resulting chief importance in the Attorney General and Solicitor General who sat in that house.

It might seem curious that the King appeared in the courts and was advised on the law by an attorney and a solicitor at a time when the profession of attorney was being sharply divided from that of barrister and when a solicitor was coming near to the position of an attorney but was still inferior to one. The explanation lies in exceptional position of the King with respect to appearing by attorney, and the doctrine that in the theory of the law the King was always present in his courts, the judges being only his deputies to administer justice. The King was said to be "praerogative." He could not only appear by attorney but also plead by attorney. For him it was the same thing as pleading for himself. At first the King appointed an attorney for a particular court or for a particular occasion or time or place. But this attorney was more than an ordinary attorney. He was the representative of the King, looking after the interests of the King in the King's own court, where he was present in the eyes of the law. Thus the King's Attorney had superior standing, especially when later the King came to appoint an attorney to represent him generally in all courts.

In time it became the practice for the King to appoint a barrister to be his Attorney General.[21] Under the Tudors and Stuarts there was a great development of public law. The King's litigation became of the first public importance. Hence men of the first ability were needed to fill the positions of Attorney General and Solicitor General.[22] The King's Serjeant could only act when specially instructed by the Crown. But the Attorney General had a general authority to represent the Crown in all tribunals. The Tudors and Stuarts pushed their general representatives over the heads of the medieval leaders of the bar. Perhaps the serjeants were too learned in the medieval common law; too tenacious of the idea of the King ruling under God and the law for the purposes of Kings aiming at absolute authority.

As the King's business in the common-law courts increased, with the expansion of trade and commerce, the colonizing projects and activities, and the development of administration under the Tudors and Stuarts, the King's Attorney and King's Solicitor could no longer do all the work involved in their offices. Hence the rise of a body of "King's counsel learned in the law" or "King's learned counsel."[23] Those are the originals of the modern

21. As to the rise of the Attorney General, see Plucknett, Concise History of the Common Law, 217–218.

22. As to the Solicitor General, see 6 Holdsworth, 462–472.

23. As to the rise of King's Counsel, see id. 472, 475.

King's (or now Queen's) counsel. A body of such counsel under that name was known at the beginning of the reign of Elizabeth. Also they are referred to in an order of the judges in 1564 in a way which makes it reasonably certain that there were a number of counsel permanently retained by the Crown and regarded as ranking next to the serjeants. They were continued by James I when he came to the throne and seem usually to have been appointed by the Crown on the nomination of the Attorney General to act as his assistants. Francis Bacon was constantly appointed by Elizabeth as counsel in special cases. On her death, Bacon was not at first reappointed by James I, but in 1604 he succeeded in getting from the King a permanent appointment as King's Counsel with a salary of £40 a year for life and precedence after the law officers of the Crown. From this time on the King's Counsel, instead of being informally created by the Attorney General and Solicitor General, were appointed directly by the Crown by patent. Thus they became an established order in the legal profession comparable to the serjeants who were appointed by royal writ. At the end of the seventeenth century this new order of barristers was ceasing to be in any real sense a body of counsel for the Crown. It became a body of counsel to whom precedence had been given either because of their professional eminence or because of political influence. By the eighteenth century it became simply a class of counsel who for one reason or another had been given a rank superior to ordinary counsel.[24]

But those to whom this rank was given were still subject to certain disabilities which came down from the time when they really were the King's counsel. For one thing, they could not appear against the King without obtaining a license from the Crown. Also, as it was an appointed office, although the pay was nominal, appointment to it vacated a seat in Parliament and necessitated a new election. Hence in the eighteenth century and earlier part of the nineteenth century barristers frequently, instead of becoming King's counsel, obtained a patent of precedence. This gave them the same precedence as a King's counsel without the disabilities of that office. What had formerly been done by the King's counsel came to be done by the Solicitor to the Treasury and by counsel retained by the Treasury.

The matter of precedence requires explanation. When motions or applications were to be heard, the Chief Justice or presiding judge addressed the senior counsel present as follows: "Mr. ——— do you move?" He then called upon others in succession in order of precedence. Thus those having patents of precedence were first heard, which is sometimes very important to a client who requires an order as soon as may be. In America, instead of this,

24. Id. 475–476.

motions and applications are usually docketed and are heard in the order in which they appear on the docket. Moreover, in England the leader has immediate control of the hearing; the junior does what the leader leaves to him. At the trial the junior counsel opens the pleadings, i. e., states what the issues are as set out in the pleadings. The senior opens the case, i. e., states what he expects to prove and how, and examines the important witnesses. He might sometimes leave it to the junior to examine less important ones. The junior is there to assist him.

In the Middle Ages the King's Serjeant had the first rank.[25] Then came the serjeants in order of seniority, and then the barristers. At first in the seventeenth century there were no clear rules. In the Court of Common Pleas the serjeants had precedence over the Attorney General and Solicitor General unless they were appearing for the Crown. By the end of the seventeenth century and in the eighteenth century the order was settled as follows: (1) The King's Serjeant took precedence of the Attorney General and Solicitor General; (2) the Attorney General and Solicitor General took precedence of King's counsel and holders of patents of precedence; (3) the King's counsel and holders of patents of precedence took precedence of the serjeants; (4) the serjeants took precedence of ordinary barristers. In fact, long before, the Attorney

25. Id. 477.

General and Solicitor General had been the leaders of the bar. But it was not till 1814 that by royal warrant they were given precedence over the King's Serjeant.

Gradually the serjeants lost more than precedence.[26] They had a monopoly of practice in the Common Pleas. But from Tudor times when a judge was to be appointed he was made a serjeant *pro forma*. Thus the bench came to be filled with judges who had never really been serjeants and cared little about the order. Also in the seventeenth century barristers not serjeants were allowed to make side-bar motions in the Common Pleas. In practice the judges were chosen from the King's counsel. Thus the latter steadily got the upper hand. In addition, the King's counsel made good a claim to be benchers in the Inns, so that the King could now make a barrister a bencher by appointing him King's counsel. This had much to do with the decline of the system of education in the Inns of Court. By the middle of the nineteenth century any barrister of a certain number of years' standing could apply to be made a King's counsel as a matter of course. Thus the number of benchers became too unwieldy for the good government of the Inn.[27]

26. Id. 477–478; Pulling, Order of the Coif, 189–210.

27. 6 Holdsworth, 478–480. As to the effect on legal education see id. 480–481, 490–492.

3. The Circuits and the Circuit Bars.[28] Trials outside of London—i. e., trials of causes depending in the courts at Westminster which were not at bar, that is, before the courts themselves—were held in the courts of assize and nisi prius at circuit. These courts were held before two or more commissioners who were sent out twice each year, by the King's special commission, all round the kingdom except London and Middlesex, where courts of assize and nisi prius were held in and after every term before the Chief Justice or one of the justices of the three superior courts. The courts of nisi prius in London and Middlesex were called sittings. These nisi prius courts tried by jury the issues settled by the pleadings in the courts at Westminster.

As far back as the reign of Henry II, justices in eyre (itinerant justices) were appointed to go about the kingdom once in seven years to try cases. Magna Carta prescribed that they should be sent into every county once a year to receive verdicts of jurors instead of jurors having to go to Westminster to give their verdicts as witness triers. Sometimes these itinerant justices had a commission from the King to determine all manner of causes.

By the Statute of Westminster II (13 Edw. I, 1285) it was provided that these justices should be assigned

---

28. Plucknett, Concise History of the Common Law, 157–158; 1 Holdsworth, 276–284.

from the justices of the King's courts associated with one or two "discreet knights of the county." By a later statute trials at nisi prius might be before any justice of the court in which the action was pending associated with a knight or other approved man of the county. Finally a statute of Edward III (fourteenth century) allowed verdicts at nisi prius to be taken before any justice of either of the courts, although the action was not pending in his court, or before the justices of assize.

In Blackstone's time [29] the judges went circuit in the vacation after Hilary and Trinity Terms. There is no need of going into the details of the circuits. There were nine and are now seven. Some of the more important were: The Home Circuit (vicinity of London), the Northern, the Western, the Norfolk, the Oxford. The names explain themselves.

A digression is called for to explain "term" and "nisi prius." In the Middle Ages the church insisted that certain holy days and seasons should be "exempt from being profaned by the tumult of forensic litigations." Particularly these were the time of Advent and Christmas, which gave rise to a winter vacation of the courts; Lent and Easter, which led to a spring vacation; the time of Pentecost and the long vacation between midsummer and Mi-

29. 3 Blackstone, Commentaries on the Laws of England, 57–59.

chaelmas, which allowed for hay time and harvest. Out of this by custom and acts of Parliament grew four terms [30] at which the courts sat, each named for some festival of the church which immediately preceded it. Down to the nineteenth century, when the dates were changed by legislation, the terms were: Hilary Term (following the feast of St. Hilary) began January 23 and ended on February 12 unless either day was Sunday, when it began or ended on the day following; Easter Term, beginning on Wednesday, two weeks after Easter Sunday and ending Monday three weeks later; Trinity Term beginning the Friday after Trinity Sunday and ending on Wednesday two weeks later; and Michaelmas Term, from the sixth to the twenty-eighth of November. Trials in the vacations were provided for by a statute of Edward I, made with the consent of the Bishops.

Terms of court were abolished by the Judicature Act in 1873 and have been done away with in many common-law jurisdictions. They ought to be abolished everywhere, but still obtain in many states and in the federal courts. They are usually fixed by statute, but in the federal judicial system are fixed by rules of court.

As to "nisi prius" those words come from the writ by which the jury was summoned when a cause was ready

30. Id. 276–277.

for trial in the courts at Westminster. The sheriff of the county where the venue lay was commanded to cause twelve good and lawful men of the vicinage to come to Westminster to give their verdict on the issue by a certain date unless before that time (*nisi prius*) the justices of assize came into the county. As the date was so fixed that the justices would be there before it arrived, the sheriff summoned the jury to appear at the assizes.

The judges who went circuit sat by virtue of commissions from the Crown. In Blackstone's day (on the eve of the American Revolution) they sat by virtue of five: (1) The commission of peace—to inquire into the keeping of the King's peace—by virtue of which they charged the grand jury at circuit, since it was the original function of the grand jury to make a general inquiry into all infringements of the King's peace; (2) a commission of oyer and terminer—to hear and determine certain criminal cases; (3) a commission of jail delivery, to deliver the jail of a county, i. e., try persons committed to jail awaiting trial; (4) a commission of assize, directed to judges and serjeants named in the commission to take the verdicts of juries in real actions, which, however, had become obsolete in the seventeenth century; and (5) a commission of nisi prius to try all questions of fact issuing out of the courts at Westminster and then ripe for trial. There was also a special writ which went out with these commissions authorizing any two named in the commissions, if all could not be present, to proceed to execute the commissions so long as one was a judge or a serjeant.

As was said above the judges proceeded twice a year to the assize towns in the circuit to which they were assigned, in order to try civil and criminal cases in the locality. In the seventeenth century when a judge was appointed he chose a circuit and was sent on that one until some other which he preferred became vacant, so that the same judge always went the same circuit. Lord King, who became Chief Justice of the Common Pleas in 1714, broke over this custom and visited all the circuits in turn. The serjeants continued to be associated in the commissions, as they were in the Middle Ages, until the order became extinct in England (it held on longer in Ireland) in the nineteenth century. In one case, near the beginning of this century, a retired judge who could not be sent circuit as a justice, which he had ceased to be, was sent as a serjeant in an emergency.[31] But as the serjeants had been losing ground since the seventeenth century, objection was often made by laymen to being tried by serjeants instead of judges. The story is told of a criminal, who was tried before a serjeant at circuit because the Lord Chief Justice had been taken suddenly ill, that when asked whether he had anything to say why sentence should not

31. Pulling, Order of the Coif, 39, 109.

be passed upon him, he answered: "Yes. I have been tried before a journeyman judge."

In the old days the etiquette of the bar was very strict as to going circuit. Before the coming of railroads, the barristers were not allowed to use public conveyances or stay at hotels. Even now there is much strictness as to associating with solicitors and public at the assize towns. The leaders used to travel with their clerks in their own carriages. The juniors combined in twos or threes to hire dilapidated postchaises. At a still earlier day, when the bar went on horseback, a junior might ride circuit on a pony given him by a relative.[32]

It was customary for the judges to come to the assize town before the bar and, as it was called, open the commission, that is, have it read publicly. They then went to church and were preached to by the sheriff's chaplain. While they were at church the bar of the circuit came into town in their own or in hired carriages and hired lodgings. The next day a flourish of trumpets announced that the judges would take their seats in half an hour. Another flourish announced that they had done so.[33]

32. 3 Campbell, Lives of the Chief Justices (Library ed.) 8.

33. Serjeant Ballentine, Some Experiences of a Barrister's Life (6 ed.) 41–42.

One judge sat in the Crown Court to try criminal cases and one in the civil court. If there were no criminal cases to be tried, the sheriff presented the judges with white gloves.

Every barrister who practiced in the common-law courts was required by the custom of the bar to choose a circuit and he then belonged to the bar of that circuit. He could not go to try a case on another circuit except on a special retainer for which he had to receive a special fee. He could only change circuits once, and it was the settled custom that a barrister who had not joined any circuit could not wait till he had made a reputation in London and then step into a circuit full fledged. Lord Loughborough, when Mr. Wederburn, tried this unsuccessfully in the eighteenth century.[34] There was no legal way of preventing a barrister from appearing on any circuit he chose. But where one flagrantly violated the customs of the bar in such ways he was excluded from the bar mess and no other barrister on the circuit would hold a brief with him.

It was also a rule that a barrister could only change circuits while he was a junior. Change of circuits was made occasionally. Lord Campbell, when a junior, after four years on the Home Circuit, when he made slow prog-

---

34. 2 Halsbury, Laws of England (Hailsham's ed.) § 658.

ress, changed to the Oxford Circuit, where he made rapid progress and rose to be a leader, Solicitor General, Attorney General, Lord Chief Justice of the Queen's Bench, and finally Lord Chancellor.[35]

There were many curious old customs at circuit. One was that only King's counsel or such juniors as had had a bag given them by a King's counsel could carry bags to hold their briefs. The bags were given to such juniors as had progressed so far that they could not conveniently carry their briefs in their hands. Those were a visible sign of advancement. The bags of that time were purple, not green as now. Today any barrister may carry a bag if he chooses.

It remains to say something of the social activities of the bar at circuit. There is good reason for speaking of this. Although much that was done was by way of joke and good fellowship, the traditions of the circuit have been a real force for maintaining and preserving professional spirit and standards of conduct and discipline.

As the barristers dined together at circuit they chose an Attorney General and Solicitor General of Circuit Grand Court,[36] as it was called, and preferred indictments for such offenses as carrying a bag with no briefs, going

35.   3 Campbell, Lives of the Lord Chancellors, 75–76.
36.   1 Hardcastle, Life of Lord Campbell, chap. 9.

special to other circuits, and the like. Indictments were in Latin till the reign of George II, and the Circuit Grand Court kept to Latin indictments for a long time afterwards. A bumptious junior who got prematurely a purple bag from a King's Counsel to whom he was related by marriage was indicted for carrying *unam purpuream baggam flaccescentem omnino inanitatis causa*—one purple bag wholly collapsing by reason of emptiness.[37] Another made a long speech in the course of which a boy fell asleep in the gallery and fell into the well of the court and broke his neck. At common law the instrument with which a murder was committed was forfeited to the Crown. Hence the indictment had to charge and the jury had to find its value. The barrister was indicted in the Circuit Grand Court for murder with a certain dull instrument, to wit, a long speech of no value. The reminiscences of English lawyers are full of such stories [38] of fun at circuit. Indeed such stories are characteristic of lawyers when they get together at bar association meetings or at terms of court, or, as it used to be in the last century, at circuit. There is an endless telling of stories, some traditional, some new, all based on the queer experiences of a lawyer's life.[39] This good spirit, a part of the professional tradition, enables them to contest with their professional breth-

37. Id. 249; 6 Campbell, Lives of the Lord Chancellors, 72.

38. 3 Campbell, Lives of the Chief Justices (Library ed.) 105.

39. 1 Hardcastle, Life of Lord Campbell, 250.

ren all day in the forum, and meet outside on the friendliest of terms and with respect for those with whom they have been engaged in the strife of litigation.[40] This spirit in the advocates who practice in a court is an important element in an effective administration of justice. The tradition handed down from the circuit bars has been a real force for preserving the spirit of a profession under the trying conditions which had developed in America in the last century.

We are now at the point where the organization and customs of the profession in England cease to influence the bar in America. After independence American students ceased to go to the Inns of Court for study of law, and American lawyers looked to their books which told of the English institutions of the eighteenth century and to the traditions which had been inherited from the profession as it was in seventeenth-century England. Hence we leave the development of the profession in England as it was when Blackstone wrote (1765–1769) and turn next to its development in America.

40. 2 Campbell, Lives of the Chief Justices, 281 note, 281–282.

VI.

The Rise and Organization of Lawyers in Colonial America

VI.

The Rise and Organization of Lawyers in Colonial America

1. Law in the Colonies. Law depends upon lawyers and lawyers are little needed in a new community until there is a considerable economic development. Hence there was little in the way of law in the American colonies in the greater part of the seventeenth century. Many things concurred to hold back the development of law and lawyers in the seventeenth and even in the early part of the eighteenth century.

(1) The fourth year of James I (1607) is often taken as the date of colonization. At that time the common law was still in the stage of the strict law. The equity jurisdiction of the Court of Chancery became established in the seventeenth century, and the seventeenth and eighteenth centuries are the era of equity and natural law in our system as they are also in the civil law. The common law, as the first colonists knew of it, was the law of the age of Coke, not the law of the age of Mansfield. To the plain Puritan who emigrated to America it seemed "a dark and knavish business." Its records were in Latin and its re-

ports in Law French—a barbarous jargon in which the reporter's ignorance of French was eked out by Gallicized Latin, Gallicized English, and offhand analogies.[1] Also it was heavily burdened with the formalism of the strict law, and its ideals were those of the relationally organized society of the Middle Ages, and so not in accord with those of pioneers opening up the wilderness. Moreover, English law of the time was hard on the dissenters, who were colonizing America because it spoke from an era of organization while the colonists represented an incoming age of individualism.

(2) It has been urged that the earlier colonists were of a class which had had little to do with the courts at Westminster and knew only the local and borough courts in which the proceedings were had by personal presentation of a plaint or bill or petition in English in the tribunal.[2] Hence such institutions as tended to develop in the earlier colonial period were likely to take form from the local courts rather than from the common-law courts at Westminster. But, on the other hand, the charters required colonial legislation to conform to the common law of England.

1. Speech of James B. Thayer, Record of the Commemoration, November fifth to eighth, 1886, on the Two Hundred and Fiftieth Anniversary of the Founding of Harvard College, 319, 320-321 (1887).

2. Cohen, History of the English Bar, 173 ff.

(3) Lawyers as a class were very unpopular in the earlier colonial history. The era of the Puritan Revolution was hostile to lawyers in England and this hostility was exaggerated in the colonies. It was long before legal learning was held necessary in a judge.[3] It must be remembered that in the seventeenth century education and discipline in the Inns of Court were decaying. The attorneys were being excluded from the Inns and left to themselves. But it was the attorneys with whom the public came chiefly in contact.

(4) Law books then were few even in England. Little printed information as to English law was available in the colonies until the Revolution. Coke's Institutes were published in England between 1628 and 1644. Those who came to America in the first half of the seventeenth century had little to which they could turn when they sought to learn the law. The first American law book, a reprint

3. Seven of the eleven chief justices of New York from 1691 to 1778 were not trained lawyers. 1 McAdams, History of the Bench and Bar of New York, 17 (1897). In appointing judges "it was considered an object to embrace as many various callings in life as the number of judges would admit." Washburn, Judicial History of Massachusetts, 255. Of the 33 who sat on the bench of the highest court of Massachusetts from 1692 to 1775, as appears from the individual sketches in Washburn, chap. 12, only nine had some degree of legal training. In 1764 the Governor of New Jersey wrote that the "gentlemen sitting as judges in the courts of the colonies were not and could not be expected to be lawyers learned in the law." Warren, History of the American Bar, 9. Until the era of the Revolution it was not "deemed necessary or even advisable to have judges learned in the law." Ibid. 3. See also the opinion of Daniel Dulany, West v. Stegars, 1 H. & McH., 247, 248 (1767).

of Magna Carta and the great statutes of Edward I and of the Pennsylvania charter, was printed in 1687.[4]

(5) The supremacy of the clergy in the magistracy and so in the tribunals, especially in New England must also be considered. The clergy were the men of learning in the colonies in the seventeenth century, and were looked to as guides where the public looked to lawyers in the nineteenth century. In New England the clergy strove hard for two generations to govern their communities from the Bible and their individual sense of justice.

---

4. James, A List of Legal Treatises Printed in the British Colonies and the American States Before 1801, Harvard Legal Essays, 160. Down to 1774 there were forty-eight. Professor James says of these: "In the hundred years between the publication in 1687 of William Penn's gleanings from Lord Coke and the issuance of the American editions of Buller's Nisi Prius and Gilbert's Evidence in 1788, not a single book that could be called a treatise intended for the use of professional lawyers was published in the British Colonies and the American States. All of the books within this period which by any stretch of definition might be regarded as legal treatises were for the use of laymen. The merchant, the farmer, the artisan, might at any time be called upon to serve as a justice of the peace, or even, in some colonies and states, in a high judicial capacity. As lawyers were not numerous, the layman frequently and perhaps generally drafted his own instruments, contracts, deeds, and wills, without professional assistance. He was also called upon frequently to serve as a juryman. Practically all of these books were designed to assist him in the performance of his judicial and other public duties, and to enable him to satisfy legal requirements in the everyday matters of business and affairs." Even as late as 1781 students' notes might have to be used for important English decisions. See Clayton v. Clayton, 3 Binney (Pa.) 476, where counsel read in argument a note of a decision of Lord Mansfield taken by Edward Tilghman in June 1773 while he was a student in the Inns of Court. He was admitted to the bar in Philadelphia in 1774. Martin, Bench and Bar of Philadelphia, 317.

(6) The royal governors frequently interfered with the administration of justice so as to make it a personal justice rather than a justice according to law.[5] This went on more or less down to the Revolution. In England in the seventeenth century, the courts and the Crown were engaged in a long and severe contest which ended only in 1688. When a bar arose in the colonies in the eighteenth century, it was in a contest with royal or proprietary governors quite analogous to that which had gone on between the lawyers and the Crown in seventeenth-century England. The Stuart Kings regularly removed judges who would not decide as the King dictated, and royal colonial governors often proceeded in imitation of their masters. There could be little legal development under such a system.

In legal theory the colonists brought the common law with them. The charters required colonial legislation to conform to the common law. Statutes could be and were annulled by the Privy Council for breach of this requirement, and decisions of the colonial courts were appealed to and reversed by the Privy Council for want of accord with the charter provisions.[6] Reception of the common law was earlier and more complete in Virginia than else-

---

5. Warren, History of the American Bar, 8.

6. As to the significance of this for American law, see Thayer, Legal Essays, 3 ff.

where.[7] In the colonies generally it begins at the end of
the seventeenth century with the setting up of courts and
judicial justice, in place of executive and legislative justice, and is not complete in all respects at the Revolution.
In a sense it is only complete at the end of the first third
of the nineteenth century.

2. **Lawyers in the Colonies.** In the development
of a bar in the colonies in the century and three quarters
from the first settlement to the Declaration of Independence we may distinguish in a general way four stages, each
somewhat longer than a generation, longer in some colonies than in others, but a traceable sequence in all. They
may be called (1) the attempt to get on without lawyers,
(2) the stage of irresponsible filling out of writs by court
officials and pettifoggers, (3) the era of admitted practitioners in permanent judicial organizations, and (4) the
era of trained lawyers—the bar of the eve of the Revolution.

(1) *The beginning—the attempt to administer justice without lawyers.* Although Virginia received the
common law early in its colonial history, it produced no
trained bar for nearly one hundred years. John Barbie

---

7. 1 Story, Commentaries on the Constitution, sec. 50; The Lawes of
   Virginia now in Force, Collected out of the Assembly Records and Digest-
ed into one Volume, Revised and Confirmed by the General Assembly
   . . . the 23rd of March, 1661, London, 1662, preamble, p. 2.

Minor, than whom there can be no higher authority on such a question, considers that this was due to jealousy by the governing landed aristocracy of any other power in the community.[8] Jealousy on the part of the clergy, which saw political power passing to a profession of the law may well have played a part in the same way in New England.[9] But the phenomenon of attempt to administer justice without lawyers, a feature of all Utopias, a feature of all revolutions from Jack Cade's rebellion to the French Revolution, to the Russian Revolution,[10] is so universal that in any event we should expect to meet with it in the beginnings in the New World.

Legislation hostile to the practice of law is continuous from substantially the middle of the seventeenth century to the middle of the eighteenth century.[11] In 1642–3, an Act for the Better Regulation of Attorneys forbade pleading causes for another without license from the court where one pleads and provided that one was not to have such license from more than two courts, the Quarter Court

8. 4 Minor, Institutes of Common and Statute Law, 3 ed. 199–200 (1893). He tells us that "the landed gentry of the colony of Virginia waged against the lawyers through the 'grand assembly' a relentless war for more than a century, of which, indeed, some practical vestiges survived until a very recent period."

9. See Pound, The Lay Tradition as to the Lawyer, 12 Michigan Law Review, 627 (1914).

10. 1 Gsovski, Soviet Civil Law, 853–855.

11. The details may be found in 4 Minor, Institutes of Common and Statute Law, 3 ed., 199–204.

and one County Court.[12] Fees (in tobacco) were fixed very low with a heavy penalty for taking more. A licensed attorney was forbidden to refuse retainer unless already retained on the other side of the same controversy. But the Act was not to apply to special attorneys within the colony nor to "such as have letters of procuration out of England."[13] An Act of 1645 recites that many troublesome suits have multiplied by the unskilfulness and covetousness of attorneys and provides that all "mercenary attorneys" be "wholly expelled from that office" except as to cases already undertaken or depending.[14] This Act was repealed in 1656 and it was enacted that the Governor and Council were to appoint attorneys in the Quarter Courts and the Commissioners to nominate attorneys for the County Courts. No attorney was to be admitted to practice until he had taken an oath. Also it was provided that "only those be called counsellors at law who have already qualified thereunto by the laws of England, and those so qualified shall have all the privileges those laws give them." That is, barristers admitted by the Inns of Court, were to be barristers in the courts of the colony without

12. The Governor and Council, sitting four times a year to dispose of judicial business, were the Quarter Court. The County Courts sat once a month (later six times during the year) and had general jurisdiction of first instance. The judges were commissioned by the Governor and Council.

13. Act LXI of 1642–43, 1 Hening, Statutes at Large of Virginia, 275–76.

14. Act VII of 1645, 1 Hening, 304.

more.[15] In 1657–58 it was enacted that no attorney and no other person should plead in any court or give counsel in any cause or controversy for any kind of reward or profit directly or indirectly, under penalty for every breach.[16] However, fees were allowed and fixed by an Act of 1680, but no one was to practice in the General Court (formerly called Quarter Court) unless licensed by the Governor.[17] This statute was repealed in 1682.[18] Of this, Minor says: "For thirty-six years after this apparent *extinction* of the profession no legislation appears to have occurred upon the subject. The craft, however, seems to have lived and flourished; the necessities of society proving more than a match for the stolidity of the Grand Assembly, so that that body, abandoning at length the vain design of suppressing it, betook itself to the not less futile attempt to *regulate the charges* of the profession." [19] Except that statutory regulation of fees went on until 1849,[20] the chapter of legislative attempt in Virginia to get along without attorneys ends with a statute of 1748 which will be considered in a later connection.

15. Act VI of 1656, 1 Hening, 418.

16. Act CXII of 1657–58, 1 Hening, 482.

17. Act VI of 1680, 2 Hening, 479.

18. 2 Hening, 498.

19. 4 Institutes of Common and Statute Law, 3 ed., 203. An Act of 1718 fixed fees in detail, 4 Hening, 59.

20. 4 Minor, Institutes, 203.

Although by the time of the Revolution Philadelphia had become an outstanding center of legal learning and forensic ability, the development of the profession in colonial Pennsylvania was retarded and was complete much later than in the colonies generally. The experience of the Quakers with the administration of justice in the English courts in the seventeenth century had been such that the general aversion to lawyers in the early colonies was exaggerated and prolonged. Penn had planned that the laws in his colony should be so plain and the statements of the parties to controversies so simple, that every one could plead his own case, and his "Laws Agreed Upon in England," embodied in the first legislation, so provided.[21] But, as has always happened, the event showed that lawyers were necessary to the administration of justice according to law. The statutes establishing the courts after 1710 [22] provided for the admission of attorneys by the judges of the respective courts. A small group of practitioners had sprung up already. But the number of attorneys was so small that in 1708 and again in 1709 complaint was made to the Council that all the authorized

21. Laws Agreed Upon in England, art. 6, Charter and Laws of the Province of Pennsylvania (George, Nead, and McCamant) 100; Laws of 1682–1700, chap. 66, Charter and Laws of the Province of Pennsylvania, 128.

22. Act for Establishing Courts of Judicature (1710) 2 Statutes at Large of Pennsylvania, 301; Act for the Establishment of Courts of Judicature, 3 id. 298.

practitioners had been retained by the petitioner's adversary, so that he prays to have counsel assigned to him or to have leave to bring in counsel from New York.[23] During the first twenty years in Pennsylvania there were not more than three or four English-trained lawyers in the province. Twenty-three are known who were called attorneys. But almost all seem to have had no training in law.[24] We are told that in 1706 three were the whole bar of Philadelphia.[25] A system of conciliation by "common peacemakers," whose award was to be a final judgment, was provided by statute in 1683.[26] An Act of 1705 allowed parties with accounts against each other to refer them to a person agreed upon in open court whose award was to stand as equivalent to the verdict of a jury.[27] This practice was extended to other actions as well as Account, so that as late as 1766 there were records of elaborate decisions of these referees. We are told that at that time "a very great share of the administration of justice" was

23. Lloyd, The Courts of Pennsylvania in the Eighteenth Century Prior to the Revolution, 56 Univ. of Pa. Law Rev. 28, 46–49 (1908).

24. Martin, Bench and Bar of Philadelphia, 236–237.

25. McCall, Discourse Before the Law Academy of Philadelphia, 14 n. 3 (1838).

26. Laws of Pennsylvania, 1682–1700, chap. LXV, Charter and Laws of the Province of Pennsylvania (George, Nead, and McCamant) 128.

27. 2 Statutes at Large of Pennsylvania, chap. CL of the Laws of 1705–06, p. 242.

entrusted to them.[28] Such things did not tend to promote development of a legal profession.

In New York the hostility to lawyers did not go so deep nor last so long.[29] In 1677 the Council resolved that "pleading attorneys be no longer allowed to practice." But the Supreme Court made a rule that no one be admitted to plead as an attorney unless first admitted by the court on producing a warrant of attorney from his client. At this time there does not seem to have been a body of regular practitioners. In 1695 the number of lawyers was so small that many would retain most of them on one side to the prejudice of other parties who could find no one to represent them. So a statute of that year prohibited employment of more than two on a side.[30] Chief Justice Horsmanden in 1743 tells us that there were but eight members of the bar in New York City at that time. Also we are told that between 1695 and 1769 only forty-one lawyers practiced there.[31]

---

28. 1 Dall, preface, p. iv.

29. As to lawyers in colonial New York, see McAdams, History of the Bench and Bar of New York, vol. I (1897); Wickser, Bar Associations, 15 Cornell Law Quarterly, 390 (1930); Blaustein, New York Bar Associations Prior to 1870, 125 New York Law Journal, no. 64 (1951), p. 1186.

30. An Act Regulating the Retaining Attorneys at Law, passed October 22, 1695, 1 Colonial Laws of New York, 351. This act by its terms expired in two years, but was revived for seven years by an Act of 1699, ibid. 409.

31. Warren, History of the American Bar, 96–97.

In Massachusetts we are told that because of the prejudice "there does not appear to have been a class of learned lawyers or of men exclusively devoted to that profession at any time during the colony charter," i. e., 1630 to 1684,[32] and in 1692 there was no one in the province "who had been regularly educated to the bar." [33] As is inevitable there were those who acted as agents for litigation or even as trial lawyers, as occasion allowed. But their caliber can be inferred from a law of 1656 prohibiting pleading by oneself or attorney for more than one hour under penalty.[34]

(2) *The era of irresponsible practice by court officials and pettifoggers.* While colonial America was learning the futility of forbidding representation in litigation and the wastefulness of every man his own lawyer, the work that ought to have been in the hands of trained, responsible members of a profession fell of necessity into the hands of officers of the court, sharpers and pettifoggers. In Virginia, which long refused to allow a profession, the colony was troubled almost from the beginning by a low class of petty practitioners or "mercenary attorneys." [35] The problem of how to control these irresponsible persons gave

---

32. Washburn, Judicial History of Massachusetts, 53.
33. Ibid. 148.
34. Ibid. 53.
35. 1 Hening, Statutes at Large of Virginia, 302.

more trouble to Virginia than to any other colony,[36] obviously because Virginia was slowest in allowing the development of a responsible profession. In New York in 1683 there was legislation such as had to be provided in other colonies, forbidding sheriffs, constables, clerks, and justices of the peace from acting as attorneys in their courts.[37] But our most authentic information as to this stage in the development of practice of the law in the colonies comes from the autobiography and the diary of John Adams, who set out vigorously at the outset of his career to combat the serious abuses which resulted. In 1759 he had an actual experience of the mischiefs arising "when deputy sheriffs, pettit justices, and pettifogging medlers attempt to draw writs and draw them wrong oftener than they do right." [38] In his autobiography he says of this time: "Looking about me in the country I found the practice of law grasped into the hands of deputy sheriffs, pettifoggers and even constables who filled all the writs upon bonds, promissory notes, and accounts, received the fees established for lawyers, and stirred up many unnecessary suits." [39] In 1760 he tells us in his diary that he

36. Warren, History of the American Bar, 41.

37. Chap. 7 Laws of 1683, 1 Colonial Laws of New York, 125. So in Maryland by Act of 1666. Riley, The Development of the Legal Profession in Maryland, 4 Transactions Maryland State Bar Association, 87, 90 (1899).

38. John Adams, Diary, January 3, 1759, 2 Works of John Adams, 58.

39. 2 Works of John Adams, 58, note.

found in Braintree "a multitude of pettifoggers . . . who stirred up dirty and ridiculous litigation." [40] A typical pettifogger was one Kibby, a tavern keeper. Adams says of him: "In Kibby's barroom, in a little shelf within the bar, I spied two books. I asked what they were. He said, 'Every Man His Own Lawyer and Gilbert on Evidence.' Upon this I asked some questions of the people there and they told me that Kibby was a sort of lawyer among them; that he pleaded some of their home cases before justices, arbitrators, etc." [41] What John Adams did toward improving this condition belongs to the story of bar meetings in Massachusetts.

(3) *The era of responsible, admitted practitioners before permanent courts.* By the end of the seventeenth century or in the beginning of the eighteenth century, the principal colonies had set up a real system of courts to administer justice according to law: Virginia in 1705,[42] Massachusetts in 1692, disapproved by the Crown but reenacted in 1699,[43] Maryland, say, in 1692 when judges not members of the Governor's Council were appointed on the Provincial Court,[44] New York in 1691,[45] Pennsyl-

---

40. Diary, June 19, 1760, 2 Works, 90–91.
41. Diary, Friday, June 7, 1771, 2 Works, 271.
42. 3 Hening, Statutes at Large of Virginia, 287–302.
43. Washburn, Judicial History of Massachusetts, 151.
44. 20 Archives of Maryland, 379.
45. 1 Colonial Laws of New York, 229.

vania, 1722,[46] New Jersey, 1704,[47] South Carolina, 1721.[48] In all the colonies there were now courts requiring trained and responsible agents for litigation and advocates, and there came to be systems of prescribed qualifications of admission to practice, and of responsibility of the practitioners. In general the systems of admission followed the English provisions as to attorneys.

A classification of the systems of admission to the bar in force at the time of the Revolution proposed by Mr. A. Z. Reed in the Bulletin of the Carnegie Foundation for the Advancement of Teaching, entitled Training for the Public Profession of the Law, brings out some points of significance for the organization of the profession in our formative era in the fore part of the nineteenth century. The classification is made with reference to the admitting authority. On this basis there were three types.[49]

Jurisdictions of the first type were Massachusetts, New Hampshire, Pennsylvania, and Maryland. In these jurisdictions the traditional English system as to attorneys prevailed. Each court admitted attorneys to practice be-

46.   3 Statutes at Large of Pennsylvania, 303–304.

47.   Field, Provincial Courts of New Jersey, 260–261.

48.   7 Statutes at Large of South Carolina, 167.

49.   Reed, Training for the Public Profession of the Law, Bulletin 15 of the Carnegie Foundation for the Advancement of Teaching, 67–68 (1921).

fore it. Mr. Reed presumed this to be the case in the then frontier colony of Georgia. But there is very little assured information as to this. Under this system the highest court tended to guard its own bar more jealously than did the lower courts so that there was something like the graded profession in England.

In colonies of the second type each court of general jurisdiction had authority to admit attorneys to practice but either on a principle of comity or by custom admission by one court sufficed for practice before every other. In Rhode Island admission in one court was regarded as giving a right to practice in any other. In Connecticut the rule was that any County Court, and only a County Court, could admit to general practice. Delaware had a like system except that it maintained a distinction between general practitioners at common law and those in equity, corresponding to the then English distinction between attorneys and solicitors.

In the remaining colonies there was a principle of centralized control over admission to practice. In some the control was in the highest court, either directly as in South Carolina or through an examining board appointed by the court, as in Virginia. In New York, New Jersey, and North Carolina all attorneys were appointed by the royal governor, although usually in practice upon the recommendation of a judge or a court. Under this system grades might be distinguished, e. g., in New Jersey, attorneys, counsellors, and serjeants.

Where each court of general jurisdiction admitted specially to its own bar those so admitted felt of themselves as members of that bar and had a feeling of unity so that bar meetings and bar control over the training and qualifications of those seeking admission developed. On the other hand, where one could be admitted in any court to practice in all or where one was admitted by a central authority to practice in all courts there was no consciousness of membership in a particular bar and only some urgent special circumstances could evoke unity of action among the attorneys.

Taking up the jurisdictions in detail, in Virginia those who had been admitted to the bar of one of the Inns of Court were entitled to practice as counsellors or barristers and as general practitioners without more.[50] This was repeated in the Act of 1748, an Act for Regulating the Practice of Attorneys, which provided for appointment of examiners by the General Court (the highest court) and licensing by that court after examination. The General Court was empowered to suspend or disbar.[51] The recog-

50. Act of 1656, 1 Hening, Statutes at Large of Virginia, 418; Act of 1732, chap. 13, 4 Hening, 357, 362.

51. Chap. 47, Laws of 1748, 6 Hening, 140–143.

nition of counsellors or barristers as distinct did not survive the Revolution.[52]

In Massachusetts a law of 1701 required an oath of office before admission to practice and attorneys were recognized as officers of the court.[53] How the mode of admission brought about a feeling of membership in a bar, instead of a general license to practice, is brought out in the account of the admission of John Adams in 1758. "In open court Gridley [the leader of the bar] said: 'May it please Your Honor, I have two young gentlemen, Mr. Quincy and Mr. Adams, to present for the oath of an attorney. Of Mr. Quincy, it is sufficient for me to say that he has lived three years with Mr. Pratt [Benjamin Pratt, one of the leaders of the bar—in 1761 appointed Chief Justice of New York]. Of Mr. Adams, as he is unknown to Your Honor, it is necessary to say that he has lived between two and three years with Mr. Putnam of Worcester [James Putnam who as Washburn tells us "attained very high rank in the profession." Judicial History of Massachusetts, 237], has a good character from him and all others who know him, and that he was with me the other day several hours, and I take it he was qualified to study the law by his scholarship [he graduated A.B. 1755 from Harvard] and that he has made a considerable, a very

52. 4 Minor, Institutes of Common and Statute Law, 198.

53. Washburn, Judicial History of Massachusetts, 189.

great proficiency in the principles of the law, and, therefore, that his clients' interest may be safely intrusted in his
hands. I . . . recommend him, with the consent of
the bar, to Your Honor for the oath.' Mr. Pratt then
said two or three words, and the clerk was ordered to
swear us." [54]

It should be noted that Gridley recommended the two
candidates "with the consent of the bar."

Adams' Diary shows that there were three grades in
the profession in his time: lower court attorney, upper
court attorney, and barrister. He became an attorney of
the Superior Court in 1761.[55] In 1775 he referred to himself as a barrister [56] and at the head of the list of subscribers to the American edition of Blackstone in 1771
next to the Governor is "John Adams, Esq., Barrister at
Law, Boston." [57] In 1768 there were twenty-five barristers in Massachusetts. Sixteen others, including John
Adams, had been made barristers before the Revolution,
and at the time of the Revolution there were thirty-six.
At that time at least ten eminent attorneys had not been
made barristers.[58] The distinction between attorney and

54. 1 Works of John Adams, 49-50.

55. 2 Works, 133.

56. 3 Works, 27.

57. The list of subscribers is prefixed to volume II, 1772.

58. Washburn, Judicial History of Massachusetts, 200-201.

barrister was introduced by rule of court by Chief Justice Hutchinson in 1761. Only barristers were to argue in the Superior Court, then the highest court. But this was not enforced. Three years of practice as an attorney were a prerequisite, afterward changed to two years, so that it came to three years of study under a preceptor, two of practice in the inferior court, and two of practice as an attorney in the Superior Court.[59]

So far as appears, attorneys were recognized in Maryland from the beginning, and there was little of the prejudice and hostility shown elsewhere. In 1669 a committee of the lower house of the General Assembly asserted that "the privileged attorneys are one of the great grievances of the country" and the house brought an impeachment proceeding against an attorney on specification that he had taken fees on both sides of a case and that he had taken retainers at unreasonable fees for a period of a year. On trial before the upper house it held the proceedings bad and that the charges had been completely answered.[60] In 1674 it was enacted that a "certain number of honest and able attorneys" should be nominated, admitted, and sworn by the Governor. In 1715 a

59. 2 Works of John Adams, 197; Warren, History of the American Bar, 83–86.

60. Riley, The Development of the Legal Profession of Maryland, 4 Transactions Md. State Bar Association, 87, 87–90 (1899). See also 1 Sams and Riley, The Bench and Bar of Maryland, chaps. 1–5.

statute provided fully as to admission, discipline, and professional conduct, and that statute stood in substance till an Act of 1898.[61]

In New York after the English took over the colony of New Amsterdam from the Dutch a code known as the Duke of York's Laws was promulgated in 1665 as the basis of the government. It provided a more elaborate system of courts than existed at that time in the other colonies. One hundred years later the Chief Justice of the Province laid down that the Supreme Court in the main proceeded according to the practice of the courts at Westminster, and that the common law of England with the statutes explaining it or altering it before a legislature was established in the colony, and those passed since expressly extended to the Province, as well as the local legislative acts, which were not to be repugnant to the laws of England, constituted the law of New York.[62] Thus New York had by the middle of the eighteenth century a good organization of courts and an accepted reception of the common law of England. But until the eve of the Revolution there was not the bar that should have gone along with them. Substantially from the beginning the Governor had the power of appointing attorneys. Lawyers were

61. Ibid. 93.
62. Horsmanden, C.J. in Fomey v. Cunningham, reported in N.Y.Hist.Soc. Collections.

not liked by royal governors and the number of licensed attorneys down to the Revolution was small. Only 41 practiced in New York City between 1695 and 1769.[63]

For reasons set forth above the bar was slow of development in Pennsylvania. "From what I have been able to learn of the early part of the history of Pennsylvania," wrote a Chief Justice in the first quarter of the nineteenth century, "it was long before she possessed lawyers of eminence. There were never wanting men of very strong minds very well able to conduct the business of the courts without much regard to form. Such in particular was Andrew Hamilton.[64] But Mr. Francis [65] appears to have been the first of our lawyers who mastered the technical difficulties of the profession." [66] However, the two decades before the Revolution developed an exceptional bar in Pennsylvania, many trained in England and men not only of general culture and legal learning but of distinguished ability. They gave the bar of Philadelphia such standing that the term "Philadelphia lawyer" became current for a lawyer who knew his business thoroughly.

---

63. Warren, History of the American Bar, 95–96.

64. Andrew Hamilton, 1676–1741, called to the bar in Gray's Inn in 1713, Attorney General of Pennsylvania in 1717, famous for his defense of John Peter Zenger in New York in 1735.

65. Tench Francis, brother of the author of Maxims of Equity, came to Pennsylvania about 1740, Attorney General of Pennsylvania in 1745.

66. Tilghman, C.J. in Lyle v. Richards, 9 Serg. & Rawle, 322, 332 (1823).

In South Carolina legislation in 1712 made the English statute of Henry IV as to examination of attorneys by the justices and swearing them and enrolling them [67] the law of the Province.[68] This was taken to centralize control of admission and discipline in the Supreme Court. Although small in numbers, only fifty-eight having been admitted to practice before the Revolution and not more than twenty in 1761,[69] it was the best educated bar in America, both generally and in the law. Of those at the bar at the Revolution fifteen were trained in the Inns of Court and a number were as well graduates of English universities. There were no less than forty-seven students from South Carolina in the Inns of Court before the Revolution. But there seems to have been no pressure on them in this country to lead them to organize as in Massachusetts, New York, and Maryland.

In New Hampshire there was the same system of admission as in Massachusetts. But there were no regular "bar meetings" till after the Revolution.[70] One of the lawyers practicing in New Hampshire at the Revolution

67. 4 Hen. IV, chap. 18 (1404).

68. An Act to Put in Force in this Province the Several Acts of the Kingdom of England or South Britain Therein Particularly Mentioned, December 12, 1712, 2 Cooper, Statutes at Large of South Carolina, 401, 447.

69. O'Neall, Bench and Bar of South Carolina (1859) gives the details.

70. Warren, History of the American Bar, 138–139.

had been in practice as a barrister in England and later in the West Indies.[71]

A bar developed in Connecticut much later than in Massachusetts. In 1708 a statute required authority from the court for each particular case before any one could act as attorney for another.[72] In 1730 a statute limited the number of attorneys to eleven, to be appointed from time to time by the County Courts as there should be occasion.[73] This was later repealed. But until the time of the Revolution there were few lawyers of any legal training. Here, as elsewhere, however, on the eve of the Revolution there was a group of strong lawyers, almost all college graduates.[74] No bar meetings are known.

Little is known as to Rhode Island lawyers in the eighteenth century. The Attorney General seems to have been the only trained lawyer.[75] Apparently the real bar

71. As to the bar in colonial New Hampshire, see Belknap, History of New Hampshire (1792); Plumer, Life of William Plumer (1857); Parker, C.J. in Pierce v. State, 13 N.H. 536, 554 ff.

72. An Act for the Better Regulating Proceedings and Pleas at the Bar, Acts and Laws of His Majestie's Colony of Connecticut in New England, 1715, p. 135.

73. An Act Relating to Attorneys, Acts and Laws of His Majestie's Colony of Connecticut in New England, Passed by the General Assembly May 1716 to May 1749, 373.

74. Warren, History of the American Bar, 133–134.

75. Warren, History of the American Bar, 140–143. See also Durfee, Judicial History of Rhode Island, in 4 Davis, The New England States, chap. 63, pp. 2362–2397.

of Rhode Island begins after the Revolution. There is, however, record of a bar meeting which will be spoken of in another connection.

Whitehead [76] gives no names of lawyers practicing in New Jersey in the seventeenth century. In 1698 attorneys practicing for fee or hire were required to be admitted by the Governor. In 1740 there was a statute going into detail as to the practice of law and prescribing fees. In 1755 the Supreme Court set up an order of serjeants. There were twelve. They were recommended to the Governor by the judges and were called up by writ as in England. They conducted examinations for admission to the bar. In 1767 provision was made for a grade of counsellor. No one was to practice as counsellor until he had been in practice three years and had been examined in court for promotion. The order of serjeants was abolished in 1839.[77] A bar meeting in 1765 will be spoken of in another connection.

Delaware, the three "lower counties," united with the Province of Pennsylvania in 1693, got a separate legislature in 1704 and a separate executive council in 1710, but the Governor of Pennsylvania was its chief executive till

76. Judicial and Civil History of New Jersey (1897).

77. Warren, History of the American Bar, 111–113; Clevenger and Keasbey, The Courts of New Jersey, also some account of their origin and jurisdiction (1903); Field, The Provincial Court of New Jersey, with sketches of the Bench and Bar (1849) in 7 New Jersey Historical Collections.

1776. A state government was organized after the Declaration of Independence. As in Pennsylvania, each court admitted to its own bar, but admission in any county court admitted to practice in all.[78]

In North Carolina the English statute of James I,[79] as to admission of attorneys, was in force. But there is little in the sources as to North Carolina lawyers before the time of the Revolution. There was nothing in the way of organization of the profession.[80]

When Georgia became a crown colony in 1752 the Chief Justice was required to be an English barrister. There was a small bar in the eighteenth century; a few English barristers practiced in Savannah. At the time of the Revolution there were a few American trained lawyers. But the history of the bar in Georgia begins at the Revolution.[81] After 1731 the English statute of George II [82] governed admission to practice.

(4) *The era of trained lawyers—the bar of the eve of the Revolution.* Barristers admitted by the Inns of

---

78. Scharf, History of Delaware (1888).
79. An Act to reform the multitudes and misdemeanors of attornies and solicitors at law, and to avoid unnecessary suits and charges at law, 3 James I, chap. 7 (1605).
80. Hawks, History of North Carolina (1889).
81. Miller, Bench and Bar of Georgia (1858).
82. An Act for the better regulation of attorneys and solicitors, 2 Geo. II, chap. 23 (1729).

Court in England, as we have seen, were generally regarded as qualified to practice in the colonies as such. In Virginia and South Carolina especially they were recognized as the best trained and best qualified type of practitioner. At that time the only advantage which the student in one of the Inns of Court, whose real study was in the chambers of an English barrister, had over the American student, who "read law" in the office of a practitioner at home, was in access to more complete libraries and in the opportunity of taking notes in the courts at Westminster, which we know was made use of profitably by a Philadelphian in 1773.[83] But the influence of these English trained lawyers, as preceptors of those who later became preceptors of many practitioners was great and wholesome.[84] In the eighteenth century it became more and more the custom for parents who could afford it to send their sons to study law in the Inns of Court. From 1760 to the Revolution there were more than one hundred Americans studying law in London. We know of forty-seven from South Carolina, twenty-one from Virginia, sixteen from Maryland, eleven from Pennsylvania,

83. Clayton v. Clayton, 3 Binney, 476, 482 (1811).

84. As to English barristers in the colonies see Reed, Training for the Public Profession of the Law, Bulletin 15, Carnegie Foundation for the Advancement of Teaching, 68.

and five from New York, and there were one or two from more than one of the other colonies.[85]

Moreover, in the course of the eighteenth century a continually greater proportion of the lawyers came to be college educated. Beside the two seventeenth-century colleges in the colonies, Harvard (1636) and William and Mary (1696), there were many founded in the eighteenth century before the Revolution: Yale (1700); College of New Jersey, now Princeton (1746); King's, now Columbia (1754); College of Philadelphia, now University of Pennsylvania (1756); Brown (1764); Queen's, now Rutgers (1766); Dartmouth (1769). In the generation of the Revolution the majority of the lawyers were graduates of colleges.[86]

Of Maryland lawyers trained in the Inns of Court outstanding in the earlier period were Daniel Dulany, Sr., a barrister of Gray's Inn (1716), leader of the bar in the fore part of the eighteenth century and Charles Carrol, barrister of the Inner Temple, who came to Maryland in

---

85. Lloyd, The Courts of Pennsylvania in the Eighteenth Century Prior to the Revolution, 56 University of Pennsylvania Law Review, 28, 49 (1908), citing Stillé, Life and Times of John Dickinson, 28. From the latter we learn that from twenty-five to fifty American born lawyers had been educated in England before 1760. It is said that one hundred and fifteen Americans were admitted to the Inns of Court from 1760 to the close of the Revolution. Warren, History of the American Bar, 188.

86. See Warren, History of the American Bar, 194–196. Substantially all of the barristers created in Massachusetts were graduates of Harvard. Ibid. 81–83 note.

1687. The Maryland bar on the eve of the Revolution was of exceptional quality. The three leaders had been trained in the Inns of Court: Daniel Dulany, Jr., barrister of the Inner Temple (1747), who was of such repute that his opinions as counsel were regarded as authoritative,[87] Charles Carrol (the second) Inner Temple (1757), and William Paca, who had studied at the Middle Temple.[88]

Massachusetts had relatively few English trained lawyers: Benjamin Lynde (Harvard, 1686, Middle Temple, 1692), Judge of the Superior Court, 1712, Chief Justice, 1728; John Gardner (Inner Temple, 1761) appointed Chief Justice of New York in 1761, and Paul Dudley (Harvard, 1690, Inner Temple, 1702) Attorney General, 1716, Chief Justice of the Superior Court, 1745. But three home trained lawyers of great ability brought up a generation of lawyers who made an outstanding bar at the time of the Revolution. John Read (Harvard, 1697) was admitted to the bar in New Haven in 1708. He had, at his death in 1749, the reputation of the greatest lawyer

---

87. They are to be found in 1 Harris & McHenry (Md.) 247, 248, note *a.*
"There are no reports of Maryland decisions till 1809. In that volume the opinions of Daniel Dulany are published along with the decisions of the Court of Appeals. The high reputation of this great lawyer stimulated ambition of the Maryland bar, while his opinions were models of legal discussions for their imitation." Tyler, Memoir of Roger Brooke Taney, 133 (1872).

88. Warren, History of the American Bar, 55–56.

of New England.[89]   Jeremy Gridley (Harvard, 1725) is called "the father of the Boston bar."   He was Attorney General in 1742 and again in 1761 and was the great legal scholar of his time.   His eminence in his profession rendered his office a favorite place of resort for students and some of the most distinguished lawyers in Massachusetts had him for preceptor, e. g., Benjamin Pratt, afterwards Chief Justice of New York, James Otis, Oxenbridge Thacher, and William Cushing, Chief Justice of Massachusetts after the Revolution.[90]   Edmund Trowbridge (Harvard, 1728), Judge of the Superior Court in 1767, was the most learned real property lawyer of his time in New England.   He had as students, among others, Francis Dana and Theophilus Parsons, who became Chief Justices after the Revolution, James Putnam, the preceptor of John Adams, Royal Tyler, Chief Justice of Vermont, Rufus King and Christopher Gore.[91]

New York had only a small bar at the time of the Revolution, but we have the testimony of Chancellor Kent that in this small group there was a "constellation of learned and accomplished men." [92]   At least fifteen were

89.   There is a life by George B. Read (1903).

90.   Washburn, Judicial History of Massachusetts, 211–212.

91.   Id. 308–311.

92.   Address by James Kent Before the Law Association of the City of New York (1836), 1889 reprint, 10.

notable—a high proportion out of forty-one. Three were graduates of Yale and two graduates of Columbia.

In New Jersey at the time of the Revolution there were two who are noteworthy. David Ogden (Yale, 1728) Judge of the Supreme Court in 1772, and his pupil, Richard Stockton (Princeton, 1748) Judge of the Supreme Court in 1774.[93]

Except South Carolina, no colony at the time of the Revolution had at the bar so many who had been trained in the Inns of Court as did Pennsylvania. The Pennsylvania bar of that time stands out in American legal history. Six deserve special mention as the founders of a great legal tradition: Benjamin Chew, Attorney General, 1755, Chief Justice, 1777; Thomas McKean, Chief Justice in 1777; Edward Shippen, Chief Justice after the Revolution; John Dickinson; Francis Hopkinson, one of the signers of the Declaration of Independence and United States District Judge after the Constitution; and George Read, a signer of the Declaration of Independence and later Chief Justice of Delaware. Except Francis Hopkinson, each was a barrister of the Inner Temple.

North Carolina had some outstanding lawyers on the eve of the Revolution, one of whom, James Iredell became later a Justice of the Supreme Court of the United States.[94]

93. Warren, History of the American Bar, 114.

94. McRee, Life and Correspondence of James Iredell (1859).

As was said above, South Carolina at the time of the Revolution had the best educated bar in America. Fifteen of them had studied in the Inns of Court, three were graduates of English Universities, and one was a graduate of Princeton. John Rutledge (Inner Temple, 1761) was regarded as the ablest lawyer of the Province. He headed the opposition to the Stamp Act, became Chief Justice of the State in 1791 and Chief Justice of the Supreme Court of the United States in 1795. All four of the South Carolina signers of the Declaration of Independence were lawyers.[95]

In Virginia the bar between 1750 and the Revolution included a group of lawyers educated mostly at Princeton, William and Mary, or in the English universities and trained in the Inns of Court, whose exceptional political talent and legal attainments put that colony in the position of leadership which it maintained for a long time after the Revolution. The names of those who stand out particularly in the Virginia bar of the time speak for themselves: Peyton Randolph, graduate of William and Mary, and of Oxford and barrister of the Inner Temple, the Attorney General of Virginia, 1748, President of the first Continental Congress, 1774; John Randolph, graduate of William and Mary, and barrister of the Inner Temple, Attorney

95. Warren, History of the American Bar, 122. Mr. Warren erroneously puts John Rutledge instead of Edward Rutledge as one of the signers.

General in 1766; Edmund Pendleton, Chief Justice of the Virginia Court of Appeals after the Revolution; John Blair, graduate of William and Mary, student in the Middle Temple 1755, Chief Justice of the Virginia Court of Appeals in 1789, and a Justice of the Supreme Court of the United States in 1789; John Lewis, preceptor of George Wythe; George Wythe, Chancellor of Virginia, 1788, the preceptor of Jefferson, John Marshall, Madison and Monroe; Thomas Jefferson; John Tyler; George Mason, author of the Virginia Bill of Rights, the prototype of the Bills of Rights in all American Constitutions; Richard Henry Lee, a student in the Inner Temple; and Patrick Henry.[96]

(5) *Organization of lawyers at the time of the Revolution.* By the time of the Revolution the legal profession in most of the colonies had become well established in public estimation, well educated, and well qualified by study of law. How or how far was it organized? As has been seen, barristers admitted in the Inns of Court were generally recognized as entitled to practice as such and were not subject to the restrictions upon attorneys imposed by local legislation. Also a few jurisdictions sought to set up grades after the English system. But these attempts came to naught.

---

96. There is a striking account of this group of lawyers in a letter of St. George Tucker, April 4, 1813, to William Wirt. 1 Kennedy, Memoirs of William Wirt, 353–355 (1849).

A significant and well established institution in the New England colonies was the bar meeting—meetings of the whole bar, not merely an associated group of members of the bar of a particular court, either at regular intervals or when called specially on some urgent occasion. We have the fullest account of these meetings in Massachusetts in the diary and the autobiography of John Adams. We first hear of them in connection with Adams' campaign against the pettifoggers a year after his admission as an attorney. He says under date of January 3, 1759, after reciting the bad conditions which he found: "I mentioned these things to some of the gentlemen in Boston, who disapproved and even resented them very highly. I asked them why some measures might not be agreed upon at the bar and sanctioned by the court which might remedy the evil. They thought it not only practicable but highly expedient, and proposed meetings of the bar to deliberate upon it. A meeting was called and a great number of regulations proposed, not only for confining the practice of the law to those who were admitted to it and sworn to fidelity in it, both to introduce more regularity, urbanity, candor and politeness, as well as honor, equity and humanity among the regular practitioners." [97]

97. 2 Works of John Adams, 58, note. The extract is from the autobiography.

We next hear of these meetings two years later when Benjamin Pratt, one of the leaders,[98] was appointed Chief Justice of New York. Adams says: "Many of these meetings were the most delightful entertainments I ever enjoyed. The spirit that reigned was that of solid sense, generosity, honor and integrity; and the consequences were most happy for the courts and the bar, instead of scenes of wrestling, chicanery, quibbling and ill manners, were soon converted to order, decency and candor. Mr. Pratt was so delighted with these meetings and their effects that when we all waited on him in Dedham, on his way to New York to take his seat as Chief Justice of that state, when we took leave of him after dinner, the last words he said to us were, 'Brethren, above all things, forsake not the assembling of yourselves together.' " [99]

From then on until the Revolution the references to bar meetings are frequent and are so illuminating that they are given verbatim.

Saturday, February 5, 1763. At a meeting of the bar "The bar agreed upon these four rules—(1) that the clerk call the plaintiff and if anybody answer except the plaintiff or some sworn attorney, his power be demanded, and no general power in such case be admitted. (2) That no attorney's fee be taxed for the future, where the

98. Washburn, Judicial History of Massachusetts, 224.
99. 2 Works of John Adams, 58, note.

declaration was not drawn by the plaintiff himself or some sworn attorney. (3) That no attendance be taxed, unless the party attend personally, or by some sworn attorney. (4) That no attorney be allowed to practice here, unless sworn in this court or in the superior court. Mr. Gridley read these rules to the court, as unexceptionable regulations agreed upon by the bar. Mr. Otis opposed the rules and the court said that if the bar was not agreed it could do nothing. It was agreed to postpone action." [100]

Monday, May 28, 1766, at Boston. "A meeting of the bar at the Coffee House for the admission of three young gentlemen . . . and another meeting appointed next Friday sevennight, to consider some measures for limitation, making a pause, etc. They swarm and multiply—*sed* the country grows amazingly, and the time will not be long ere many who are now upon the stage will be in their graves. Four years must pass before the three young gentlemen admitted this night will assume the gown. . . . But the bar has at last introduced a regular progress to the gown, and seven years must be the state of probation." [101]

May 1, 1771, Wednesday. "This evening at the bar meeting I asked and obtained the unanimous consent of

100. Ibid. 142. The extract is from the diary.
101. Ibid. 197. The quotation is from the diary.

the bar to take Mr. Elisha Thayer of Braintree, son of Captain Ebenezer Thayer, Jr., as a clerk." [102]

Thursday, July 4, 1771. Meeting of the bar at Shattuck's Tavern. "Agreed unanimously to recommend Tim Langdon to be sworn." [103]

Tuesday, March 29, 1774. "At a meeting of the bar, a doubt of Brother Lowell was mentioned, upon the law of the Province for the relief of poor prisoners for debt. Questions were asked, whether appealing an action was not fraud? whether trading without insuring was not fraud? etc. A question also about the duty of the sheriff. Whether a party plaintiff could control the King's precept, etc., by ordering the sheriff not to serve it? etc. Mr. Wetmore was agreed to be recommended for the oath, etc." [104]

Here we see the bar meetings suggesting rules to the court, passing on recommendations to the court to admit applicants (note the consent of the bar when John Adams was admitted [105]), consenting to members taking in particular students as clerks, and discussing improvements of the law by legislation.

---

102. Ibid. 258. The extract is from the diary.

103. Ibid. 287. The extract is from the diary.

104. Ibid. 337. The extract is from the diary.

105. *Supra*, note 54.

In Rhode Island in 1745 there was a bar meeting at which the eight members entered into an agreement as to conduct of the profession.[106]

Also in New Jersey a meeting of the state bar was called in 1765 to consider the Stamp Act.[107]

In Maryland in 1725 there was a statute regulating fees strictly and allowing planters to pay in tobacco or in currency at a fixed rate. Three lawyers headed by Daniel Dulany, Sr., petitioned against this Act in the Upper House claiming it infringed their rights as British subjects. In 1729 the statute was extended for three years and the lawyers petitioned against it to the Proprietor in London. It was disallowed on an opinion by the Attorney General, Sir Philip Yorke, afterward Lord Hardwicke.[108] But this does not seem to have been action by the bar as an organized body but rather the action of a number of individual lawyers. There is one case of something which suggests bar action as such. In 1679 there is record of a deed by the Proprietor to three "attorneys of our Provincial Court" of an acre in the City of St. Mary's "on their petition for them to build and erect chambers for the more commodious dispatch of their clients' business and af-

---

106. Updike, Memoirs of the Rhode Island Bar, 55, 294–295 (1842).

107. Warren, History of the American Bar, 113–114.

108. Ibid. 54.

fairs." [109]   But by that time the number of attorneys before the Provincial Court had become considerable. This evidently was neither a bar association at one pole nor a partnership at the other. It was something like the law buildings and medical buildings we see in some cities today, a private building in which lawyers might have their individual offices.

In addition to the bar meetings there are accounts in John Adams's diary of bar dinners, dinners of the bar as a whole. [110]

A bar association (the New York Bar Association) as distinguished from an organized bar, is known to have been in existence in New York City as early as 1747 and to have continued until 1770. [111] Whether it was organized in 1744 or 1745 or 1741 is in dispute and unhappily we have little information about it. We know that at first it sought to prevent members from taking in as clerks students preparing for practice. [112] What chiefly occasioned the organization, however, and gave it strength and continuity, was the long and bitter controversy between the lawyers and the royal governors as to tenure and inde-

109. Riley, The Development of the Legal Profession in Maryland, 1669–1715, 4 Transactions Maryland State Bar Association, 87, 93 (1899).

110. 2 Works of John Adams, 221. From the diary.

111. Wickser, Bar Associations, 15 Cornell Law Quarterly, 390, 394 (1930).

112. Blaustein, New York Bar Associations Prior to 1870, 125 New York Law Journal, no. 64, April 3, 1951.

pendence of the judges—whether judges should hold during good behavior only at the pleasure of the King and the Governors. Also from 1763 to 1765 the Governor sought to compel the courts to allow an appeal to the Governor and Council on the facts as well as on questions of law. The united bar prevailed in this controversy, and perhaps we should think of an organized bar analogous to the bar meetings in Massachusetts rather than of a voluntary association of such lawyers as chose to adhere to it. But Governor Colden wrote of it as an association.[113] At any rate the royal governors considered that domination of the colony by lawyers was threatened and wrote much and vigorously to the home government about the dangerous influence of the lawyers and the menace to the authority and prerogatives of the King which their activities involved. Mr. Warren has brought together extracts from the letters of the Governor to his superiors at Westminster which bring this out.[114] When the controversies as to the tenure of judges and as to the Stamp Act came to an end the association came to an end or the bar ceased to act as an organized body. But in New York as in the other colonies individual lawyers were among the leaders in the assertion of the rights of the colonists which led to the Revolution.

113. Warren, History of the American Bar, 100.

114. Ibid. 99–100.

Two clubs of lawyers which cannot be brought into the category of bar associations deserve mention. In 1765 there was formed a law club or junto, a "small sodality" of seven to read in concert the feudal law in the appendix to Gothofredus' edition of the Corpus Juris, and Cicero's orations. They also were to read Coke on Littleton and the English statutes reign by reign. Gridley said: "I hope to see at the bar, in consequence of this sodality, a purity, an elegance, and a spirit surpassing anything that ever appeared in America." [115] But he died two years later and the sodality did not continue.

A similar club called "the Moot" was founded in New York in 1770 "to encourage a more profound and ample study of the civil law, historical and political jurisprudence, and the law of nature." Among its members were John Jay, afterward Chief Justice of the Supreme Court of the United States; Egbert Benson, the preceptor of Chancellor Kent, and Robert R. Livingston, afterward Chancellor of New York. "It is said that a Chief Justice of the Superior Court once sent an issue of law to the Moot for its advice." [116] Its last meeting was on January 6, 1775.

115. 2 Works of John Adams, 146–150. From the diary.

116. Warren, History of the American Bar, 203.

Such clubs as Gridley's Sodality and the Moot show the spirit of the profession as it was on the eve of the Revolution.

Why was organization so far advanced as shown by the bar meetings in some colonies and so wholly wanting in others? Two conditions seem to have made for consciousness of the bar as an entity and for action by the bar as a unit. What seems to have been chiefly effective was control of admission and so over training and qualifications by the local bar through the system of admission by the local court of general jurisdiction of first instance. This seems to explain the general custom of bar meetings in New England. Secondly, controversies with royal governors called for united action in New York, New Jersey, and Maryland. On the other hand, two conditions operated to hold back and even prevent organization. Minor tells us that the dominant landed proprietors as a class in Virginia were jealous of a profession which might challenge their power. Very likely they would not have tolerated an organized body of lawyers. The royal governor in New York had the same objection to an organized profession. But what seems to me likely to have been decisive is that in Pennsylvania, Virginia, and South Carolina, where the lawyers had achieved a high degree of development at the time of the Revolution, a large and

[172]

probably most influential element in the profession had been admitted in the different Inns of Court and practiced by virtue of this and not by virtue of admission by the local court. Hence they did not think of themselves as members of a local bar but as members of their Inn.

3. The Effect of the Revolution on the Profession. The conservatism characteristic of lawyers, led some of the strongest to take the royalist side and so in some jurisdictions the Revolution decimated the profession. Washburn names twelve Massachusetts lawyers who went to Halifax when the British evacuated Boston or went out of the country during the war.[117] Among them were two members of Gridley's sodality [118] and the preceptor of John Adams.[119] Two, Timothy Ruggles [120] and Benjamin Kent [121] had been counted distinguished contemporaries of Gridley, and two more, David Leonard [122] and Sampson Salters Blowers [123] were rated as distinguished contemporaries of John Adams. According to Washburn there were thirty-six barristers and ten attorneys in Boston at

117. Washburn, Judicial History of Massachusetts, 226–227, 231–239, 312–313.

118. Samuel Fitch, ibid. 232, and Benjamin Gridley, ibid. 236.

119. James Putnam, ibid. 237.

120. Ibid. 226–227.

121. Ibid. 232.

122. Ibid. 237.

123. Ibid. 239.

the outbreak of the Revolution.[124]   Between one third and
one fourth left after the evacuation.   We have a like story
as to New Jersey.[125]   There are no such full statements
available from other jurisdictions as Washburn gives for
Massachusetts.   But forty-eight lawyers are listed in the
most complete general list available.[126]   The Revolution
left a huge gap in what had become a great body of lawyers.

124.   Ibid. 201.

125.   Warren, History of the American Bar, 114.

126.   2 Sabine, Biographical Sketches of Loyalists of the American Revolution (1864).

VII.

Bar Organization in the Formative Era

*

VII.

Bar Organization in the Formative Era

1. General Survey of Professional Organization from the Revolution to the American Bar Association. Both for American law and legal institutions and for the legal profession in America, the formative era is the period from the Revolution to the Civil War. As has been seen the reception of the common law and reshaping it to a law of America and the development of a legal profession were well begun at the time of the Revolution. After the Revolution a reaction set in. There were many reasons for this. One was economic conditions which gave rise to widespread dissatisfaction with law and distrust of lawyers. Another was political conditions which gave rise to hostility toward English law and lawyers trained in the common law. A third was social conditions which gave rise to disbelief in professions and tended to bring about deprofessionalizing of all callings. Thirdly, geographical conditions gave rise to an extreme decentralizing of the administration of justice and so of the bar. These reasons were decisive in the formative era of the profession in this country.

At the time of the Revolution the old prejudice against lawyers had all but worn away. Twenty-five of

the fifty-six signers of the Declaration of Independence
were lawyers and so were thirty-one of the fifty-five members of the Constitutional Convention. Indeed, five of the
latter had studied law in England. But these men were
almost entirely of the generation which had come to the
bar under the colonial regime. Unhappily, a large number
of the older and stronger lawyers were loyalists and left
the country or ceased to practice.[1] Thus one result of the
Revolution was to leave or put the practice of law chiefly
in the hands of lawyers of a lower type and of less ability
and training. Except in a few centers of legal culture,
the bulk of the profession came to be made up of men who
had come from the Revolutionary armies with many bitter
feelings and but scanty knowledge of the law.[2] Alexander Hamilton's preparation for the bar was three months'
reading.[3] His less gifted contemporaries at the bar, who
came before the courts with the same hasty preparation,
could not have been expected to have much acquaintance
with the principles and doctrines of the common law nor
with the traditional ethics of the profession, Moreover,
the judges in many jurisdictions were often little better

1. Maryland lost two of her strongest lawyers, including Daniel Dulany,
Jr. It is claimed that at least one hundred and thirty of the loyalists
who left the country listed by Sabine were lawyers, though only forty-
eight are expressly stated to have been such. Warren, History of the
American Bar, 213.

2. Kent, Memoirs of James Kent, 31, 284–290.

3. Lodge, Alexander Hamilton, 289–290.

prepared.[4] Naturally courts for a time resented any serious investigation of English law books and frequently sought to palliate their lack of information by a show of patriotism.

After the Revolution a deep and widespread economic depression set in. Business had been wholly deranged. The ports had been closed and the British Navigation Acts cut off the once profitable West Indian trade. Public debts were enormous and required ruinous taxation. Those who had property were property poor. Those who had set up enterprises were unable to pay their debts. The paper money of the government was worthless. The Tories were reclaiming their property under the treaty of peace and English creditors were seeking to recover the debts due them in spite of confiscatory legislation. Those were the days of strict foreclosures and imprisonment for debt. The chief law business was collection of debts and recovery of property held under confiscatory laws. Thus the

4. David Brearley was appointed Chief Justice of New Jersey in 1779 while he was a Lieutenant Colonel in the Continental Army. Isaac Smith, appointed Justice of the same Court in 1777 was not a lawyer, nor was Samuel Tucker, who sat in the same court. Whitehead, The Supreme Court of New Jersey, 3 Green Bag, 401, 402, 404, 405. Of the three Justices of the Superior Court of New Hampshire after independence, one was a theologian and another a physician. Corning, The Highest Courts of New Hampshire, 2 Green Bag, 469, 470. Charles Brayton, Judge of the highest court of Rhode Island, 1814–1818, was a blacksmith, and Isaac Wilbour, a farmer, was Chief Justice of that state from 1819 to 1826. Edwards, The Supreme Court of Rhode Island, 2 Green Bag, 525, 532, 533. The first Chief Justice of North Carolina was admitted to the bar in 1788 before he was twenty years old. Clark, The Supreme Court of North Carolina, 4 Green Bag, 457, 461.

lawyers were largely debt collectors, a type that has never been of the best. While almost every one else was perforce idle, the lawyers were busy, and they had a monopoly of practice in the courts and would do nothing without a retainer. In consequence there was some radical legislation which undid much of the best which had been achieved in the eighteenth century, and little that was good was put in its place. For a generation after the Revolution law and lawyers labored under the ill effects of this period of depression.[5]

Political conditions after the Revolution had a like influence. Naturally the public was very hostile to England and it was impossible for the English law to escape the odium of its English origin. The books are full of illustrations of the hostility toward English law at the end of the eighteenth and in the earlier years of the nineteenth century.[6] Pennsylvania,[7] New Jersey,[8] and Ken-

---

5. This is well brought out in Warren, History of the American Bar, 214–217.

6. See, e. g., the argument of Mr. Sampson on the motion to quash the indictment in The Journeymen Cordwainers' Case, Yates, Select Cases (N.Y.) 111, 147–156 (1809). During the attempt to impeach the judges of the Supreme Court of Pennsylvania in 1803 "one of the staple theories of those who opposed the judges was 'the hated and exploded English common law'." Wister, The Supreme Court of Pennsylvania, 3 Green Bag, 58, 68. John Dudley, who sat in the Superior Court of New Hampshire, used to say: "They would govern us by the common law of England. Common sense is a much safer guide. . . . It is our duty to do justice between the parties, not by any quirks of the law out of Coke and

---

7. See page 181.
8. See page 181.

tucky,[9] legislated against citation of English decisions, and there was a rule of court against such citations in New Hampshire.[10] It is significant that almost nothing of the decided cases of the time in most of the states was thought worthwhile to report and that Kent, Marshall, and Story and the great judges who presently came upon the bench found themselves without help or hindrance from reported decisions of their predecessors.[11] This period of distrust of the common law was prolonged by the rise of Jeffersonian democracy at the beginning of the nineteenth century. That large and influential party not only heartily detested things English, but looked more than favorably upon things French. There was agitation for an American code on French lines and a temporary cult of French law books.[12] In the end nothing came of this so far as it affected reception of the common law. But the development of a legal profession was held back.

Blackstone—books that I never read and never will." Corning, The Highest Courts of Law in New Hampshire, 2 Green Bag, 469, 470. ,

7. Act of March 19, 1810, P.L. 136, repealed in 1836, Act of March 29, 1836, P.L. 224.

8. Act of June 13, 1799, sec. 7, Patterson, Laws of New Jersey, 436.

9. Act of February 12, 1808, Acts of Kentucky, 1807, p. 23. See preface to 1 Litt. (1823).

10. Corning, The Highest Courts of Law in New Hampshire, 2 Green Bag, 469, 470.

11. Kent, Memoirs of James Kent, 112–113.

12. See Pound, The Influence of French Law in America, 3 Illinois Law Review, 354, 354–356, 361–362 (1909).

Social conditions played a part also. The idea of a profession was repugnant to the Jeffersonian era. The feeling was strong that all callings should be on the same footing, the footing of a business, a money-making calling. To dignify any one calling by styling it a profession seemed undemocratic and un-American. Distrust of things English, pioneer distrust of specialists, for versatality is a characteristic article of the pioneer's creed, and what we must pronounce false ideas of democracy, led to general rejection of the common-law idea of an organized, responsible, self-governing profession. Some states threw the practice of law open to non-lawyers, with bad effects long manifest in our legal procedure.[13] All states made admission easy with a minimum of qualification. Also, as has been said, the lower branch of the profession in England was made the model for an undifferentiated body of general practitioners. No doubt this was inevitable. If for no other reason, the extreme and strict differentiation which had grown up in England was too expensive to be adopted in the new world. But putting the whole on the basis of the unorganized branch, as it then was, of the profession in England, with no tradition of responsibility for the conduct of its members, called the more for provision for responsible organization. The attorney con-

13. E.g., Mass. Act of March 6, 1790, 1 Laws of Massachusetts 1780–1807, 493.

ducts something very like a business, but ought to carry it on in the spirit of a profession. The advocate certainly does not conduct a business. There is danger to professional ideals and to the spirit of practice of a profession as a public service in the legal department of a great public utility or industrial enterprise or legal staff of an administrative agency or even the great law office in a metropolitan city where there is temptation to operate as a business organization in which the advocates are simply employees.

Geographical conditions and conditions of travel completed the process of decentralization and deprofessionalization. In a country of long distances and in a time of slow communication and expensive travel it was a prime necessity to bring the administration of justice to every man's door. The general tendency was to set up independent courts of general jurisdiction in every locality and to give to each local court its own local unorganized bar. Every member of a local bar, after a certain number of years, was taken to be competent to practice in the highest court on application. The system of distinct local bars for each local court, with no more than a nominal organization, as cities grew large was subjected more and more to deprofessionalizing influences which the professional tradition inherited from England could only feebly counteract.

[183]

As to the law, the formative era is one of upbuilding. As to the profession it is one of a vain struggle to maintain what had been achieved at the time of the Revolution.

At first, the influence of the strong bar in many centers on the eve of the Revolution and of those trained in the offices of the lawyers of that era kept up a high level in spite of the general letting down of the bars as to education and admission to practice. Also for a time the institution of the circuit bar, going about with the Circuit Judge from one county seat to another, in constant contact in court and during term time, had a good effect in maintaining standards of what is done and what is not done and in keeping alive a tradition of professional ethics.[14] But with the rise of metropolitan urban centers and the increasing importance of client-caretaking, the circuit bars substantially disappeared in the latter part of the nineteenth century. By that time a new, unofficial but practical differentiation of the profession was growing up, a most unfortunate one, into (1) habitual client-caretakers, (2) habitual defendant's lawyers, (3) habitual plaintiff's lawyers, and (4) habitual practitioners in criminal cases, usually ranking in the large cities about in that order. The

---

14. Biographies and Reminiscences of the time before the Civil War are full of accounts of the circuits. See, e.g., Caton, Early Bench and Bar of Illinois, chap. 7; Taylor, Bench and Bar of Indiana, 127-148; Willis, History of the Law, the Courts, and the Lawyers of Maine, chap. 8; Mann, Bench and Bar of Saratoga County (N.Y.) 269-270 (1876).

effect on practice in the courts, especially in criminal cases was bad. Discipline by the courts was invoked only in rare and extreme cases. Effective discipline by bar associations was in the future. Loose and even bad forensic practices came to obtain, especially in the larger cities, with no real checks upon them. Economic conditions turned the leaders of the profession more and more away from the courts. Neither the judges nor the professional opinion of an unorganized bar were equal to maintaining the standards required for an effective administration of justice by court aided by counsel.

There is another side to the picture. The period from the Revolution to the Civil War is in a sense the golden age of American law.[15] The creative legal achievements of that period will compare favorably with those of any period of growth and adjustment in legal history. In seventy-five years at most, the English seventeenth-century legal materials were made over into a common law for America, which became controlling for every state but one and has largely affected the law in that state. This was the work of great judges and great lawyers practicing before them, for there was a high type at the upper level of the profession throughout this period. Of ten outstanding names in the judicial history of the United States, six,

15. I have discussed this at length in The Formative Era of American Law (1938).

James Kent,[16] John Marshall,[17] Joseph Story,[18] Lemuel Shaw,[19] John Bannister Gibson,[20] and Thomas Ruffin,[21] belong to this formative era. Five of these six were college graduates and two studied under great lawyers of the period before the Revolution.

Nine great lawyers who practiced in this era deserve mention also: Luther Martin[22] (1748–1826) acknowledged leader of the American bar for two generations; William Pinkney[23] (1764–1822); William Wirt[24] (1772–1834); Jeremiah Mason[25] (1768–1848); Daniel Webster[26] (1782–1852) counsel in many of the great cases that made American constitutional law; Rufus Choate[27] (1799–1859) by general consent the greatest advocate that has been at the bar in this country; James Louis Peti-

16. William Kent, Memoirs and Letters of James Kent (1898).

17. Beveridge, Life of John Marshall, 4 vols. (1916–1919).

18. W. W. Story, Life and Letters of Joseph Story, 2 vols. (1851).

19. Chase, Lemuel Shaw, Chief Justice of the Supreme Judicial Court of Massachusetts (1918).

20. Porter, Memoirs of John Bannister Gibson (1890).

21. Graham, Life and Character of the Honorable Thomas Ruffin, Late Chief Justice of North Carolina (1871).

22. Didier, Luther Martin, 3 Green Bag, 149 (1891).

23. Pinkney, Life of William Pinkney by his Nephew (1853).

24. Kennedy, Memoirs of William Wirt, 2 vols. (1849).

25. Hillard, Memoirs and Correspondence of Jeremiah Mason (1872).

26. Fuess, Daniel Webster (1930).

27. Brown, Life of Rufus Choate, 2 ed. (1870).

gru [28] (1789–1863); Horace Binney [29] (1780–1875); and Reverdy Johnson [30] (1790–1876). All of these were born before 1800 and were at the height of their careers before the Civil War. Seven of the nine great lawyers were college graduates and all were trained in the offices of lawyers who had their training in the great era of the colonial bar on the eve of the Revolution. Thus these great lawyers handed down a great tradition. They were the product of that tradition, not of the system or want of system that grew up from the end of the eighteenth century.

2. **Organized Bars and Bar Meetings.** The régime of bar meetings, meetings of the whole bar of a court, which obtained in colonial New England survived the Revolution. Admission to its bar continued to be in the hands of each court and the bar of the court had come to think of itself as a unit and through its recommendations, and its rules by which those recommendations were governed, prescribed the educational qualifications and professional training of candidates for admission. Its rules prescribed how many students a member could have at one time, so as to insure real instruction, and required good character in those who could be taken in as students. [31] It made recom-

---

28. Carson, Life, Letters, and Speeches of James Louis Petigru (1920).

29. C. C. Binney, Life of Horace Binney (1903).

30. 1 Sams and Riley, The Bench and Bar of Maryland, 330–337 (1901).

31. Warren, History of the American Bar, 196–201.

mendations as to rules of practice. It sought to uphold the ethics of the profession.[32]

All this is brought out fully in the Bar Book of Suffolk County (1770–1805).[33] In 1836 the Bar of Suffolk County (Boston) was dissolved and a bar association took its place.[34]

Maine, which until 1820 was part of Massachusetts, continued control of education, training and admission to practice, recommendations as to rules of court, and professional ethics and discipline as in colonial Massachusetts. This is shown in detail in The Old Bar Record Book, found among the effects of the late Samuel Titcomb, Esq., of Augusta, Maine, and presented by his widow to the Supreme Judicial Court of Maine on Tuesday, May 8th, 1951.[35] The book begins with a record of "a barr meeting of the gentlemen usually practicing in the District of Maine, at Spring's Tavern at Biddeford, on the fifteenth day of October, anno domini 1789." [36] It was voted that

32. Ibid. 209.

33. As to this see ibid. 196–200.

34. See, infra, under 3.

35. Through the courtesy of Hon. Harold H. Murchie, Chief Justice of Maine, I was allowed to have a copy made of this book of 119 pages and two loose leaves, giving a list of "Lawyers Practicing in the District of Maine from 1789 to 1829–40 yrs." The list ends with two admitted in 1823. I have used the copy which has been given to the library of the Harvard Law School.

36. Old Bar Record Book, 1.

(1) "The gentlemen of the Barr usually practicing in the District of Maine form themselves into a Society for the purpose of conforming their practice in Court & the admission of students to that of the Gentlemen in the other parts of the Commonwealth of Massachusetts. . . . 4thly, that the Secretary be directed to procure from the several Secretaries of the Bar in the Counties of Suffolk and Essex a copy of the rules & proceedings of the Barr in their several counties to be laid before the Bar in the District of Maine. 5thly, That such rules as shall be adopted by the Barr of the District of Maine, shall be fairly transferred into the said District, & by every attorney hereafter admitted within the same, at the time of their admission" (the rest of the page is illegible).[37]

The "society" thus formed seems very like a bar association. But it was fundamentally different in that it was formed by and of the whole body of practitioners, those who were thereafter admitted became members as members of the bar and its rules were binding upon all who practiced in the District by their membership in the bar. This was brought out at the very beginning. At a meeting held in Portland on the 27th of October, 1789, it was voted: "That George Thatcher, Esq. be requested to wait on Mr. Salmon Chase, a person lately removed from the State of New Hampshire to this place, and opened an

37. Ibid. 1–3.

office here without having produced a certificate of his regular admission as an attorney at the Court of Common Pleas, and acquaint him with the Rules and Regulations of the Bar of this Commonwealth, and that the Bar expect a strict compliance therewith on his part before they shall consider him as a member of the Bar." Mr. Chase asked a reasonable time "to procure the proper evidence that he had studied the usual time in the State of New Hampshire & had been regularly admitted an attorney at the Court of Common Pleas in that State" and said that when he had procured that evidence he would "then request of this Bar an admission according to the rules and regulations thereof & the Laws of the Commonwealth." [38]

There are records of refusing to recommend candidates for admission to practice before the court of Common Pleas,[39] of a vote that to qualify a person to be admitted as a student he must have a university education or the equivalent,[40] of rules as to length of study,[41] rules as to requiring continuous full time study.[42] There are nu-

---

38. Ibid. 5–7. Mr. Chase's name appears among those present at a bar meeting in York in 1796, ibid. 32, and on the first loose leaf list of practitioners as admitted in 1795.

39. Old Record Book, 11, 13, 40.

40. Ibid. 13.

41. Ibid. 17, 20.

42. Ibid. 21, 28.

merous records of consent to taking students into offices and of recommendations for admission to practice.[43] At a meeting in 1800 it was voted that a secretary be chosen in each county who was to communicate to each other secretary all rules and regulations adopted at any meeting and providing what should be done in case of "a temporary diversity of rules in unessential points," but the rest of the entry is illegible.[44] This seems to mark a time of separate bar meetings in the different counties. Up to this time meetings had been held at different places: one at Biddeford, nine at Portland, eight at Pownalborough, two at Hallowell, one at York, one at New Gloucester, two at Waldoborough, two at Augusta, and one at Topsham. From now on (1800) the meetings are held at Augusta and are called meetings of the bar of the county of Kennebec until 1811 [45] after which the phrase is "meeting of the members of the Kennebec Bar." The significance of this will appear in connection with the Cumberland Bar Association later.

A number of rules with respect to professional ethics deserve notice. One was intended to prevent using students as runners. No member of the bar was to allow any student to receive or appropriate any part of the fees or

43. Ibid. 16, 17, 18, 19, 29, 31, 32, 33, 36, 42, 44.
44. Ibid. 54.
45. Ibid. 71.

bills of costs for business done in the offices as perquisites. But the student might be paid a gross sum, not dependent on or connected with the work of the office for work done.[46] Also no member of the bar. was to permit any person not qualified under the rules to do the work of an attorney in his office and in his name or under his countenance.[47]

At the August Term, 1827, of the Court of Common Pleas, the bar "proceeded to consider the Bar Rules agreed upon and recommended for adoption by a convention of delegates from all the Bars in this State (two excepted) holden in Portland on the first day of February, 1827." It was voted to communicate adoption of the rules to the other bars in the state.[48] The record comes to an abrupt end with a short notice of a meeting on April 14, 1829.[49] According to Hill's list, there was a Kennebec County Bar Association, claiming to date from 1841, in existence in 1887.[50]

46. Ibid. 88.

47. Ibid. 90.

48. Ibid. 111. The rules adopted by the convention appear on pages 112 to 115. But only a small part of page 115 is legible. The rules so far as they appear have to do with education and qualifications for admission to practice.

49. Ibid. 119.

50. 5 Rep.Ga.Bar Ass'n, 51, 89 (1889).

Claim has been made for the Cumberland Bar Association, incorporated in 1917 [51] that it is the successor of a bar association said to have been in existence in Cumberland County, Maine (Portland) since 1790. The great fire at Portland in 1866 probably destroyed the older records of the Association and those that may have been replaced from the library of Simon Greenleaf were destroyed in the burning of the county building in 1909. The present association has records from 1866 (after the great fire). But there is a statement in the History of Cumberland County that there was there as early as 1790 an association of members of the bar which had formulated bar rules as bar meetings were doing at that time, in Massachusetts.[52] I am satisfied, however, that this refers to the Bar of the District of Maine above described. Its first recorded meeting, in which an organization was effected, was at Biddeford in 1789. But its second meeting was at Portland the same year and it met nine times at Portland between 1789 and 1800.[53] What seems conclusive is that the History of Cumberland County names Samuel C. Johonnot and Salmon Chase as members of the Cumberland Bar in 1789. The Old Record Book shows Samuel C.

---

51. Private and Special Laws of Maine, 1917, chap. 30.

52. W. W. Clayton, History of Cumberland County, Maine, chap. 16, p. 84 (1880).

53. *Ante*, note 35; Old Record Book, 48.

Johonnot as present at the second meeting [54] and regularly at meetings thereafter, and we have seen how at this second meeting Salmon Chase's admission was taken up.[55] It is clear that about 1800 the county bars began to act separately and hence the Cumberland County Bar was to that extent a successor of the old Bar of the District of Maine. We next hear of the Cumberland County Bar in 1829, the year with which the Old Record Book comes to an end, in a pamphlet "Rules and Regulations of the Bar in the County of Cumberland adopted March 13, 1829," of which there is a photostat reproduction in the library of the Harvard Law School. Article 8, sections 1 and 2 of this pamphlet are so like rules 2 and 3 adopted by the convention of delegates of the county bars in 1827 [56] that the pamphlet of 1829 seems almost certainly a Cumberland County version of those rules. But the manuscript of the Old Record Book is illegible and deficient as to most of them. The succession from 1789 to 1829 is pretty well established. Thus far we have been dealing with the Bar of Cumberland County, in accordance with the old New England system of Bar Meetings. In 1864 the Cumberland Bar Association published a pamphlet, "Rules and Regulations of the Cumberland Bar Association" of which there is a photostat reproduction in the library of the

54. Ibid. 4.
55. *Ante*, note 37.
56. Old Record Book, 113–114.

Harvard Law School. This pamphlet recites: "That it appears by the records that the Association formed in 1805 by the then practitioners in the County of Cumberland was duly preserved and maintained until the year 1835—since which time under the hostile system of legislation that has prevailed in this State, the members appear to have yielded in despair to the spirit of reckless innovation upon old and well established principles, and the organization (formed by illustrious predecessors) to have fallen into decay, leaving no record even of its dissolution." A reorganization of the Bar is then recited showing organization of The Cumberland Bar Association on March 5, 1864.[57] The "spirit of reckless innovation" is so far yielded to that a Bar Association has replaced the Bar and it is provided how members of the Bar may become members of the Association "with the consent and approval of the general committee." This is clearly the present association of which the records begin in 1866. The hiatus of almost a generation from 1835 to 1864 stands in the way of the claim to be the oldest of our bar associations.

There is said to have been a "bar association" formed in Essex County, Massachusetts, in 1770 [58] and we know that the Essex County Bar had adopted a rule as to the members taking students into their offices and as to the

57. Rules and Regulations of the Cumberland Bar Association, 1864, 1.
58. Warren, History of the American Bar, 87–88.

time of study as far back as 1768.[59]   In the sketch of the
history of the Essex Bar Association published by that
Association in 1900 we are told that the first Essex Bar
Association was formed in 1806.[60]   But the printed rules
of 1806 show that there was not a bar association but an
organized bar, comprising all the members of the bar.   The
title is: "Rules and Regulations of the Bar in the County
of Essex."   The first article begins: "There shall be two
stated meetings annually of the members of the bar." [61]
There are records of bar meetings in 1812, but how much
longer they were held is not known.   There is a printed
copy of rules under a new organization in 1831, but that
organization lasted only a few years.[62]   The record of the
organization of the present Essex Bar Association in 1856
is illuminating.   It is headed: A record of the proceedings
of the Essex Bar preliminary to the organization of the
Essex Bar Association."   The record recites a meeting
of the "Essex Bar" on two days and the adoption of a
"Constitution of the Essex Bar Association," and the first
article tells how members of the Bar of Essex County may
become members of the association.   The preamble states

59.   Ibid. 196–197.

60.   Memorials of the Essex Bar Association, iv (1900).

61.   Rules and Regulations of the Bar in the County of Essex. Agreed upon at March Term, 1806, art. 1. The original is in the Essex County Law
Library in Salem, Mass. I have used a photostat reproduction in the
library of the Harvard Law School.

62.   Memorials of the Essex Bar Association, iv.

as the purposes of the association: "To promote fraternal feeling, and ensure conformity to a high standard of professional duty, to establish a more uniform method of practice and to discountenance and prevent the abuse of legal process either by members of the bar or by unsuitable and unqualified persons." [63] It is significant that the bar meetings characteristic of the New England lawyers of the colonial era and earlier era of independence should be assumed by the lawyers at Salem in 1900 and by Mr. Warren in 1911 to have been bar associations or meetings of groups of local lawyers to form bar associations. So complete was the break of continuity in the period of decadence after the first third of the nineteenth century till the revival in the 1870s.

I have had access to a bound photostat copy of a manuscript of Bar Rules for the County of Franklin (Mass.) and record of meetings from 1812 to 1835. It begins with "a meeting of the Gentlemen of the Bar in the County of Franklin" on August 3, 1812. Not, it will be noticed, a meeting of certain members of the bar choosing to be organized, but meeting of *the* gentlemen of the bar—of the bar as a whole. The meeting voted at once that "the Bar Rules for the County of Hampshire be adopted for the government of the bar in this county, until a new code for

---

63. MS Record of the Proceedings of the Essex Bar, preliminary to the organization of the Essex Bar Association, 1856, pp. 1, 2, 5, 6.

that purpose shall be accepted by the bar." [64]   The rules later adopted (December 16, 1812) have the provisions as to students usual in bar rules in Massachusetts at the time, provide against connection in any way in professional practice with persons not admitted to the bar and in particular require a member of the bar to have "no partnership connection in business or participation in profits with any sheriff, deputy sheriff, broker or party creditor" nor "be concerned in purchases of securities and debts for the purpose of instituting suits thereon, nor advance money to creditors to induce them to commence suits against their debtors." [65]   The records of meetings to the end recite meetings of the bar, and follow the lines above indicated in the Bar Meetings elsewhere.

For a time the bar in the federal courts in the first circuit seem to have held bar meetings. Also, in Massachusetts at the time of the Revolution, rules of court provided for grades in the bar—attorneys, counsellors, barristers, and serjeants, [66] and in 1812 Judge Story, as Justice of the Supreme Court of the United States, sitting in the United States Circuit Court for New Hampshire ordered that "the honorable degree of serjeant at law" be

64. Franklin County Bar Rules, MS, p. 1.

65. Ibid. 5–9, 11–12.

66. Warren, History of the American Bar, 242. Barristers and Counsellors as well as attorneys were admitted at the first sitting of the United States Circuit Court for Connecticut in 1790. Ibid. 244.

conferred upon Jeremiah Smith and Jeremiah Mason and that of barrister at law upon Daniel Webster, then at the New Hampshire bar, and three others.[67] A rule of court providing for the calling of barristers by the Superior Court of Judicature was adopted in Massachusetts in 1781. In 1806 counsellors were to be called by the court instead.[68]

When the bar in New England lost substantial control of preliminary education, professional training and admission to practice the reason which had chiefly brought about the régime of bar meetings ceased. The power to constrain professional conduct went with the power to control admission. A responsible profession was no longer possible when an increasingly large proportion of the practitioners were out of the reach of the responsible organization. Hence bar meetings as a substantial institution came no longer to be held. But a remnant persisted and exists today as meetings of the bar as a whole, or at least in which any member of the bar, although not a member of any organized body of lawyers, may participate, on the occasion of the death of some eminent judge or lawyer. Such meetings have been held regularly by the bar of the Supreme Court of the United States to this day.[69] Dur-

---

67. Ibid. 243; Bell, The Bench and Bar of New Hampshire, 60 (1894).

68. Warren, History of the American Bar, 307–308. But after 1784 no barristers were called.

69. In 1822 on the death of William Pinkney, 7 Wheat. xix–xx; in 1830 on the death of Mr. Justice Washington, 3 Pet. ix. In these and all the

ing our formative era such meetings were held frequently by the bar of the Federal Circuit Courts.[70] As to the state courts, in 1849 on the death of Charles Chauncey, and in 1852 on the death of John Sergeant, meetings, said in the one case to be "of the members of the Bar of the city and county of Philadelphia," and in the other case to be of "the Bar of Philadelphia" were held at which memorials were adopted. In each case the memorials included a resolution that "with the leaves of the Supreme Court of Pennsylvania and of the Circuit Court of the United States they be inserted in the next volume of their printed decisions." The proceedings are headed: "Proceedings of the bar of

---

earlier cases we are told of "proceedings of the bar of the court." But today the sense of action by the bar as a whole has been lost. We now read of a "meeting of members of the bar." See the proceedings on the death of Mr. Justice Rutledge in 1951, 341 U.S. v.

70. In 1820 by the bar of the United States Circuit Court for the District of Kentucky on the occasion of the death of Mr. Justice Todd. Johnson, History of Franklin County Bar (Frankfort, Kentucky) 21–22 (1932). Said to have been a meeting of the bar of the court. In 1835 in the United States Circuit Court for the District of Ohio a member of the bar addressing the court said: "I am constituted the organ of a bar meeting held yesterday" to present resolutions on the death of Chief Justice Marshall. He moved that they be entered on the journals of the court. In responding Judge MacLean said: "The Court feels great satisfaction in directing the proceedings of the members of the bar shall be placed upon the Court's records." 1 MacLean, 355–356. Query—Did Judge MacLean mean to make a distinction between the bar and an unofficial and unorganized number of members of the bar? In the Circuit Court for the District of Maine, as might be expected, we read of "Proceedings of the Bar of the Circuit Court for the District of Maine" on the death of Joseph Story in 1845. 1 Woodbury & Minot, ix–xx. When Judge Ware died in 1873 the proceedings were reported as those of the Cumberland Bar Association, although in the federal court. 3 Ware, 357 (1874).

Philadelphia." [71]   The meetings were held in the Federal
Court room.   They were not meetings of the bar of the
United States Circuit Court, which would certainly not
expect them to be published in the Pennsylvania State Reports, nor of the Bar of the Supreme Court of Pennsylvania.   The Law Association of Philadelphia was the
local bar association at the time.   Mr. Wallace does not
seem to have been certain whether these were meetings of
the Philadelphia bar or of an unorganized body of members of the bars of the courts sitting in Philadelphia. [72]
After 1835 adoption of resolutions on the death of eminent
judges and lawyers seemed all that was left for a local
bar to do.

It will have been seen that bar meetings in their day
did what we now expect of Bar Associations, or, rather,
Bar Associations do now what Bar Meetings did and was
long left undone upon their decay.

3.   Bar Associations.   Warren tells us of a "State
Bar Association" in New Hampshire which "as early as
1788 and later in 1805 adopted elaborate" regulations for

---

71. 2 Wallace, Jr. xi–xxxi (1854). The address of Horace Binney on John
Sergeant is reprinted in The Law Association of Philadelphia Centennial
Book, 1902, 185, reciting a meeting of the bar of Philadelphia.

72. The proceedings or resolutions do not seem to have been published in
the Pennsylvania State Reports. In 1853 on the occasion of the death
of Elijah Paine, one of the judges of the Supreme Court of New York, the
Chief Justice of the Superior Court presided. The resolutions recite that
they are those of "the bar of New York." 2 Paine, x–xiii (1856).

the Bar.[73] What really happened, however, is shown by the Records of the Bar of the County of Grafton.[74] They begin with something that sounds very like organization of a State Bar Association: "At a meeting of the members of the Bar throughout the State of New Hampshire, on the third Wednesday of June, 1788 . . . voted that the Society will consider themselves as a corporation, and *bound by the votes and proceedings at any regular meeting of the Bar,* in the same manner as the individuals of any society regularly incorporated. Voted that this society be styled an Association of the Bar throughout the State of New Hampshire. Voted that the Gentlemen of the Bar in their respective counties, at their first meeting after these rules are adopted, form themselves into a county society." The record then goes on to show Bar Meetings of the Bar of Grafton County, exactly like and doing the same things as the Bar Meetings in Maine and Massachusetts, with which we have become familiar, from 1793 to 1805. Nothing further is said about the "Association of the Bar throughout the State of New Hampshire." The first meeting adjourned to meet at Concord on the first Wednesday of June 1790.[75] There is no record of any such

73. History of the American Bar, 200.

74. Grafton County Bar Records, Proceedings of the Grafton and Coos Counties Bar Association for 1891, 2 Grafton and Coos Counties Bar Association, 185.

75. Ibid. 187.

meeting. The rules adopted at the first meeting were evidently recommendations to the County Bars. At a "regular Bar Meeting" of the Bar of Grafton County at the May Term of the Superior Court, however, it was voted that General Regulations for the Gentlemen of the Bar in the State of New Hampshire, *"which had been laid before this Bar"* be adopted.[76] These regulations which follow the general lines we have seen heretofore, were "unanimously voted to be recommended to the Gentlemen of the Bar in the several counties in this state for their adoption and practice by delegates from four counties,"[77] exactly as we have seen elsewhere. If there had been the state association proposed in 1788 this convention of delegates of the county Bars would not have been necessary. There is no suggestion anywhere but of action by each local Bar as a whole. It should be noted, however, that from 1805 on the meetings are said to be meetings of the "Grafton County Society," as the County Bars were requested to be called in 1788. We saw the same use of the term "society" in the vote of the "gentlemen usually practicing in the District of Maine" in 1789.[78] After 1814 we read sometimes of regular meetings of the Grafton County Society, and sometimes of "regular Bar Meetings."[79]

76. Ibid. 201–202.

77. Ibid. 207.
78. *Supra*, note 35.
79. Grafton County Bar Records, 219, 228, 231, 232, 233, 234, 236, 238.

Sometimes it says "regular Bar Meeting of the Grafton County Society," [80] or simply "regular meeting." [81] Once it says "meeting of the members of the Bar." [82] From 1820 on the term is almost always "Bar Meeting." [83] There is nothing to show any difference in these meetings of the Bar of Grafton County from 1788 to 1838, when the record ends.

May we not say that the attempt in 1788 to set up an organization of the entire bar of New Hampshire was at any rate prophetic of what was to be achieved by the movement for the integrated bar in the third decade of the present century?

Mr. Warren tells us that the first Bar Association in Connecticut was formed in 1783. [84] But this was what we have seen already in Massachusetts from colonial times and in New Hampshire and Maine after the Revolution. It was the whole bar at Hartford holding Bar Meetings and adopting Bar Rules. [85]

In Vermont the régime of Bar Meetings and Bar Rules prevailed before 1787. [86]

---

80. Ibid. 220.
81. Ibid. 230, 234.
82. Ibid. 232, 237, 244.
83. Ibid. 238–262.
84. History of the American Bar, 200.
85. See Ibid. 322.
86. Ibid. 201.

Discussion as to which is the oldest of existing Bar Associations in the United States is futile. There are solutions of continuity in many cases of old organizations and changes of form and purpose in others. Often records have been lost and there is much as to which we have no assured information. But although the Philadelphia Bar Association cannot in a strict sense make out its claim to date as a Bar Association from 1802, since in the earlier part of its existence it was engaged in maintaining a library and in promoting social intercourse between bench and bar rather than in the activities which we must consider the characteristic marks of a Bar Association, yet it is at any rate the oldest continuously existing organization of lawyers in the United States and has long been an active Bar Association of the modern type. Philadelphia lawyers were pioneers in starting organized activity by an unofficial organization, and, at a time when the régime of organized local bars had developed in but a few states and could not spread nor in the end even maintain itself in New England where it had been strongest, and the Bar Association in New York had not survived to the Revolution, were steadfast in preserving continuity of organization during the long era of decadence. The Philadelphia Bar Association was quite justified in celebrating a hundred and fiftieth anniversary in 1952.

The history of this organization is set forth in detail in the address of Chief Justice Mitchell on the occasion

of the celebration of its centennial in 1902.[87] It begins
with the Law Library Company, a corporation with stock
fixed at $20 a share to be held by members of the Bar of
Pennsylvania. The articles of association were signed on
March 13, 1802, but incorporation was not complete till
May 13, when they were enrolled.[88] The articles were
signed by seventy-two lawyers "including all the prominent members of the bar of that day." [89] While this corporation was building up and maintaining a law library,
a movement began to improve legal education. In 1784
and again in 1798 there were societies of law students to
conduct moots. They were short lived but out of them
grew The Law Academy of Philadelphia (1821) an institution to supplement practical office work with moots
and lectures which still survives as a moot court society.[90]
A "Society for the Promotion of Legal Knowledge" incorporated in 1821 lost its charter.[91] But some time before 1821 a society including the leading lawyers of the
day was formed. It published Constitution and By-Laws
in 1821 under the name "The Associated Members of the

87. Historical Address by Hon. James T. Mitchell, Chief Justice of the
     Supreme Court of Pennsylvania, The Law Association of Philadelphia,
     Addresses Delivered March 13, 1902, and Papers Prepared or Republished
     to Commemorate the Centennial Celebration of the Law Association of
     Philadelphia, Pennsylvania (1906).

88. Ibid. 16–17.

89. Ibid. 20.

90. Reed, Training for the Public Profession of the Law, 432.

91. The Law Association of Philadelphia Centennial, 25–26.

Bar of Philadelphia Practicing in the Supreme Court of Pennsylvania." It provided censors who were "to give special attention to the practice of the bar and report on unprofessional conduct; were to suggest to the Association alterations or rules of practice which, if approved, might be presented to the proper court for adoption by rules; and "generally to aim at maintaining the purity of professional practice." [92] The Constitution was signed by sixty-seven members, nearly all the then principal members of the bar and largely the same as the membership of the Law Library Company at that time.[93] Thus the connection of the two organizations was very close. In 1821 negotiations for a union began and in 1827 the charter of the Law Library Company was amended and the new charter established The Law Association of Philadelphia.[94] The charter was again amended in 1880, the objects being stated as follows: (1) The general supervision of the conduct of members of the Bar, and of all persons connected officially with the administration of the law or in charge of the public records, and, in cases of any breach of duty on their part, the institution of such proceedings as may be lawful in respect thereto. (2) The improvement of the law and its administration; the protection of the Bar and of judicial tribunals, their officers and members from in-

92. Ibid. 29.
93. Ibid. 31.
94. Ibid. 32.

[207]

vasion of their rights; and the maintenance of their proper influence. (3) The keeping up of a Law Library." [95] In 1931 the name was changed to "The Philadelphia Bar Association." [96]

In 1835 lawyers in New York City attempted to form a "Legal Alliance," but the attempt failed.[97]

A letter to the secretary of the Detroit Bar Association brought an answer that the Association was formed in 1835 and has had a continuous existence since that time. It was said further: "The chief promoter of the Detroit Bar Association was the Honorable William Woodbridge; for the purpose of creating a bar library and disciplining any attorneys guilty of professional misconduct." As evidence of the date, 1835, there is a manuscript Record Book, 1835–1842, in the Detroit Public Library of which I have a photostat copy. It begins with an entry of a "Bar Meeting" on November 19, 1835, at which it was voted (1) To appoint a committee to investigate the conduct of a member of the bar; (2) to appoint a committee to consider the propriety of "a fee bill for professional services;" (3) to appoint a committee to consider the expediency of forming a law library for the use of the Bar and Court; (4) that a committee be appointed to report

95. Ibid. 430–431.

96. 126 The Legal Intelligencer (Philadelphia) 315.

97. Wickser, Bar Associations, 15 Cornell Law Quarterly, 390, 394, note 7.

upon the propriety of this Bar holding quarterly meetings for the transaction of business; (5) that the Hon. William Woodbridge, chairman of the meeting be invited to deliver a eulogy on Chief Justice Marshall and that a committee report resolutions on his death. "The Bar adjourned to meet again the first day of the next term of the Wayne Circuit Court." The next entry is of a "meeting of the Bar" on December 21, 1837, more than two years later. It was resolved that "in the opinion of the members of this Bar the infirm health of the Presiding Judge of the First Circuit of the State of Michigan is such as to disqualify him for the performance of his official duties" and that a committee be appointed and instructed to inform the chairman of the Select Committee of the Judiciary of the resolution. No report of the committees appointed at the first meeting are recorded. Next there is an entry of a "meeting of the Bar on August 5, 1839 at which a committee was appointed to investigate the professional conduct of two members of the bar who were partners, and there follows a record of a "meeting of the bar" on March 16, 1840 at which the committee to investigate the conduct of the partners reported covering pages 5 to 11 of the record book. It was voted to acquit the partners of misconduct. From then on there are short reports of meetings to arrange for a Bar Dinner in 1841, to vote resolutions on the death of Judges and members of the bar, to consider a communication from the Bar of Philadelphia as to a monument to Chief Justice Marshall, and to vote resolutions of regret at the resignation of Chancellor Farnsworth. The last entry, April, 1842, is of a "meeting of the Bar to adopt resolutions on the resignation of Chief Justice Fletcher." Evidently it ceased to be felt necessary to keep a record of such occasional Bar meetings for the only matters which the Bar had come to be able to deal with.[98]

What we have here is a record of Bar Meetings held under the pressure of charges of professional misconduct or inability of a judge to perform his judicial duties, at the time when the old type of Bar Meeting was coming to an end, tapering off into meetings upon the death or retirement of eminent judges. It is significant that the proposal for regular quarterly meetings came to nothing. This is very far from showing a Bar Association in the sense of today from 1835.

Meetings of the Bar of Suffolk County, Massachusetts (Boston) and Bar Rules, especially as to education

98. William Woodbridge studied law in the famous school of Tapping Reeve at Litchfield, Conn. He was a judge of the Territorial Supreme Court of Michigan, 1828–1832, Governor of Michigan in 1839, and United States Senator, 1841–1847. Except for presiding at the first Bar Meeting he is not recorded as present at any subsequent meeting. He is said to have been very energetic and his activities diverted to politics (delegate to the Constitutional Convention, 1835, State Senator, 1838–1839, and Governor, 1839) no doubt were wanting to bring about the permanent organization he proposed. 20 Dictionary of American Biography, 483.

and admission to practice, are known from 1761.[99] From 1770 to 1805 the proceedings of this Bar are recorded as we have seen in the case of other Bar Meetings in New England.[100] But these meetings seem to have been continued till 1836 when a committee appointed February 27 of that year made a report reciting, "That the revised Statutes by abolishing the ancient distinction between Counsellors and Attornies and by making essential changes in the terms of admission and practise require corresponding alterations in the Rules of the Bar." [101] The committee reported recommending, as the marginal note puts it, the "dissolution of the Bar of Suffolk" and formation of "an Association of Gentlemen of the legal profession to be called and known by the name of the 'Fraternity of the Suffolk Bar.'" It also recommended seven articles of association. Article 2 provided for membership: "The Fraternity shall consist of all such persons as have heretofore signed the Bar Rules and are Attorneys or Counsellors at Law usually practising in the courts of this county *who may choose to sign these articles* on or before the 1st October next." It is further to consist of "such other persons practising law in this county *as from time to time shall be*

99. Warren, History of the American Bar, 83–85, 87. Mr. Warren speaks of a Bar Association. But his authority is the Diary of John Adams.

100. Ibid. 146. Here Mr. Warren properly speaks of "Massachusetts County Bars" instead of Bar Associations. The rules as to education and professional training are well set forth pp. 196–200.

101. MS Record Book of Fraternity of the Suffolk Bar, 1.

elected members of the Fraternity in manner hereinafter prescribed and who shall subscribe these articles." Article 4, entitled "Objects of this Association" reads: "The object of the Fraternity is to cultivate a spirit of friendship, kindness and good will towards each other—to preserve the purity of the legal profession—to discountenance all abuse of legal process and all such practises as might bring odium or disgrace on the administration of the Law." The remaining articles have to do with fees, with expulsion from the Fraternity for "illegal, ungentleman-like, or unwarrantable practices" and for dues. They are signed by sixty-seven members.[102] The record shows a public dinner in 1837, an "annual meeting", an "annual dinner", a meeting called by the standing committee, and two meetings of the standing committee in 1838, an annual meeting which only elected officers in 1839, like annual meetings in 1840 and 1841, and end with a meeting to adopt resolutions on the retirement of Judge Davis, United States District Judge for the District of Massachusetts in 1841.[103]

It will have been seen that we have here a clear account of transition from an organized bar to an association of such members of the bar as choose to join in forming the association and such others as may be subsequently

102. Ibid. 2–14.
103. Ibid. 32.

elected. The purposes were those of the old Bar Meetings, except that the Bar had lost all control over education, professional training and admission to practice. Deprived of this and with no control over professional conduct of nonmembers it soon found itself with little to do but adopt resolutions on the retirement or death of judges and went out of existence.

A small pamphlet in the Massachusetts State Library, of which there is a photostat copy in the Library of the Harvard Law School, shows an attempt to form a State Bar Association in 1849. It is entitled "The Association of the Bar," and recites that at a meeting of members of the Bar from all parts of the State on January 4, 1849, "it was resolved that an association be formed and a committee was appointed to prepare a plan of organization to be reported at an adjourned meeting to be held on January 18." On that date the committee, consisting of twenty members, seven from Suffolk County, one from Essex, two from Middlesex, two from Worcester, and one each from Franklin, Hampshire, Hampden, Berkshire, Norfolk, Bristol, Plymouth, and Barnstable Counties, reported nine articles of association. The preamble recites the importance of maintaining a high standard of professional duty and character and of "distinguishing those who recognize and desire to sustain the true position of members of the Bar and exonerating them from all com-

[213]

munion in reputation with those who disgrace it," and the first article provides that: "The purpose of the Association, to which all its efforts and influence are to be directed, are declared to be the cultivation of social and friendly intercourse among its members, and the elevation of the standard of professional duty, education and character." Perhaps the most striking provision was one for a "Solicitor," whose duty it was to be to "receive all complaints in writing signed by any member or members of the Association and report them to the Executive Committee." If the Executive Committee directed a hearing he was to prepare and produce the evidence "and render such aid in the trial as ordinarily devolves upon a prosecuting officer." On January 18 the adjourned meeting, said to be a meeting of the "Bar of Massachusetts," considered the proposed articles of association and made two significant amendments. Article 3 had spoken of the "Bar in this State." These words were stricken out and the article was made to read, "persons admitted to practice in the courts of the Commonwealth." This giving up of the idea of an organized bar is characteristic of the transition to the era of decadence. The other amendment provided that where complaint was made of any misconduct within the provisions of the Revised Statutes the Solicitor was to represent it to the Court of the County where the attorney complained of resides in order that the Court, if it sees fit, may direct the necessary legal proceedings. This and an

[214]

amendment providing for signing of the complaint by a complainant instead of "by any member or members of the association," show a tendency to weaken discipline by imposing an invidious task on a complainant. It was voted that the Articles of Association with the amendments be laid upon the table and that the committee be requested to cause them to be printed and a copy forwarded to every member of the Bar in the Commonwealth with notice of a future meeting for final action upon the proposed constitution and organization of the Association. Accordingly the six-page pamphlet was printed dated February 5, 1849, notifying that the proposed meeting would be held in the Court House in Boston on February 22. But the times were not propitious for such an organization.

4. Law Library Associations. The Law Library Association of Philadelphia, 1802, which was the starting point of a bar association, has been described above. A like organization is the Social Law Library in Boston (1804) still existing, which might have merged with the Fraternity of the Suffolk Bar.[104] Another is the New York Law Institute, a membership corporation incorporated in 1930, but founded in 1828 "for literary purposes, the cultivation of legal science, the advancement of jurispru-

---

104. Report of the Committee of the Fraternity of the Suffolk Bar, Record Book of the Fraternity of the Suffolk Bar, 21, 23, 24.

dence, the providing of a seminary of learning in the law, and the formation of a law library." [105] It only developed the last of its five announced purposes, but "for many years served as the sole meeting grounds for the legal profession of New York, and its Junior Bar Group was particularly active in providing for instructive forms and lecture programs." [106] The proposal for a Bar Association in Detroit in 1835, as we have seen, involved providing a Bar Library.[107] But the project was not realized. In Massachusetts an Act of 1842 provided: "The counsellors and attorneys at law, duly admitted to practice in the Courts of this Commonwealth, resident in the several counties thereof, except Suffolk, are hereby constituted corporations for the purpose of holding and managing the law libraries belonging to said counties, by the name of the Law Library Association of the County in which it is formed." It was further provided that the by-laws to be adopted in each County should be approved by the Justices of the Court of Common Pleas, that within sixty days after the Statute took effect the clerks of the several courts should call the first meeting of the corporation in their respective counties

105. Charter of the New York Law Institute, chap. 48, Laws of 1830, sec. 1.

106. Blaustein, New York Bar Associations Prior to 1870, 125 New York Law Journal, no. 64.

107. *Supra*, note 98.

by posting notices in the Court House.[108] Accordingly
"the Counsellors and Attorneys at Law (in Berkshire
County) held their first meeting under the Act of March
3, 1842" and elected officers and appointed a committee to
draft by-laws. The by-laws were adopted at an adjourned
meeting on June 30, 1842, and the corporation has had a
continuous existence ever since.[109] Here, near the end of
the era, is a legislative recognition of the county Bar as
an entity. But no bar association grew out of it.

Another law library association of this era did grow
into a bar association. The records of the Wilkes-Barre
Law Association, a photostat copy of which is in the library of the Harvard Law School, was organized on June
18, 1850, as the Wilkes-Barre Law Association, the name
evidently suggested by the Philadelphia Law Association.
Neither the constitution, adopted at the organization meeting, nor the by-laws adopted at the semi-annual meeting on
August 9, 1852, make any statement as to the purposes
of the organization. But the minutes of the meetings,
fairly continuous but very sketchy, show nothing beyond
the maintenance of a law library and meeting place for
lawyers for a generation. The only suggestion of anything more is a provision in section 11 of the by-laws of
1852 that "each member is required to procure a green bag

108. Massachusetts Acts and Resolutions, 1842, chap. 94, secs. 1, 2.
109. Letter of Irving H. Gamwell, Esq. of Pittsfield, May 24, 1951.

of the common professional shape, and to use the same in his practice, in the professional manner as usual elsewhere, after the present term." From 1858 to 1860 there are only short notes of unimportant matters. In 1865 it was voted to remit the dues of members who had served in the Union Army. In 1866 a committee was named to promote legislation for establishing a sitting of the Supreme Court at Wilkes-Barre. This was renewed in 1868. Before this in 1865 it had been voted to apply for a charter, and it was granted one under the name of the Wilkes-Barre Law and Library Association in 1866.[110] For some years less than half of the stated meetings had a quorum present. But occasionally there were things done that are properly the work of a Bar Association—sending a committee to attend a conference of judges at Pittsburgh (1873), to consider holding courts at other places than the county seat (1874), to consider the time for filing exceptions (1874).[111] In other words, it was not until after 1870 that the organization began to function as a bar association. But it must be said that in its continuous functioning from 1850 it furnished a nucleus about which a true bar association could form gradually in the begin-

110. Pa. Act of April 11, 1866. See also Acts of 1887, P.L. 1460.

111. Woodruff, Lawyers of Olden Days, 40 Luzerne Legal Register Reports, 470, 471, 473–475, 476–477 (1949). Mr. Woodruff was secretary of the Luzerne Bar Association, which the Wilkes-Barre Law and Library Association used as an alternative name, until his death in December 1949.

nings of the era of bar associations in the last third of the nineteenth century.

Looking back over the period from Independence to the Civil War, we see in the end the disappearance of the organized local bar and the small beginnings of what were to become the Bar Association of a later generation.

*

VIII.
The Era of Decadence
1836-1870

VIII.

The Era of Decadence—1836–1870

**1. The Breakdown of Organization, Education
and Professional Training.** Mr. Brand has pointed out
a cycle from recognition at first that the legal profession as
a whole had problems, functions, and obligations tran-
scending those of the individual lawyer and groups of
lawyers, to gradual loss and finally all but giving up of
the professional idea, thence to gradual regaining of that
idea, and final achievement of it again in the integrated
state bar of today.[1] The high point at the beginning is
on the eve of the Revolution. The lowest point is immediately after the Civil War. The rise begins with the
present-day type of bar association in 1870 or certainly
in 1878, and the high point has been regaining since 1921
and is attained once more in the integrated bar in half of
the states.

It is significant to note the dates at which the bar meetings in New England came to an end: The Bar of the
District of Maine, 1829, but continued by the Bar of Ken-

---

1. Brand, Bar Organization and Judicial Administration, 34 Journal,
American Judicature Society, 38, 39 (1950).

nebec County till the end in 1841; The Bar of Franklin County, Massachusetts, in 1835; the Suffolk Bar (Massachusetts) dissolved in 1836; The Bar of Cumberland County, Maine, replaced by a selective Bar Association in 1836; The Bar of Grafton County, New Hampshire, Bar Meetings cease in 1838. The Bar of Essex County, Massachusetts, held on longer but the Bar Meetings cease in 1856. Also the abortive attempt to form a State Bar Association in Massachusetts in 1849 tells a story.

We are told that the Suffolk (Boston) Bar dissolved "because of the Revised Statutes making essential changes in the terms of admission to the Bar." [2] The record of the Bar Meetings at Concord, New Hampshire, gives the same reason. [3] Almost from the beginning there had been legis-

---

2. Record Book of the Fraternity of the Suffolk Bar, 1.

3. The Massachusetts statute reads: "Sect. 19. Any citizen of this Commonwealth, of the age of twenty one years, and of good moral character, who shall have devoted three years to the study of the law, in the office of some attorney, within this state, shall, on application to the supreme court, or court of common pleas, be admitted to practise as an attorney in any court of this Commonwealth, on complying with the other requisitions contained in this chapter [e.g., an oath to support the Constitution of the United States and of the Commonwealth and the usual attorney's oath].

"Sect. 20. Any person, having the other qualifications, required in the preceding section, but who shall not have studied the term therein prescribed, may, on the recommendation of any attorney within this Commonwealth, petition the supreme court, or court of common pleas, to be examined for admission as an attorney in said courts, whereupon the court shall assign some time and place for the examination, and if they shall thereupon be satisfied with his acquirements and qualifications, he shall be admitted, in like manner as if he had studied three full years."

lation authorizing litigants to be represented by attorneys in fact whom they specially appointed. But for a long time such legislation had little practical result. Litigants for obvious reasons preferred regularly admitted attorneys. The attack on the profession called for taking away the standing of the admitted attorney by admitting every one freely irrespective of education and professional training. The Michigan Constitutional Convention of 1850 voted, as a section in the article on the Judiciary: "Every person of the age of twenty-one years, of good moral character, shall have the right to practice in any court in this State." Although strongly resisted by a small minority, this proposed section was twice adopted by an overwhelming vote.[4] Ultimately the section was made to read: "Any suitor in any court of this state shall have the right to prosecute or defend, either by his own proper person or by

---

"Sect. 23. Every person, admitted to practise in any court, may practise in every other court, in the state, and there shall be no distinction of counsellors and attorneys.

"Sect. 24. Any person, who shall have been admitted an attorney or counsellor of the highest judicial court of any other state, of which he was an inhabitant, and shall afterwards become an inhabitant of this state, may be admitted to practise here, upon satisfactory evidence of his good moral character and his professional qualifications." Mass.Rev.Stats. 1836, chap. 88, sects. 19, 20, 23, 24. The New Hampshire statute reads: "Any citizen of the age of twenty one years, of good moral character, on application to the Superior Court, shall be admitted to practice as an attorney." New Hampshire, Rev.Stats.1842, chap. 177, sect. 2.

4. Report of Proceedings and Debates in the Convention to Revise the Constitution of the State of Michigan, 1850, 388, 395.

an attorney or agent of his choice."[5] In Indiana, the Constitutional Convention of 1850, in the address submitting the proposed constitution to the electors, called special attention, as a measure of law reform, to the following provision: "Every person of good moral character who is a voter is entitled to practice law in any of the courts of this state."[6] This provision has stood in the Constitution of Indiana, despite frequent attempts to amend or remove it, beginning in 1880.[7] But the courts have modified its operation by holding that practice of the law in that state is not an unqualified constitutional or natural right but that the courts may make reasonable rules and regulations for admission.[8] In the convention which adopted this provision there was a further proposal for a section prohibiting the use of "technical terms in Latin or in any other than the English language," in legislative acts. The member who introduced it said: "From the use of verbiage with which the law is encumbered and technical terms in Latin and other languages, it requires a lawyer to inter-

5. Ibid. 477.

6. 2 Debates and Proceedings of the Convention for the Revision of the Constitution of the State of Indiana, 1850, 2044. It became Art. 7, sect. 21 of the Constitution.

7. 2 Indiana Historical Collections, Constitution Making in Indiana (1916): 195–196 (1880), 248 (1885), 259 (1889), 281 (1891), 321 (1897), 325 (1899), 351 (1901), 357 (1903), 364 (1905), 368 (1907), 380 (1909), 529–530 (1913).

8. In re McDonald, 200 Ind. 424, 428, 164 N.E. 261, 262 (1928).

pret every enactment that is made by the legislature.
. . . Now then I want the kind of language made use
of that will put the meaning of these laws within the reach
of justices of the peace and private citizens." [9] In the
course of debate on this proposal one of the delegates said:
"I have been a lawyer for some years, and I have no hesi-
tation in telling gentlemen that I never studied Latin; and
I will tell you further that any man who studies Latin for
the purpose of making himself a lawyer, is a fool for his
pains." [10] The debates of the time are full of such pronouncements and give some understanding of the caliber
and attainments of the lawmakers who persisted in breaking down the organization, educational qualifications, and
professional training of the bar.

From the first third of the nineteenth century increasingly there was legislative breaking down of the requirements as to education and professional training of lawyers.
In 1800 a definite period of preparation for admission to
the bar was prescribed in fourteen of the nineteen states or
organized territories which then made up the Union. In
1840 it was required in but eleven out of thirty jurisdictions. In 1860 it had come to be required in only nine of

---

9. 2 Debates and Proceedings of the Convention for the Revision of the
Constitution of the State of Indiana, 1850, 1128. The resolution propos-
ing this provision was adopted by a vote of 109 to 21, ibid. 1129, and later
voted to be incorporated in the draft submitted, ibid. 1196–1197.

10. Ibid. 1136.

the then thirty-nine jurisdictions. The number of juris-dictions preserving the requirement had shrunk from fourteen to nine. The proportion of those requiring it had shrunk from three fourths of the whole number to less than one fourth. North Carolina was the only south-ern state and Ohio the only state or territory west of the Alleghenies to retain the requirement even nominally.[11] Reed is no doubt right in saying that attacks on the re-quirement of a prescribed period of preparation for the practice of law "represented a general attitude toward governmental problems rather than peculiar hostility to lawyers as such. The essentially governmental privilege of practicing law is thrown more widely open for the same reason that qualifications for governmental office were reduced. The movement was grounded in the politi-cal philosophy of an insurgent democracy, which was fighting its way into control of our governmental machin-ery, and was less concerned with making sure that priv-ileges bestowed by the state should be well bestowed than with guarding against their again becoming a monopoly of a favored class in the community." [12]

That thinking of this sort was behind much of it is brought out in the remarks of one of the judges of the

11. The details are in Reed, Training for the Public Profession of the Law, 86–87. I have verified them and can vouch for their accuracy.

12. Ibid. 85–86.

Supreme Court of Indiana, in passing upon eligibility for admission to the bar long afterward: "Whatever the objections of the common law of England, there is a law higher in this country, and better suited to the rights and liberties of American citizens, that law which accords to every citizen the natural right to gain a livelihood by intelligence, honesty, and industry in the arts, the sciences, the professions, or other vocations." [13]

Along with the legislation in many states to do away entirely with the requirement of a definite period of professional training there went a tendency to reduce the length and quality of professional training in the states which still retained it. The requirement of preliminary general education, which the New England Bar Meetings had insisted upon, was abandoned. Moreover, the administrative regulations, needed for enforcement of such requirements as survived were relaxed. Formal apprenticeship, such as the New England Bar Rules had demanded, gave way to what was called "reading law" in the office of a practitioner. In Ohio the only requirement was an attorney's certificate that the applicant had "regularly and attentively studied law." The study was not required

13. Hackney, J., in In re Petition of Leach, 134 Ind. 665, 668, 34 N.E. 641. 642 (1893). How differently men think today is shown by the language of the same court a generation later: ". . . the practice of the law in this State is not an unqualified constitutional or natural right. It should be termed a privilege." Per Curiam, in In re McDonald, 200 Ind. 424, 428, 164 N.E. 261, 262 (1928).

to have been under the attorney's personal direction, as had been the rule in the Territory by adoption from the old Bar Rules. Also whereas the old Bar Rules required notice to the Bar when a student was taken into an office, so that there was some assurance of his term of study, in 1860 Pennsylvania was the only state which required students of law to register at the beginning of their period of study.[14] It is well known that such rules as there were lacked vigorous administration anywhere. Good natured lawyers gave certificates of "regular and attentive study" liberally to the asker with little or no inquiry.

In the movement to facilitate admission to the bar under the theory of a natural right to pursue a lawful calling, an idea which made much trouble in our constitutional law even in the present century [15] there was often mandatory legislation to prevent the courts from using their examining power to defeat the policy of easy admission. Massachusetts in 1836 provided that admission might be had by "taking one's chance" with the courts without previous training, but if an applicant was of good moral character and had read law for three years in an attorney's office the courts were obliged to admit him.[16]

---

14. Reed, Training for the Public Profession of the Law, 87.

15. Pound, Liberty of Contract, 18 Yale Law Journal, 454, 470 (1909).

16. Reed, Training for the Public Profession of the Law, 87.

Later came legislation abolishing all educational requirements. After 1842 every citizen over twenty-one years of age in New Hampshire,[17] every citizen of Maine after 1843,[18] every resident of Wisconsin after 1849,[19] every voter in Indiana after 1851, might practice law without more.[20] New Hampshire, Maine, and Wisconsin later repealed this legislation. But Indiana still retains the constitutional provision shorn of effect.

Not only did legislation of this era seek to open practice of the law to all, but there was strong objection to an organized Bar. A writer in 1834 spoke of the "secret trade union of the Bar."[21] The proponent of a proposition to the Michigan Constitution Convention in 1850, to allow any person of age and good moral character to practice in any of the courts, said in the course of debate: "This profession of the law is the only class that has the privilege of making their own rules—of saying who shall or who shall not practice in their courts. The practice of medicine, that is fully as important, is not subject to the

---

17. N.H.Rev.Stats.1842, chap. 177, sect. 2.

18. Maine, Acts and Resolves of 1843, chap. 12.

19. Wisconsin, Laws of 1849, chap. 152.

20. Const.Ind.1851, Art. 7, sect. 21. In Kentucky in 1847 there was a proposal of a constitutional amendment against lawyers as a profession. Wickser, Bar Associations, 15 Cornell Law Quarterly, 390, 393 (1930).

21. Frederick Robinson, A Program for Labor (1834) in Social Theories of Jacksonian Democracy, edited by Blau, 330, 339 (1947).

restriction; the practice of divinity is not so restricted. Any man may give either medicine or gospel and collect his dues. I have no objection to this; I think that each should stand upon his own merits. I want the lawyers to stand upon the same platform with the priests and the doctors. A man's property is no better than his life or his soul. We allow a man to tamper with soul and body, but not with property." [22] In 1838, a writer in the Southern Literary Messenger denounced Bar Associations saying that they "were wrong in principle, betray competition, delay professional freedom, degrade the bar." [23] Thus in this era of decadence it was assumed for the first time in Anglo-American law that the bar was not to be regarded as a profession, with requirements for admission such as public policy may prescribe, but as a mere private, money-making occupation. The harm which this deprofessionalizing of the practice of law did to the law, to legal procedure, to the ethics of practice and to forensic conduct has outlived the era in which it took place and still presents problems to the promoters of more effective administration of justice.

2. Causes of the Movement for Deprofessionalizing Practice of Law. Many things operated from

22. Report of the Proceedings and Debates in the Convention to Revise the Constitution of the State of Michigan, 1850, 812.

23. Quoted by Wickser, Bar Associations, 15 Cornell Law Quarterly, 390, 393 (1930).

the fourth decade of the nineteenth century to the Civil War to promote antagonism to an organized profession, faith in a natural right of every man to pursue any calling of his choice, distrust of specialization and requirements of special training for particular callings, and fear that recognition of professions might create a privileged class not open equally to all citizens.

For one thing the attacks upon lawyers and organized bars, which grew strong in the depression following the Revolution, continued into the succeeding decades and furnished abundant material for those who came to oppose an organized profession on other grounds. In the Maine legislature [24] in 1790 a speaker "objected to the association of members of the bar and the formation of bar rules" as "illegal and unwarrantable usurpation." [25] Town meetings in Massachusetts during the period of depression called for abolition of "the order of lawyers." [26] For a generation after the Revolution there was constant agitation in many states to abolish the system of call to the bar by the courts or by Bar Meetings.[27] In particular the writings of Benjamin Austin, an Anti-Federalist politician, of Boston, whose pamphlets had wide influence, at-

24. Although Maine was part of Massachusetts till 1820 it had a separate legislature.
25. W. W. Clayton, History of Cumberland County, 84 (Everts and Peck, 1880).
26. Warren, History of the American Bar, 214–215.
27. Ibid. 218.

[233]

tacked "the order of lawyers." "The question is," he wrote, "whether we will have this order so far established in this Commonwealth as to rule over us." Continuing he wrote: "The order is becoming continually more and more powerful. . . . There is danger of lawyers becoming powerful as a combined body. The people should be guarded against it as it might subvert every principle of law and establish a perfect aristocracy. . . . This order of men should be annihilated." [28] In 1803 Charles Jared Ingersoll of Philadelphia wrote: "Our State rulers threaten to lop away that excrescence on civilization, the Bar." [29] In Philadelphia William Duane, editor of the *Aurora*, the organ of Jefferson's party, was no less vigorous in his attacks upon the bar as a "privileged order or class." [30] McCall in 1838 tells us that the profession was still "regarded with distrust." [31] As it has been put, "The Bar was regarded as too 'aristocratic,' the law was deemed too 'feudal.' " [32]

In the next place, organization of the Bar had not taken a strong hold in some important states. Virginia

---

28. Observations on the Pernicious Practice of the Law, by Honestus (Benjamin Austin) as published occasionally in the Independent Chronicle in Boston in 1786 (1819) 11–12.

29. Meigs, Life of Charles Jared Ingersoll, 14.

30. See the long quotation in Warren, History of the American Bar, 220.

31. McCall, Discourse before the Law Academy of Philadelphia, September 5, 1838, 35.

32. Blaustein, New York Bar Associations Prior to 1870, 125 New York Law Journal, no. 64, 3 (1951).

and the Carolinas had no tradition of a state or local bar, in Virginia partly because of hostility of the planters to organizations and both in Virginia and South Carolina because the English trained barristers, who practiced without admission by the local courts, felt themselves members not of a local Bar but of the Bar of the Inns of Court where they had studied.

Third, account must be taken of the somewhat rapid admission of new states and consequent strengthened influence of the frontier and reinforcing the ideas of the extreme Jeffersonians, as we have seen them in the writings of Benjamin Austin and Duane, by those of frontier democracy. Ten new states were admitted between independence and 1830 and nine between 1830 and 1860, or in all nineteen in the formative era of American law from the Revolution to the Civil War. In many of these the growth of the law was slow. Even in one of the original thirteen states, Georgia, the first volume of law reports was published in 1824, forty-eight years after independence, and reports decisions from 1805. The Tennessee reports begin seventeen years after admission. In Ohio the interval is twenty-two years; in Indiana, fourteen years; in Mississippi, seventeen years; in Illinois, thirteen years; in Alabama, ten years. Thus by the time of the Civil War more than half of the states had been admitted since the generation that fought the Revolutionary War and had been repeating the experience of developing law and lawyers in new communities. It was no accident that by 1860 North Carolina was the only southern state and Ohio the only state or territory west of the Alleghenies to require a definite period of training before admission to practice law.[33] The prime characteristic of the pioneer is versatility. When anything is to be done he must do it himself. Thus he develops faith in the ability of any man to do anything. He would leave every one free to change his occupation as and when he likes and to take up freely such occupations as he likes. A pioneer society does not believe in specialists nor in an organized profession. The pioneer sees no reason to suppose that judges need any special training or that either judge or party needs the help of a lawyer to argue the law or to present a case adequately on the facts. He prefers to believe that he can prosecute and defend his own law suits and judge competently the law suits of others. Each new state down to the time of the Civil War repeated or at least threatened to repeat the attempts of the colonies in their earlier polities to make every man his own lawyer.

A closely connected cause is to be found in the political ideas of the Jacksonian era.[34] The good side of that

---

33. Reed, Training for the Public Profession of the Law, 87.

34. As to these ideas, see Peck, The Jacksonian Epoch (1899); MacDonald, Jacksonian Democracy (1907); Ogg, The Reign of Andrew Jackson (1919).

era in political, economic, and social development is another matter. The development of American law and even more the development of the legal profession was retarded and warped by the frontier spirit surviving the frontier. The opposition to an educated, adequately trained Bar and to an independent, experienced, permanent Judiciary which marked what Dickens described as the Jefferson Brick frontier community, left a mark upon our law and procedure which we have been striving hard to erase in the present century.

James Fenimore Cooper, one of the exponents of frontier democracy, in his story "The Pioneers" gives a striking picture of an American pioneer community in 1833. He tells us of a homogenous population jealous of its rights and in sympathy with the institutions of popular government. Such a community is intrinsically law abiding, even if inclined under provocation, under its theory of popular sovereignty, to vindicate public justice by rough and ready methods. Its polity presupposes a people which characteristically will conform to rules of law when ascertained and made known and expects legislation to determine what is law. Its polity presupposes a people which in the jury box may be relied upon to enforce law and vindicate justice between man and man intelligently and steadfastly. It presupposes an American farming community of the first half of the nineteenth century, not the

[237]

great urban, industrial community in which justice has had to be administered at the end of the nineteenth and in the present century.

John Adams noted that a main reliance of the pettifogger of his time was procedure, as a means of taking advantage of a defendant or stalling off a plaintiff. The uneducated, untrained practitioner of the era of decadence had the same reliance on procedure, and our legal procedure as it had developed by the end of the nineteenth century showed the hand of the pioneer almost everywhere. Taking the country as a whole, many of the features were adapted to the conditions of rural communities of the time of the Civil War. As I have said elsewhere, our procedure as it stood even fifty years ago was largely moulded to the demands of the rural agricultural community where before the days of motor vehicles and television the farmer found his theater in the court house and looked to politics and litigation for amusement. No small part of the exaggerated importance of the advocate in many of our states, of the free rein, one might almost say the license afforded him, while the trial judge must sit by as an umpire to administer the rules of the combat, is to be explained by frontier conditions and frontier modes of thought. The farmers who had tied their wagons to posts in the court house square resented direction of a verdict on a point of law cutting off the anticipated flood of eloquence. The audience was to be considered as well as the court and the litigants. Legislation tying down the trial judge in the interest of untrammeled advocacy had its origin on the frontier.

In a book of reminiscences of an eminent lawyer there is a chapter entitled "Country Practice of the Law" which describes the writer's experience in the western part of Massachusetts in 1861. He describes a prosecution for malicious injury to real property in which it appeared that a wooden pump had been removed from a well in mere wanton mischief. Counsel for the accused argued that the land was not injured and the pump was personalty so that the prosecution should have been for malicious injury to personal property. To clinch his argument he submitted that a deed of conveyance was not needed when a pump was sold. The accused having been acquitted was rearrested upon a new complaint for malicious injury to personal property. The same counsel then produced conclusive authority that the pump in the well, annexed to the land for permanent use, was a fixture and so realty. He tells us that a trial was then regarded as a contest of wits. The ethics of such a contest were at least no higher than those of a professional base ball game.[35] For a long time our procedure was too much in the spirit of frontier advocacy.

35. Torrey, A Lawyer's Recollections, 117–122 (1910).

At the same time with the unchecked advocacy and want of ethics in the conduct of litigation which was aggravated by frontier modes of thought, there was much in the legal procedure of the time, the eve of the codes of civil procedure, to make the man of affairs, the promoter of enterprises and the business man profoundly dissatisfied with the law and inclined to put the blame upon the lawyers. Adaptation of the inherited English common-law procedure to the conditions of the new world was not an easy task and a bench and bar made over to the frontier pattern and reliance upon legislation to do the work of setting up a new procedure in detail were by no means equal to it. But the effect upon the administration of justice was serious and complaint was justified and general. Thus in the debates in the Indiana Constitutional Convention in 1850, a speaker quoted a judge as saying: "During the fifteen years that I practiced law, I can say with safety that not one half of the suits with which I was familiar were decided upon their merits, or upon principles of substantial justice. This was hardly in any degree attributable to the courts, but was to be attributed principally to the system of pleading and practice." [36] But most of the speakers were not so understanding of the cause of the hypertrophy of procedure as was the judge. One speaker said the legal procedure was "a cunningly devised machine

36. 2 Report of the Debates and Proceedings of the Convention for the Revision of the Constitution of Indiana, 1850, 1738.

to make money and deceive the people." [37] Another said that many believe that if the laws were made more certain and definite the lawyer's trade, "like the shrine maker's spoken of by St. Paul, would be at an end or at least rendered less profitable than it is at present".[38] Another said: "Gentlemen of the Bar seem to think that hard things are said here of those of them who oppose this statutory reform. But let me say to these gentlemen that this is a reform for which the people call—a reform that the people's interest demands, and those gentlemen will hear a voice from the people ere long, which will tell them in tones of muttering thunder that 'the day of their powers that be are numbered.' " [39] The proceedings of the Michigan Constitutional Convention the same year are filled with speeches of the same sort showing the temper of the time. There was undoubtedly ground for much dissatisfaction with many features of the administration of justice at that time.[40] But an uneducated untrained Bar and short-term elected Bench simply fastened some of its worst features upon us for a long time to come.

37. Ibid.

38. Ibid. 1748.

39. Ibid. 1822.

40. I have discussed them at length as they had developed at the end of the nineteenth century in a paper, "The Causes of Popular Dissatisfaction with the Administration of Justice," 29 Rep. American Bar Association, pt. 1, 395 (1906); 40 American Law Review, 729 (1906).

It must be added that after the Civil War the development both of the law and of the lawyers was further affected by the growth of large cities with so many courts sitting, often with no real coordination, and so many lawyers practicing with no real even if some nominal organization, that there could no longer be any collective opinion of the Bar to bring pressure to bear upon the individual lawyer. The lawyer no longer met his fellow lawyers day by day in court. He was not likely to know more than a few of the judges and they could only know the few who came regularly before their particular court. The checks that had operated in the formative era before the Civil War had ceased to exist.

3. The Beginnings of Bar Associations. When the Bar Meetings, the meetings of the Bar of a local court as a whole, to do the things incumbent upon a professional body as expected of it as a matter of professional duty, came to an end, as we saw in the preceding chapter, attempt was made to replace them by associations of a voluntary, selective, non-inclusive, unofficial type. We have seen how some of those which arose upon the dissolution of the local Bars in New England continued for some time as social organizations or to meet upon the occasion of some flagrant wrongdoing affecting the honor and credit of lawyers as a class or to adopt resolutions upon the death of a leading practitioner or a highly respected

[242]

judge. We have seen also how some of these kept a certain tenuous continuity, without attempting the functions we now attribute to a real Bar Association, until the rise of true Bar Associations in the last quarter of the nineteenth century. Some associations of the voluntary selective type, however, were organized in the fore part of the last century without any previous holding of regular Bar Meetings before them. A check list published in 1923 [41] enumerates five. There was, it is said, an organization of the Bar in Mississippi in 1825, in Arkansas in 1837, in Louisiana (Association of the Bar of New Orleans) in 1847 and 1855, and in Kentucky in 1846. Also the list includes a Bar Association in Massachusetts in 1849. This refers to the attempt to organize a Massachusetts State Bar Association in 1849 which, we have seen, came to naught. The times were not ripe for such associations between 1836 and the time of the Civil War. We have seen how violently organization of lawyers in any form was objected to in that era. If they could have succeeded in maintaining themselves anywhere it would have been in New England where there was a long tradition of local Bars. But even there there was no tradition of a state bar, although there had been a project for one in New Hampshire which failed. None of the associations listed as organized before 1850 left permanent records and they all seem to have had only a temporary existence.

41. Small, Check List of Bar and Allied Associations (1923).

Another list made in 1887 includes a number of Bar Associations organized before 1870 and claiming continuous existence to the date of the list.[42] Eleven claiming continuous existence from a date before 1870 are included. Arranged according to priority of date they are: 1802, Law Association of Philadelphia, heretofore considered; 1841, Kennebec County, Maine, heretofore considered; 1843, Berkshire Law Library Association, one of the associations provided for by the Massachusetts Act of 1842,[43] heretofore considered; 1847, New Orleans Bar Association; 1849, The Wilkes-Barre Law Library Association, heretofore considered; 1853, Association of the Bar of Bucks County, Pennsylvania; 1856, Essex Bar Association, Salem, Massachusetts, heretofore considered; 1862, West Chester Bar Association, Pennsylvania; 1864, Hampden County Bar Association, Springfield, Massachusetts; 1866, Cumberland County Bar Association, Portland, Maine, heretofore considered; 1867, Plymouth County Bar Association, Massachusetts.

Of these the Law Association of Philadelphia, now the Philadelphia Bar Association, makes reasonably good its claim of continuous existence since 1802, and has come

42. Hill, Bar Associations, 5 Rep. Georgia Bar Association, 51, Appendix A, pp. 89–90. Mr. Hill, President of the Georgia Bar Association, sent out a circular inquiring as to existing Bar Associations and listed those whose officers responded, with the date of organization claimed.

43. Mass. Acts and Resolves of 1842, chap. 94, p. 543.

more nearly to functioning continuously as an organization of the profession for maintaining its professional character during the era of decadence than any other. The Essex Bar Association of Salem, Massachusetts, The Cumberland Bar Association of Portland, Maine, and the Kennebec County Bar Association of Augusta, Maine, have a certain not wholly continuous succession from the organized local Bars of colonial New England. But they can show no clear continuous active existence through the era of decadence. Moreover, for a long time they did not function as we expect the Bar Association of today to do. The several Massachusetts Law Library Associations, apparently organized under the Act of 1842, are not at first true Bar Associations and show no continuity from before 1870 as such. The Pennsylvania county associations, apparently organized along the lines of the Law Society of Philadelphia, do not furnish evidence of continuous existence as true Bar Associations from before 1870. The Plymouth Bar Association, Massachusetts, has records as far back as 1867. But in answer to the questionnaire says: "Our Association . . . started out as a county association, and then later on dwindled to a Brockton Bar Association. Then about twenty years ago we went back on a county basis, but in the meantime, for a great many years, there had been a town of Plymouth Bar Association, which still continues side by side with the county association." For the rest we are referred to "some menus of Bar Association banquets held in the early days of the Association." [44] It is sufficiently clear that this association merely held dinners from time to time and was long not an active Bar Association in the sense of today.

In other words, of the eleven Bar Associations which in 1887 claimed organization before or during the era of decadence and survival continuously through that era to the present, only one appears able to make good that claim, and even that association can do so only with some qualifyings.

In answer to the questionnaire the Secretary of the Milwaukee Bar Association wrote: "Our records are very clear that, after some preliminary or informal meetings of the Milwaukee County lawyers, a formal meeting was held of the Association of the Bar of Milwaukee on May 23, 1858. The Minutes of that meeting refer to the constitution previously adopted and to which some slight changes were made at the meeting. The constitution was adopted as corrected and is copied in full into the minute book in longhand and certified by the Secretary and three members under date of May 18, 1858. From the foregoing, it is evident that the constitution was adopted on May 18, 1858, but there are no minutes that could be as-

44. Letter of George L. Wainwright, Esq., of Brockton, Mass. of May 17, 1931.

sociated with the meeting on that date. The minute book subsequently discloses minutes of meetings held at more or less frequent intervals after the meeting of May 23, 1858, and there is nothing of record to indicate that the Association ceased operation. Under date of August 10, 1881, a new constitution was adopted and the organization named therein appears the same as that of the present organization. It is possible . . . that there may have been a lull in activities and it is quite likely that some bar associations discontinued operation entirely, but that is not the situation with reference to the Milwaukee Bar Association. The activities of our Association are only meagerly indicated by the minutes. . . . It is our position that the Milwaukee Bar Association has been in continuous existence since early in the year 1858." [45] It is evident that the Milwaukee Association was not functioning as a bar association in the sense of today continuously before 1881. It did not respond to Mr. Hill's questionnaire in 1887, but did respond to the American Bar Association call for information, giving the name of a secretary in 1886. [46]

Also a letter in answer to the questionnaire tells us that "the law order books of the [Monongalia] County [West Virginia] Bar Association indicate that the local

45. Letter of L. G. Barnes, Esq., of Milwaukee, of November 6, 1950.
46. 10 Rep. American Bar Association, 446.

attorneys met as a group as far back as 1869, though they had no formal organization." [47]

Bar associations as social organizations kept a certain degree of professional organization alive in some communities until the revival in the last quarter of the nineteenth century. Also in some states county Bars had occasional dinners with an address or were sometimes called to a special meeting to adopt resolutions on the death of a judge or leading lawyer or when some scandal of jury fixing or of flagrant misconduct called for exceptional action. That this is the most that can be said, testifies to the thorough deprofessionalizing of the Bar in the era of decadence. There had come to be, not a Bar, but "so many hundred or so many thousand lawyers, each a law unto himself, accountable only to God and his conscience—if any." [48] Dean Wigmore put it even more vigorously: " . . . the profession was a complacent, self-satisfied, genial fellowship of individual lawyers— unalive to the shortcomings of justice, unthinking of the urgent demands of the impending future, unconscious of their potential opportunities, unaware of their collective duty and destiny." [49]

47. Letter of September 8, 1951.

48. Pound, A Task for a University Law School, St. Lawrence University, Exercises at the Dedication of Richardson Hall, 10 November, 1928, 15.

49. 20 Journal, American Judicature Society, 176 (1937).

4. The Transition to True Bar Associations. Revival of professional organization for promoting the practice of a learned art in the spirit of a public service and advancing the administration of justice according to law got its impetus as a country wide movement from the organization of the American Bar Association in 1878. But the movement definitely began with the organization of the Bar Association of the City of New York in 1870. One association seems to mark the transition. The Franklin County Bar Association, Columbus, Ohio, now called the Columbus Bar Association, is not in Mr. Hill's list but is in the American Bar Association list with the name of the secretary in 1886. I have seen in photostat the minutes of the first meeting and adoption of a constitution on April 20, 1869. Continuous existence since that date is claimed.[50] Continuous activity as a Bar Association in the sense of today would put that Association among the few with which the era of Bar Associations begins. I do not think its purposes and activities at the outset entitle it to be placed at the first of the new era. But it marks the transition. For a full account reference may be made to Mr. Morris' report,—a part of the Survey. It is today one of the most active and fruitful of local bar associations. In 1949 it was given an Award of Merit by the American Bar Association.

---

50. Letter of the Secretary to Reginald Heber Smith, Esq., of February 20, 1951.

IX.

The Revival of Professional Organization

*

IX.

The Revival of Professional Organization

1. Beginnings of the Revival: Bar Associations 1870–1878. At the outset we must recur to a distinction often referred to hereinbefore, between Bar, Bar Meeting, and Bar Association. Except where the integrated Bar obtains, the term Bar in a strict sense can only mean the aggregate of lawyers admitted to Practice in a given jurisdiction or before a given court. Bar Meeting in Colonial New England meant a meeting of the lawyers admitted to practice in a county or district without formal organization but considering themselves a unit for maintaining and promoting the standards of the profession. In the era of decadence it came to mean any meeting of the lawyers in practice in a given locality who, without definite organization, chose to attend to take part in memorial services or for adoption of resolutions in case of matters of grave consequence for the local administration of justice or the standing of the profession, or at a Bar dinner. The term Bar Association, which came into use on the cessation of the old Bar Meetings and especially in the era of decadence, means a definite and permanent organization of lawyers for purposes of the profession,

[253]

which has usually been both selective and non-inclusive but, without being inclusive, as in case of an integrated Bar, may no longer be selective, membership being open to every one admitted to practice, on his application, without action upon the application. The Boston Bar Association and the New York County Lawyers Association are of the non-selective, non-inclusive type. It will be seen that they are an approach to the integrated bar. But since 1870, Bar Associations are expected to be more than organizations for good fellowship and social purposes.

Although the organization of the American Bar Association in 1878 undoubtedly gave a decisive impetus to the movement for Bar Associations which has carried forward the reprofessionalization of American lawyers, the era of modern Bar Associations must be held to begin with the Association of the Bar of the City of New York in 1870. At the end of the first decade of the American Bar Association, one hundred and seventy-six associations were listed as responding to the circular set out by its Secretary.[1] Thirty of them, however, were scarcely active. Of the ninety-six which were reasonably active, eleven had been organized between 1870 and 1877, and nine or ten claimed, a few rightly, continuous existence as Bar Associations since before 1870. On the whole, the

1. 10 Rep. American Bar Association (1887) 439–447.

turning point may justly be fixed at the organization of the Association of the Bar of the City of New York in 1870. It marks a decisive change in the character and objects of organizations of lawyers. William D. Guthrie rightly called it "the premier association of its kind in every sense of the word." [2] Mr. Wickser said justly that it has been a model for true Bar Associations. [3] Mr. Blaustein properly pronounced it "a major step forward in modern Bar Association history." [4]

In 1870, there were about four thousand lawyers in New York City. Early in December of 1869, two hundred and thirty-five of them, headed by William Maxwell Evarts, one of the leaders of the American Bar of the time after the Civil War, signed an agreement to form an association, reciting their belief that "the organized action and influence of the legal profession, properly exerted, would lead to the creating of more intimate relations between its members than now exist and would at the same time *sustain the profession in its proper position in the community, and thereby enable it in many ways to promote the interests of the public.*" [Italics supplied]. Pursuant to this agreement a meeting was held on February 1,

2. Address Before the Bar Association of Chicago, 2 Rep. Association of the Bar of the City of New York (1926) 8.

3. Philip J. Wickser, Esq., Bar Associations, 15 Cornell Law Quarterly (1930) 390, 396.

4. 6 Record of the Association of the Bar of the City of New York, 261.

1870, at which a committee on constitution and by-laws and a committee on nomination of officers were appointed. An adjourned meeting was held on February 15, 1870, at which a constitution and by-laws were adopted and officers were elected. Mr. Evarts was the first president. Article II of the constitution provided: "The Association is established to maintain the honor and dignity of the profession, to cultivate social intercourse among its members, and to increase its usefulness in promoting the due administration of justice." [5]

In the circular announcing the organization the committee said: "No one had any authority to call a general meeting of the Bar." [6] New York had never had the New England Bar Meetings, called by the senior members of the Bar, and such associations as it had at one time or another had long gone out of existence. The new Association was from the first and has remained non-inclusive and selective, as indeed was necessary to its objects after the breakdown of requirements of education, professional training, and admission. The members of the bar who signed the preliminary agreement were made members of the Association. Any members of the profession residing or practicing in the City of New York might become members by vote of the Association on recommendation of the

5. 1 Rep. Association of the Bar of the City of New York, 1–5, 31, 32–35.
6. Ibid. iii.

Committee on Admissions.[7]   The constitution provided for a library and reading room in this respect suggesting something of an Inn of Court and following in the tradition of Pennsylvania and Massachusetts.[8]

In addition to the objects stated in the agreement in 1869, Article 8 of the By-Laws provided for four standing committees: A committee on Amendment of the Laws; a Judiciary Committee "charged with the duty of observing the working of our judicial system;" a Committee on Grievances to hear complaints against members of the Association and complaints as to the administration of justice; and a Committee on Legal Education to consider changes in the system of education and of admission to practice.[9] It is noteworthy that the objects as set forth in the Constitution and in the provision for committees in the By-Laws are substantially those which were pursued in the old Bar Meetings. But a significant change was made when the Constitution of the Association was revised and amended in 1876. In the original Constitution cultivating of social intercourse among the members is put second among the objects stated. In the revision six years later it is put last.[10] This shows progress in the

7.   Art. III of the Constitution, ibid. 4.

8.   Ibid. 5.

9.   Ibid. 11–12.

10.   Ibid. 8.

ideals of purposes of a Bar Association toward what we now take them to be. What had been the chief and almost the only function of an association of lawyers during the era of decadence had now fallen to the last place.

What was said in the organization meeting as to the causes of the deprofessionalizing which the Association was to seek to remedy is noteworthy. Henry Nicoll, Esq., said: "The most prominent of the causes of this decline are to be found in the revolutionary changes made in our condition by the [State] Constitution of 1846. That Constitution, under which we still live, gave almost a death blow to the legal profession." So the Association was to seek to undo the mischief to the profession and to the administration of justice done in the era of decadence. The State Constitution, it is fair to say, has been amended and revised many times since 1870. Samuel J. Tilden said the Bar should organize for two objects: "The one is to elevate itself—to elevate its own standards; the other object is for the common and public good." He added: " . . . it is impossible for New York to remain the center of commerce and capital for this continent unless it has an independent bar and an honest judiciary." [11] Mr. Evarts, referring to the scandals in the Erie Railroad litigation and the Tweed frauds, said that an object of the Association was to "restore the honor, integrity, and

11. Ibid. 20–21.

fame of the profession in its manifestations of the Bench and of the Bar." [12] It should be remembered that this was said in the time of the Tweed regime, the impeachment of corrupt judges and widespread political corruption and misconduct in which judges and court officials were involved along with political officials.

A principal result of the organization of this Association was to awaken lawyers generally to the need of effective professional organization. At the outset in its address to the bar the executive committee in 1870 suggested like associations in the other cities and counties of the State as well as a State Association. The press, in the excitement of the struggle with political corruption affecting the courts, gave the new organization great publicity. Organization of the Chicago Bar Association (1874), of the Cincinnati Bar Association (1872), of the Iowa State Bar Association (1874), of the Bar Association of the City of Boston (1876), and of the New York State Bar Association (1876) is said to have been stimulated by the example in New York City. [13] In its endeavors to improve the administration of justice the Association at once came in conflict with the Tweed ring, then dominant in New York politics. The legislature refused to

12. Ibid. 29.

13. Sheldon, Historical Sketch of the Association of the Bar of the City of New York, 1870–1920, Prepared for the Semi-Centenary Celebration, February 17, 1920, 43.

enact the charter drafted by the Association and enacted a fundamentally different charter. Happily this was not signed by the Governor and a year later, April 28, 1871, the one drawn up by the Association was enacted. In the struggle with the Tweed ring which ultimately brought about its downfall, the Association played an important part. The impeachment of two judges, and resignation of a third, as a result of an investigation it had recommended, established it in public confidence, and though not uniformly successful, in the first twenty-five years of its existence it had done great things for the administration of justice in the city and state.[14] No less important and effective has been the work of its Committee on Grievances. It has done outstanding work to elevate the standard of the profession.[15] The Association also took a leading part in the struggle during the '80s over the Field Codes. The time was not then ripe for codification of the common law. Moreover, to draft an adequate Civil Code was too great a task for one man, even if as great a lawyer and skilful draftsman of laws as David Dudley Field. In the part it took in the code controversy the Association did a real service to the law.[16] It has also been active in improvement of legal education and admission to the bar.[17]

14. Ibid. 262–264.
15. Ibid. 264–266.
16. For the details see ibid. 266–267.
17. Ibid. 268.

Indeed, it is not too much to say that from the beginning the Association has gone on steadily along the lines indicated when it was organized. At the celebration of its seventy-fifth anniversary Chief Justice Stone said of it: " . . . the Association has been wisely progressive in meeting the manifold changes which, through the years, have affected the law, the courts and the Bar. With it all the Association has had no selfish aim. It has sought to promote no individual or selfish interest which was not calculated to advance the best interests of the profession and of the public." [18]

During the period from 1870 to 1877 some County Associations in Maine and in Massachusetts, the Philadelphia Law Association and County Associations, especially library associations in Pennsylvania, the Detroit, and Milwaukee and Columbus, Ohio, Associations, a County Association in Michigan and one in Iowa, which had grown up and maintained themselves with more or less continuity during the era of decadence, were developing in varying degree into what we now understand by the term Bar Association. Fourteen which grew up between the Association in New York City and the organization of the American Bar Association require brief notice.

The Allegheny Bar Association was chartered February 28, 1870, as the Pittsburgh Law Association, chang-

18. Proceedings of a Special Meeting to Commemorate the Seventy-fifth Anniversary of the Bar of the City of New York (1945) 12.

ing its name in 1882. Its object is thus stated in its charter in 1870: "The elevation of the character, superintendence of the general interests and cultivation of a fraternal feeling among the members of the profession of law in said county." [19] This does not come up entirely to the standard set about the same time by the Association of the Bar of the City of New York. The Pittsburg Association has had continuous existence since 1870, but it belongs to the group which organized between 1850 and 1870 on the model of the Philadelphia Law Association. The same may be said of the Lycoming Law Association (1870) and the Erie County (Pennsylvania) Bar Association (1875). The Bar Association of New Castle County (Wilmington, Delaware, 1871) seems to have been of the older type.

The Cincinnati Bar Association, organized February 27, 1872, with Alphonso Taft, father of Chief Justice Taft, Secretary of War and afterwards Attorney General of the United States, as President. This was one of the first fruits of the example set in New York. It was called for a time the Hamilton County Bar Association.[20]

Bar Association of the State of New Hampshire, incorporated July 2, 1873. The purposes of the corporation

19. Charter, By-Laws and Rules of the Allegheny County Bar Association (1889) 5.

20. Answers to the questionnaire, 1950.

were stated to be: "Maintaining the honor and dignity of the profession of the law, and cultivating social relations among its members, and increasing its usefulness in promoting the due administration of justice." This Association was inactive between 1878 and 1898. In 1899 the Bar Association of Grafton and Coos Counties (formed in 1882) and the Southern New Hampshire Bar Association (1891) formed an Association under the original charter granted by the legislature in 1873 [21] and that is the present Association.[22]

The Cleveland Bar Association, originally the Cuyahoga County Bar (1873),[23] was organized March 22, 1873. Its objects were stated to be "To maintain the honor and dignity of the profession of law, to cultivate social intercourse and acquaintance among members of the Bar; and to increase the usefulness of its members by aiding in the administration of justice and in the promotion of legal and judicial reforms." It claims to have had a continuous existence.[24] It has received two Awards of Merit from the American Bar Association—1940, 1945.

21. Laws of New Hampshire, 1873, chap. 115, pp. 220–221.
22. Answers to the questionnaire, 1950.
23. According to Small, Check List of Bar and Allied Associations (1923) the dates should be 1876–1882. The Association is not in Mr. Hill's list and is in the American Bar Association list in 1887 as the Cuyahoga County Bar Association with only the name of the Secretary in 1886. No President is named. This usually indicates a feeble activity or even dormancy.
24. Letter of the Secretary in answer to the questionnaire, 1950.

Chicago Bar Association (1874). This, too, followed the example of the New York City Association. It has had a continuous and conspicuously useful existence from its first organization.

Bar Association of the District of Columbia (1874). This Association, organized June 5, 1874, "to maintain the honor and dignity of the profession and to provide a library for its members" was originally of the Pennsylvania Library Association type. Until about 1930 "the Association was in the nature of an exclusive club with a small membership."[25]

Iowa State Bar Association (1874–1881). This Association was also among the first fruits of the New York City Association. It was organized May 29, 1874. The constitution declared as its objects: "To promote mutual acquaintance and harmony among the members of the Iowa Bar; to maintain a high standard of professional integrity, honor, and courtesy among them; to encourage a thorough and liberal legal education; to give expression to the deliberate and well considered opinion of the legal profession upon all matters wherein its members are expected to act as a body; and to assist in the improvement of the laws and the better administration of justice to all classes of society without distinction." In 1912, the then reorganized Association published a volume of proceed-

25. Letter of John C. Poole, Esq., July 10, 1951.

ings of the first Association compiled from newspaper accounts, from published pamphlets of proceedings at annual meetings, and from accounts of meetings and addresses published in the Western Jurist. The meeting which was to have been held in June 1882 was postponed till the following January but was never held and the first Association went out of existence.[26]

Holmes County Bar Association, Lexington, Mississippi. This Association claims continuous existence from 1875 but has no records and the exact date of its organization is not certainly known. It seems to have been of the type of association for an annual dinner and occasional meetings to adopt resolutions on the death or retirement of judges, such as existed commonly in the period before 1870.[27] It is not in Mr. Hill's list nor in that of the American Bar Association in 1887.

San Bernardino County Bar Association (California, 1875–1877). This Association was organized December 11, 1875. Its primary object was social, but included promotion of the ethics of the profession. It held meetings for two years but became inactive thereafter until reorganized October 31, 1887.[28]

26. Proceedings of the Iowa State Bar Association, held at Des Moines, Iowa, 1874–1881 (1912).
27. Answers to questionnaire, 1950.
28. Letter of Hon. Jesse W. Curtis, formerly Justice of the Supreme Court of California, June 1, 1951.

State Bar Association of Connecticut (1876–1891). The original long-hand minutes which have been preserved show an organization meeting on June 15, 1876, at which fifty-eight members of the bar were present and adopted a Constitution. At an adjourned meeting on June 30, 1876, one hundred and thirteen more members were elected. An interesting item in the minutes is: "January 3, 1878. Mr. Simeon E. Baldwin moved that a Committee be appointed to consider the propriety of organizing an association of American lawyers with power to issue a circular on the subject. Passed." The minutes show appointment of the committee. The minutes of June 21, 1878, set forth the report of the committee, a vote that the President appoint twelve delegates to the organization meeting of the American Bar Association, and appointment of the delegates accordingly. The minutes of the annual meeting on January 23, 1879, show a report of the delegates on the organization of the American Bar Association. There were no annual meetings after 1891. A meeting in 1906 resulted in a reorganization in 1907 and the association has been continuously active since that time.[29]

Boston Bar Association (1876). This Association was organized on the model of the Association of the Bar

29. Letter and copies of the minutes by Charles M. Lyman, Esq., New Haven, Conn.

of the City of New York. Originally and for a long time it was a conservative, selective group. But after 1920 it began to widen its membership and it came to make eligible for membership any person admitted by the courts. It has had a continuous and fruitful existence and publishes a Bar Bulletin which is of service in improvement of the law.[30]

Queens County Bar Association (New York, 1876). This association was organized at Garden City, New York, on July 19, 1876. Its objects were stated to be: "To maintain the honor and dignity of the profession of the law, to increase its usefulness in promoting the administration of justice, and to cultivate social intercourse among its members." For the first fifty years only the annual meetings, which were social meetings, were well attended but it has acted from the beginning on some occasions of serious questions as to the administration of justice in the locality. Since 1920 it has been active in all matters which are now the province of a Bar Association.[31]

New York State Bar Association (1876). This association was formed November 21, 1876, and was incorporated under an Act of the Legislature passed May 2, 1877.[32] Its objects were said to be: "To cultivate the

30. Nicholson, The Organized Bar in Massachusetts, (1952).

31. Letter of Samuel S. Tripp, Esq., Jamaica, New York.

32. Laws of New York, 1877, chap. 210.

science of jurisprudence, to promote reform of the law, to facilitate the administration of justice, to elevate the standard of integrity, honor, and courtesy in the legal profession, and to cherish the spirit of brotherhood among the members thereof." It has had a continuous active existence. It is the oldest of the State Bar Associations organized before 1878 with unbroken continuity. The Bar Association of the District of Columbia did not become what we now consider a Bar Association till long afterward.[33]

Illinois State Bar Association, organized January 4, 1877. The immediate occasion of the organization was the then urgent need of relief of the Supreme and Appellate Courts of the State. The objects were stated to be to improve the administration of justice in the State, to promote better relationships among individual lawyers, and to provide a forum for discussion of common problems. It at once recommended a revision of appellate practice which was adopted by the legislature. It has been active in the improvement of legal procedure. But its most fruitful activities were after 1912 when the late R. Allan Stephens became editor of the Quarterly Bulletin of the Association, the first in time of periodicals of the sort which have become common in the present generation.[34]

33. Information in answer to questionnaire.
34. Answers to questionnaire, 1950. Other periodicals of the sort are:

Shelby County Bar Association (Shelbyville, Ill.). This Association was organized in January, 1877, by Hon. Anthony Thornton, Judge of the Supreme Court of Illinois, 1870–1873, who was one of the organizers of the Illinois State Bar Association. It claims to have been in continuous existence since 1877, but was little active for many years only holding regular meetings in recent years.[35] It is not in Mr. Hill's list nor in that of the American Bar Association. An Association of the old type, it has recently been modernized.

Alabama Lawyer, Official Organ of the State Bar of Alabama, 1940; Association of the Bar of the City of New York Bulletin, 1920; Bar Bulletin, New York County Lawyers Association, 1943; The Record, New York City Lawyers Association, 1946; Bench and Bar, Lawyers Club of Detroit, 1921; Bench and Bar, Lawyers' Association of the Eighth Judicial Circuit of Missouri, 1935; The Brief, Hollywood Bar Association, 1940; State Bar Journal of California, State Bar of California, 1926; Connecticut Bar Journal, State Bar Association of Connecticut, 1927; Dicta, Denver Bar Association, 1923; Florida Law Journal, Florida State Bar Association, 1927; Journal of the Bar Association of the District of Columbia, 1934; Journal of the Bar Association of the State of Kansas, 1932; Journal of the Missouri Bar (formerly Missouri Bar Journal) 1930–1944, no more published; Kentucky State Bar Journal, Kentucky State Bar Association, 1936; Massachusetts Law Quarterly Massachusetts Bar Association, 1915; Michigan State Bar Journal, Michigan State Bar Association, 1921; Nevada State Bar Journal, Nevada State Bar Association, 1936; New York State Bar Association Bulletin, New York State Bar Association, 1928; The Journal, Oklahoma Bar Association, 1930; Pennsylvania Bar Association Quarterly, Pennsylvania State Bar Association, 1929; Texas Bar Journal, Texas Bar Association, 1938; Wisconsin Bar Bulletin, Wisconsin Bar Association, 1929.

35. Letter of A. L. Yantis, Esq., President, in response to questionnaire, 1950.

2. The American Bar Association and State Bar Associations, 1878–1936. The story of the organization of the American Bar Association has been well told by the moving spirit in bringing it about, Hon. Simeon E. Baldwin, some time Chief Justice of Connecticut and long Professor of Law at Yale.[36] But its origin, history, and achievements are the province of Professor Sunderland in another portion of the Survey, and I can only speak of them in connection with and as bearing upon the general organization of lawyers throughout the country as promoted by the activities of that Association.

At first the American Bar Association had a small and highly select membership. The programs of its meetings were good. There were excellent papers and addresses and useful reports of committees. But it had relatively little influence except in stimulating leaders of the Bar in the States and in localities to urge and promote effective Bar organizations. It was long in making its influence felt by legislatures. Down to 1893 the average attendance at its meetings, held each year at Saratoga, was from seventy-five to one hundred and fifty. It began to grow slowly after 1893 and by 1903 had two thousand members. After 1904 it began to grow rapidly, and the meetings were no longer held at Saratoga but were held instead at the larger cities in different parts of the coun-

---

36. 3 American Bar Association Journal (1917) 658.

try, so as to visit each region in turn so far as possible. In 1914 it had eight thousand members. In 1924 it had twenty thousand. In 1928, at the end of its first fifty years, it had a membership of twenty-eight thousand. In 1950, its membership was over forty-two thousand.

In its first fifty years its most useful activities had been its promotion of the Conference of Commissioners on Uniform State Laws; its work for reform of procedure; its work for improvement of conditions of admission to the bar; its work for legal education, especially in connection with the organization of the Association of American Law Schools, pursuant to an invitation extended by the Bar Association's Section of Legal Education, at the meeting in 1900. That Section of Legal Education and the Association of American Law Schools cooperated from the start in the heat of the struggle for improvement of training for the profession. Not less important was its codification of the canons of professional conduct. In all these achievements it increasingly enlisted the activities of the State and local organizations. Its achievements since 1928 would of themselves require nothing less than a book to tell adequately and are the subject of another part of the Survey.

Organization of a State Bar Association in twenty-five states in the first decade of the American Bar Association was a notable testimony to the effect of that organization. But of the twenty-five only fourteen survived the decade. Of the remaining eleven, two were reorganized before 1890, and five more before the end of 1900. The rest were reorganized by 1907. But it was not till 1923 that there was an active State Bar Association in every State or Territory of the Union.

By the time State Bar Associations had become active in substantially every State, but before the list was complete, the movement for integration of the Bar of the State as a whole had begun with the State Bar of North Dakota in 1921. Moreover, as far back as 1918 through the activities of the American Judicature Society and the American Bar Association a model form of statute for integration of a State Bar had been drafted and published.[37] Thus the American Bar Association was helping move toward the final stage before the penultimate stage was complete.

As the matter stands now, following is the list of States and Territories with active Bar organizations, date of the first organization and date of the present organization in case of breach of continuity.[38] Where the Bar is integrated, that is noted in each case.

37. Brand, Bar Organization and Judicial Administration, 34 Journal of American Judicature Society (1950) 38, 41. A full list of integrated Bars with references to the mode of integration and full citation of statutes and rules of Court may be found in 10 Alabama Lawyer (1949) 468–469.

38. Where the first organization did not persist the name of the State is

New Hampshire, 1873, reorganized 1899.

Iowa, 1874, reorganized 1895, received Award of Merit from American Bar Association, 1947.

District of Columbia, 1874, reorganized 1891, received Award of Merit from American Bar Association, 1951.

New York, 1876 (December).

Illinois, 1877 (January).

Alabama, 1878, integrated 1923.

Vermont, 1878.

Wisconsin, 1878.

New Jersey, 1878, reorganized 1899.

Nebraska, 1878, reorganized 1900, integrated 1937.

Missouri, 1880, integrated 1944, received Award of Merit from American Bar Association, 1944.

Ohio, 1880, received Award of Merit from American Bar Association, 1949.

Tennessee, 1881.

Indiana, 1881, reorganized 1886.

Texas, 1882, integrated 1939, received Award of Merit from American Bar Association, 1940.

Maine, 1882, reorganized 1891.

Arkansas, 1882, reorganized 1899, integrated 1938, received Award of Merit from American Bar Association, 1948.

put in italics with the date of the later and present organizations following.

Colorado, 1882, reorganized 1897, received Award of Merit from American Bar Association, 1941, 1949.

Kentucky, 1882, reorganized 1901, integrated 1934, received Award of Merit from American Bar Association, 1951.

Georgia, 1883.

Kansas, 1883.

Minnesota, 1884, reorganized 1904, received Award of Merit from American Bar Association, 1945.

Montana, 1885.

New Mexico, 1886, integrated 1925.

West Virginia, 1886, integrated 1945.

South Carolina, 1887, reorganized 1901.

Virginia, 1888, integrated 1938.

Washington, 1888, integrated 1933.

California, 1889, reorganized 1909, integrated 1927, received Award of Merit from American Bar Association 1942, 1943, 1946, 1948, 1950.

Florida, 1889, reorganized 1907, integrated 1949.

Michigan, 1890, integrated 1935.

Oklahoma, 1890, integrated 1939.

Oregon, 1890, integrated 1935.

Mississippi, 1892, reorganized 1906, integrated 1930.

Utah, 1894, integrated 1931.

Nevada, 1894, reorganized 1911, integrated 1929.

Pennsylvania, 1895.

Alaska, 1896.

Maryland, 1896.

South Dakota, 1897, integrated 1931, received Award
of Merit from American Bar Association, 1939.

Louisiana, 1898, integrated 1940.

Rhode Island, 1898.

Hawaii, 1898.

North Carolina, 1899, integrated 1933.

North Dakota, 1899, integrated 1921.

Delaware, 1901, reorganized 1923.

Idaho, 1901, reorganized 1909, integrated 1923.

Arizona, 1906, renewed activity 1912, integrated
1933.

Massachusetts, 1909.

Wyoming, 1915, integrated 1939.

The Bar of Puerto Rico was integrated in 1932.

Enthusiasm of leaders of the profession in many
states led to premature state organizations before the in-
ertia of the era of decadence could be overcome. Also in
states where there had been a long tradition of local associations it was long before a movement for a state association could gather momentum. In the eighteen states
in which there had to be a new organization after 1878,
some, Arkansas, California, Florida, Indiana, Kentucky,
Mississippi had to develop standards of education and

[275]

admission to bring about a Bar which could long sustain a state association. Some had not had a long enough development as states, with common law and legal and professional problems of their own, to sustain the state organization. Here I venture to put Colorado, Idaho, Iowa, Minnesota and Nebraska at the time the first State Bar Associations in those states lapsed. In both groups the meetings became social occasions and for the most part took the form of a dinner and annual address. This is well brought out by later publications in Iowa, Kentucky, Minnesota and Nebraska. It is shown also by the experience in Arizona. When the Association was reorganized in 1912, it was said:

"The Arizona Bar Association had a more or less active existence for many years prior to 1906. Tradition has it that on some occasions in the remote past, papers were read at meetings of the Association, and an effort made to give it a reason for existence extending beyond the mere social function of arranging an annual dinner. The social feature has been observed with much regularity, and has been an important factor in the formation of acquaintances among members of the Bar from widely separated parts of Arizona. The desire of many members to render the Association more efficient, crystallized in 1906 in its incorporation—which seems to have exhausted the unusual vitality so manifested, for, until the year

[276]

1911–12, the Association was no more vigorous than before. The first program of papers read in many years—since the traditional period—was read at the 1912 meeting." [39]

In Maine, New Hampshire and Delaware there had been a long development of local associations. As to Delaware, the zeal of Josiah Marvel, afterward President of the American Bar Association, effected the reorganization in 1923, overcoming the apathy of the local associations. [40] Clearly also the relatively long history of strong local associations explains the delay in organizing State Bar Associations in Pennsylvania and Massachusetts, each a Commonwealth with great legal traditions and notable lawyers. It is said that the immediate interest of Hollis R. Bailey, Esq., who was mainly active in organizing the State Association in Massachusetts, was in having a state organization to invite the American Bar Association to meet in Boston. [41] As to Connecticut and New Jersey I cannot speak with assurance. Perhaps in Connecticut the energies of Judge Baldwin were taken up in the formative years of the American Bar Association and without his unflagging zeal behind it the State

---

39. Transactions of the Arizona Bar Association at its Seventh Annual Meeting (1912) 3.

40. Such, at least, is the tenor of the answer from the present association to the questionnaire.

41. Letter of Frank W. Grinnell, Esq., January 22, 1952.

Association lapsed. I have been unable to get any response as to the cause of the hiatus in New Jersey.

Organizations which have grown out of or been formed to cooperate with or have arisen in rivalry with the American Bar Association are treated of in separate reports in the Survey and I do not go into their organization, purposes or achievements.

3. Reorganization of the American Bar Association and Cooperative Professional Activity. At the beginning of the era of Bar organization the call for organization of the Association of the Bar of the City of New York called for promotion of State Bar Associations.[42] We have seen how this Association stimulated the growth of such organizations before the advent of the American Bar Association and doubtless contributed to the formation of that Association. But, as set forth above, all but three of the present day State and Territorial Associations were organized after or, because of failure of the first organization to maintain itself, reorganized after 1878. Thus a long period of further growth was necessary before a next step of effective bringing of state and local bar associations into close cooperation with the American Bar Association, so as to make a truly representative organization of the lawyers of the whole country, could be taken.

42. Annual Report of the Association of the Bar of the City of New York (1870) 7.

In 1918, Hon. Elihu Root, then President of the American Bar Association, by authority of the Executive Committee, invited all state and local bar associations to a conference in connection with the annual meeting of the American Bar Association at Chicago. Fifty-four associations sent delegates to this conference. It became a permanent feature and in 1919 became a Section of the Association. By 1922 one hundred and forty-seven associations took part, sending two hundred and ninety-seven delegates. The purpose of the Section was thus declared: "To create a better understanding between the members of the American Bar and to bring about a better and more effective cooperation by the Bar Associations of the country in securing and maintaining high standards of character, education, fitness, ability, and conduct in the legal profession and a more speedy, efficient, and satisfactory administration of justice." [43]

The last State Bar Association was organized in 1923. Ten years later a movement for reorganization of the American Bar Association to take a decisive step toward cooperation began in earnest. At the meeting in Milwaukee in 1934 it had gone so far that the executive committee asked an appropriation of $50,000, to equal a grant of a like amount by the Carnegie Foundation, to further the

---

43. Boston, The Past, Present, and Future of the Conference of Bar Association Delegates, 48 Rep. American Bar Association (1923) 565.

program of coordinating the activities of the general Association with those of the state and local organizations.[44] The details belong to the special report on the American Bar Association. It is enough to say here that the new constitution adopted at the meeting at Boston, August 24, 1936, added as one of the objects of the Association: "To correlate the activities of the Bar organizations of the respective States on a representative basis in the interest of the legal profession and of the public throughout the United States." [45] The end was achieved by the creation of a House of Delegates, to control the administration of the Association, preserving, however, the autonomy of the state and local associations. The membership of this House of Delegates was to be composed of delegates, one from each state; State Bar Association delegates in number according to the membership of the State Association, but not more than four to any association; local Bar Association delegates, one from each such association having eight hundred or more members in good standing, twenty-five per cent. of them members of the American Bar Association; five delegates chosen by the Assembly of members of the Association at its annual meeting; and a number of ex officio members, among whom the President of the National Conference of Commissioners on Uniform

44. 60 Rep. American Bar Association (1935) 375–376.
45. 61 Rep. American Bar Association (1936) 76, 966–982.

State Laws, the Chairman of the National Conference of Bar Examiners, the Chairman of the National Conference of Judicial Councils, the President of the Association of American Law Schools, and the President of the National Association of Attorneys General, are specially significant. Thus a body was created which may well speak for the profession as a whole and be accepted as the voice of the profession in its task of making the administration of justice what it should be.

Since 1939 the American Bar Association has made Awards of Merit for the most outstanding and constructive activity to a State Bar Association or State Bar. Since 1947 two Awards are made annually, one to a larger association, the other to a smaller association.

4. The Local Bar Associations Today. Since 1936 there has been a great increase in the activities of local associations. The old type of annual-address-and-dinner association has been disappearing and has been replaced by associations with definite purposes of advancing professional aims and making for improving the law both in its substance and in the machinery of making it effective.

It has proved impossible to give a complete account or even to give an assured complete list of the local bar associations in the United States. In the spring of 1950 a simple questionnaire (four questions only) was sent to over twelve hundred associations. Less than twelve per cent. responded. Mr. Porter then published an article in the American Bar Association Journal,[46] repeating the four questions propounded a year before and asking for answers. The answers received before publication of Mr. Porter's article showed five associations claiming continuous existence since before 1860, eight claiming origin between 1860 and 1875, four between 1876 and 1879, twenty-six between 1880 and 1899, thirty-two between 1900 and 1919, and twenty-one after 1919. But this total of ninety-six is but a small fraction of the actual number. A letter from George M. Wiener, Esq., Chairman of the Junior Bar Members of the State Bar of California, tells of the difficulty in obtaining full information. He explained that to obtain answers to Mr. Porter's four questions from the local Bar Associations in California would "of itself justify the employment of a full time lawyer for a period of many weeks." [47]

All that can be done is to give a list of the local associations which responded, calling attention to interesting features of some of them.

Alabama. The Eleventh Judicial Circuit Bar, formed 1935, and in continuous existence since that time.

46. Porter, Dean Pound and Bar Association Beginnings: A Survey Request for Primary Data (1951) 37 American Bar Association Journal, 269.

47. Letter of George M. Wiener, Esq., of Los Angeles, August 3, 1952.

"The object of this Association was merely a getting to-gether of the lawyers of the Eleventh Circuit for fellow-ship." [48]

The survival of this type of association is noteworthy. In 1887 Alabama reported a Mobile Bar Association, which made only a feeble showing of existence, and a Shelby County Association apparently functioning.[49] In 1900 there was one local association, in 1911, 3, and in 1929, 15.[50]

Arizona. Maricopa County Bar Association at Phoenix. Organized 1914, continuously existing. The Association was originally founded for social reasons only. No Association was reported in 1900, but one in 1911, and 3 in 1929.[51]

Florida. Jacksonville Bar Association, organized February 4, 1897, and in continuous existence since. The question as to objects of the Association was not an-swered.

---

48. Letter of James L. Orman, President.

49. 10 Rep. American Bar Association (1887) 487.

50. Wickser, Bar Associations, 15 Cornell Law Quarterly (1930) 417.

51. Ibid.

Orange County Bar Association (Orlando), organized in 1910 and in continuous existence since. The question as to objects was not answered.[52]

Tallahassee Bar Association, formed February 17, 1933, in continuous existence. The purpose is stated to have been "to obtain the formation of an association to raise the ethics of the local bar in certain particulars, to uplift the local bar generally, and to discourage certain practices then creeping into use by members of the local bar and not considered in accord with the highest professional standards." [53]

In 1887 both the Jacksonville Bar Association and the Orange County Bar Association were on the American Bar Association list.[54] In 1900 the same two local associations were reported. In 1911, 6 local associations were reported, and in 1929, 18.[55]

California. San Bernardino County Association, organized September 11, 1875, heretofore considered.

Fresno County Bar Association, organized September 4, 1882, for the purpose of maintaining the honor

52. Letter of Charles O. Anderson, Jr., President in 1950.

53. Answers to questionnaire.

54. 10 Rep. American Bar Association (1887) 440.

55. Wickser, loc. cit.

and dignity of the profession and of the practice of the law.[56]

Mendocino County Bar Association (Ukiah), formed 1913, in continuous existence since. The occasion of the organization is said to have been a scandal in the handling of divorce actions.[57]

Pasadena Bar Association, organized 1916, in continuous existence since. The object is stated as: "To advance the science of jurisprudence, to promote the administration of justice, to encourage a thorough legal education, to maintain the honor and dignity of the profession of the law and to cultivate social intercourse among its members." It has standing committees on: Bench and Bar, which attends to all judicial and court matters of concern to the Association; on Ethics, illegal practices and grievances, charged with consideration of disciplinary action in connection with the activities of individual lawyers and in improving the standards of professional ethics, honor, and conduct; Legal Aid Committee, which attends or assigns to various members of the Association such matters as are worthy of charitable assistance by the legal profession, and the Public Relations and Publicity Committee which at-

56. Answers to questionnaire.
57. Answers to questionnaire.

tends to all matters of general civic nature and fosters maintenance of a proper and wholesome relationship between the public and the legal profession. The Association from the beginning has taken a leading part in Pasadena community life.[58]

Shasta County Bar Association (Redding), formed June 7, 1939, in continuous existence since. The object is stated to be: "Furthering of improved personal relations among members of the local bar, and the dissemination of professional information." [59]

The bar in Los Angeles and vicinity is exceptionally well organized and a special report on the organized bar in Los Angeles is a part of the Survey.[59a] Answers to the questionnaire, however, were sent by the Los Angeles Bar Association formed in 1888. Also by The Lawyers Club of Los Angeles, formed September 21, 1931 to cooperate with the State Bar of California to enable fulfilling of its purposes, to encourage the spirit of constructive usefulness on the part of the membership, and in every reasonable way to render dignity to the practice of the profession and honor to the legal fraternity, to promote the growth of better understanding between the legal fraternity and the

---

58. Answers to questionnaire.

59. Letter of Richard B. Eaton, Esq., Secretary, May 1, 1950.

59a. See Clark and Hoose, The Organized Bar in Los Angeles, reprint from Los Angeles Bar Bulletin, October 1952.

laity, concerning the ethical relation to the public of those engaged in the administration of justice; to discuss questions of legal and social importance, and take such action relative to the same as the Club may deem expedient and for the general welfare; to foster good feeling and the spirit of fraternity among the members of the bar; to aid and assist worthy members of the bar in case of legal emergencies, to stimulate the spirit of patriotism and promote the love of Americanism; to foster international good will; to cherish peace and abhor war.

The questionnaire was answered also by the Conference of Junior Bar Members of the State Bar of California, by The Lawyers Club of San Francisco, organized in 1946 with one thousand members which is the third largest bar association in the state; by the Northern California Council of Bar Associations, organized August 29, 1949, for the purpose of raising ethical standards among lawyers. The Council had been organized as The Lawyers Club of San Francisco on January 14, but was organized in 1949 to extend its aims to a larger group in Northern California and to provide a clearing house for ideas of the various bar associations, and to obtain unified action on matters affecting the profession.[60]

There is also a Council of Bar Associations of Los Angeles County, formed October 19, 1948, to make it pos-

60. Answers to questionnaire.

sible for the smaller bar associations as well as the larger bar associations to cooperate with each other in disseminating and distributing educational information and to create a means whereby each Bar Association could help the other in unified action for better relations between the Bars, the lawyer and the public, and between themselves.[61]

In 1887, three local associations, the Bar Association of Los Angeles, the Bar Association of Oakland, and the Bar Association of San Francisco were listed, but apparently only the latter was then functioning.[62] In 1900, four local associations were reported, in 1911, 18, and in 1929, 45.[63]

In the list of "the larger local Bar Associations" in the Report for 1922, the Los Angeles Bar Association, the Sacramento Bar Association, the Bar Association of San Diego, and the San Francisco Bar Association are named.[64]

In 1944 the Santa Barbara County Bar Association, and in 1949 the Beverly Hills Bar Association received the Award of Merit from the American Bar Association.[65]

---

61. Answers to questionnaire.

62. 10 Rep. American Bar Association (1887) 439.

63. Wickser, loc. cit.

64. 47 Rep. American Bar Association (1922) 440.

65. 76 Rep. American Bar Association (1951) 683.

Georgia. Lawyers Club of Atlanta, Inc., formed 1922 and in continuous existence since. "There had been much criticism among the younger members concerning the inactivity of the Atlanta Bar Association and certain unethical practices by many members of the bar. A strong undercurrent of dissatisfaction among the younger members culminated in the group which organized the Lawyers Club." [66]

No local association was reported in 1887. In 1900, 2 were reported, 23 in 1911, and 39 in 1929. In 1922 The Savannah Bar Association was listed among the larger local associations.[67]

Idaho. All presently existing local bar associations were organized pursuant to Rules 186 and 187 of the Supreme Court and of the Board of Commissioners of the Idaho State Bar. Every lawyer in the State is within the jurisdiction of the local bar associations so organized. The Rule as originally adopted is Rule 49 effective October 16, 1935, and on that date at a meeting of the Board of Commissioners at Boise an order was issued directing the organization of the First Judicial District Bar Association (Shoshone County); another order directed the organization of the Second and Tenth Judicial

66. Answers to questionnaire.
67. 47 Rep. American Bar Association (1922) 440.

Districts (Clearwater Bar Association); another order directed the organization of the Eighth Judicial District Bar; another order directed the organization of the Eleventh Judicial District Bar; the organization meetings to be held respectively October 25, 1935, November 13, 1935, October 25, 1935, and November 1, 1935. At a meeting of the Board December 2–5, 1935, an order was entered organizing the Third Judicial District Bar; the organization meeting to be held December 19, 1935. At a meeting on January 6, 1936, an order was entered organizing the Fifth Judicial District Bar, organization meeting to be held June 25, 1936. On the same date an order was issued directing the organization of the Sixth Judicial District Bar at a meeting to be held on July 11, 1936, and an order directing the organization of the Ninth Judicial District Bar, the meeting to be held July 10, 1936. Subsequently the Sixth Judicial District having failed to organize, the Board directed that it be consolidated with the Fifth Judicial District Bar and they now operate under the name of the Southeastern Idaho Bar Association. The organization meeting of the Seventh Judicial District Bar was entered April 13, 1936, the meeting to be held April 30, 1936. The Fourth Judicial District Bar Association was annexed to the Eleventh Judicial District Bar about September, 1936. On September 19, 1936, a uniform set of by-laws for all local bar associations was promulgated by the Supreme Court and is now Rule 187.

All of the local associations organized as above are stated to have been continuously active, but the degree of activity has varied with the locality.[68]

The Third, Seventh, and Ninth Judicial District Bar Associations appear to be holding regular meetings and to be quite active. Idaho had but one local association in 1911 and six in 1929.[69]

Illinois. The Chicago Bar Association, incorporated May 27, 1874, had its origin in a meeting of forty-two lawyers in November, 1873, who agreed to unite and form a bar association "to sustain the profession in its proper position in the community and thereby enable it . . . to promote its own interest and the welfare of the public." A committee of five members was then appointed to consider the organization of a bar association. This association has been spoken of above and is the subject of a special paper, part of the Survey, "The Organized Bar in Chicago," by George W. Gale, Esq., published in the Chicago Bar Record of September, 1950.

Springfield Bar and Law Library Association, organized March 28, 1892, and in continuous existence since.

68. Letter of Sam Griffin, Esq., August 29, 1951.

69. Wickser, loc. cit.

The purpose was stated to be the advancement of legal knowledge and the proper discharge of the professional duties connected therewith and to purchase, acquire, and hold a law library.[70]

Will County Bar Association, organized June 16, 1900. Originally it was known as the Joliet Bar Association, but it changed its name in 1912. It has been in continuous existence since organization. Minutes of the earlier proceedings show that a group of forty-two Joliet attorneys agreed to form an association to promote higher standards of the legal profession and combat illegal practices of certain men before the Probate Court.[71]

Jackson County Bar Association, formed 1901 and in continuous existence since. The purposes are not stated.[72]

In 1887 only the Chicago Bar Association was reported.[73]

In 1942 The Lake County Bar Association received an Award of Merit from the American Bar Association.[74]

---

70. Answers to questionnaire.

71. Answers to questionnaire May 15, 1950.

72. Letter of Isaac K. Levy, Esq., Murphysboro, who was the first Secretary of the Association.

73. 10 Rep. American Bar Association (1887) 440.

74. 76 Rep. American Bar Association (1951) 683.

In 1900, six were reported, in 1911, sixty-five, in 1929, one hundred and two,[75] yet only three answered the questionnaire in 1951.

Indiana. Wayne County Bar Association (Richmond), incorporated February 16, 1918. Its continuous existence from its organization is reported. In 1887, two associations, the Howard County Association at Kokomo, and the Marion County Bar Association at Indianapolis were listed.[76]

In 1900, 21 local associations were reported, in 1911, 26, and in 1929, 26.[77]

Iowa. Very full reports have been received from this state.

Appanoose County, 1920.

Carroll County, exact date not stated.

Cass County, 1897–1899, but inactive until 1942 when it was reorganized.

Cerro Gordo, 1859, but not in Hill's list nor the American Bar Association list in 1887.

Cherokee County, 1922, reporting three regular meetings a year.

75. Wickser, loc. cit.

76. 10 Rep. American Bar Association (1887) 440.

77. Wickser, loc. cit. 417.

Chickasaw County, organized prior to 1925 with no intermission and a present high degree of activity.

Clay County, 1899, inactive during the war years 1918 and 1941.

Crawford County, 1939.

Des Moines County Bar Association, formerly Polk County Bar Association, organized 1886, in continuous existence since, meeting for luncheon every Wednesday during the year, and given the American Bar Association Award of Merit in 1947.[78]

Dickinson County, 1946.

Dubuque County, 1884, in continuous existence since that time. Object stated to be promoting mutual acquaintance and harmony among the members of Dubuque County and vicinity, and elevating the standard of integrity, honor, and courtesy in the legal profession, facilitating the administration of justice, cultivating the science of jurisprudence, giving expression to a deliberate opinion upon all matters upon which they may properly act as a body, and cherish the fraternal spirit among the members. This organization has been continuously active.[79]

78.   76 Rep. American Bar Association (1951) 683.

79.   Letter of Walter H. Paisley, Esq., Secretary, May 17, 1950.

Floyd County Bar Association, January 29, 1918.

Franklin County Bar Association, October 25, 1948.

Hamilton County, December 28, 1906.

Howard County, date of formation not known.

Jefferson County, organized prior to 1900 to maintain a county library and "iron out legal problems when presented."

Johnson County, 1881.

Keokuk County, 1931, holding luncheon meetings.

Linn County Bar Association (Cedar Rapids) organized 1896.

Louisa County, date of organization unknown.

Monona County, organized 1922.

Pocahontas County, date of organization unknown.

Pottawattamie County (Council Bluffs), organized 1900.

Poweshiek County, organized 1915.

Sioux County (Sioux City), organized 1941.

Story County, organized 1904.

Tama County, organized 1900.

Wayne County, organized June 6, 1949.

Winnebago County, organized 1947.

Wright County, organized 1916.

Each of these except Cass County and Cerro Gordo County, and Clay County and Hamilton County report continuous existence. The purposes stated vary greatly.

Seven of the associations stress friendly association, good fellowship, and mutual acquaintance and harmony. The oldest association (Cerro Gordo) as far back as 1859 puts as its purpose upholding the principles and honor of the legal profession and furthering the practice of and profession of law. Four maintain libraries. Three put fee schedules as an object. The remainder in different ways of putting it stress the purposes which have been generally set forth since 1870.

In 1887, two associations, the Clark County Bar Association at Osceola and the Polk County Bar Association at Des Moines are listed.[80] In 1900, 26 were listed, the same number in 1911, and 62 in 1929.[81] The Linn County Association is in the American Bar Association list in 1922.

Kansas. Bar Association of Northwestern Kansas, organized 1929 and in continuous existence since that date.[82]

Crawford County Bar Association, organized 1905, and continuously existing.

---

80. 10 Rep. American Bar Association (1887) 440.

81. Wickser, loc. cit. 417.

82. Answers to questionnaire.

Labette County Bar Association (Parsons), organized 1907, and continuously existing since. No statement as to objects was made by either association.[83]

A letter from J. C. Ruppenthal of Russell, Kansas, Secretary-Treasurer of the Bar Association of Northwestern Kansas, advises that as a part of the legal history of Kansas the writing of which was committed to a historical committee created by the State Bar Association in 1939, bar associations of Kansas are under consideration but so far very little literature exists on the subject. There are a few pamphlets, a few articles in legal periodicals, and something in the newspapers, but the material is extremely limited. Mr. Ruppenthal adds: "I do not think that the Kansas bar has yet awakened to the progress and/or aim of your Survey, but I hope they will learn. In fifty years that I have been a member of the State Bar Association of Kansas there has been but slow progress in arousing interest in legal history."

In 1887 no local bar associations were reported.[84] Two were reported in 1900, 23 in 1911, and 38 in 1929.[85]

Kentucky. Kenton County Bar Association, organized February 16, 1901, and in continuous existence

---

83. Ibid.

84. 10 Rep. American Bar Association (1887) 441.

85. Wickser, loc. cit. 417.

since. The purpose is stated to be: "To raise the standards of the bar, to maintain the honor and dignity of the profession of the law, to cultivate social intercourse and acquaintance among the members of the bar, and to increase their usefulness in the administration of justice, and in promoting legal and judicial reforms. It shall not discuss or take action on questions of politics or religion." [86]

Bell County Bar Association (Pineville), organized April, 1942, and in continuous existence. The purpose is said to be: "To uphold the honor of the profession of the law; to prepare and execute programs for professional and educational improvement; to promote proper social relations among the members." [87]

Kentucky was reported as having no local associations in 1887, none in 1900, 3 in 1911, and 10 in 1929.[88]

Maine. The Cumberland Bar Association (Portland), and Kennebec County Bar Association (Augusta) have been spoken of heretofore. A Penobscot County Bar Association is in the American Bar Association list (1887) but not in Mr. Hill's list. It is said there were 7 local as-

86. Answers to questionnaire.

87. Answers to questionnaire.

88. 10 Rep. American Bar Association (1887) 441; Wickser, Bar Associations, 15 Cornell Law Quarterly, 417.

sociations in 1900, 16 in 1911, and 16 in 1929. Only the Cumberland and Kennebec County Associations answered the questionnaire.

Maryland. The Bar Association of Baltimore City, founded January 15, 1880, to aid in maintaining the honor and dignity of the profession of law, to promote sound legal science and further the administration of justice. This association is in the lists in 1887 and 1922.

The Allegany County Bar Association, founded 1878, to maintain the honor and dignity of the profession of the law, to cultivate social intercourse among its members, to increase its usefulness in promoting a due administration of justice, and to procure a library for its members.

The Caroline County Bar Association, date unknown, some time prior to 1935. Infrequent meetings until October 16, 1947. No special purposes named in the constitution.

The Carroll County Bar Association, founded February 24, 1898, to maintain the honor and integrity of the profession, the promotion of social intercourse among its members, and the maintaining of a library for the use of said members.

The Cecil County Bar and Law Library Association, founded 1904. Purposes not specified.

[299]

The Charles County Bar Association, founded June 1, 1949. The usual purposes, but with the addition of encouragement of legal education.

The Dorchester County Bar Association, founded September 11, 1945. Substantially the same as in case of the Charles County Association.

The Frederick County Bar Association, founded March 21, 1933. Substantially the same purposes.

The Garrett County Bar Association, founded approximately 1920, to promote a better fellowship and fraternal relationship among the members; to provide for a minimum fee schedule, and to provide for a better understanding and relationship with the public and the members of the bar. This statement is in rather striking contrast with the more recent ones above noted.

The Kent County Bar Association, founded May 1, 1947, has for its purposes, partly continuing legal education, partly items of a business nature from minimum fees to memorials, and in part social purposes. In other words, it is an older type of organization in respect of purposes.

The Bar Association of Washington County, founded May 16, 1896, has the recent type of statement of purposes substantially that of most recent associations with the addition of procuring a library for the use of the members.[89]

Each of the associations is stated to have had no period of quiescence except in case of The Caroline County Bar Association which had infrequent meetings until October 16, 1947.

In 1887, Maryland had one local association, namely, the Bar Association of Baltimore City.[90] In 1900 there were 5 local associations, in 1911, 11, in 1929, 12.[91]

Massachusetts. The Survey has published a pamphlet "The Organized Bar in Massachusetts," by Lowell S. Nicholson, 1952. It discloses 12 county associations and 19 city and district associations. A number of them, the Berkshire County Bar Association, the Boston Bar Association, the Essex County Bar Association, the Franklin County Bar Association, and the Plymouth County Bar Association have been spoken of in other connections. Mr. Nicholson's account does not state the objects but in all the more recent associations they are substantially those which we find in most of the constitutions of such organizations today.

---

89. Information as to Maryland Associations in a letter from Herbert R. O'Conor, Jr., Esq., Baltimore, Maryland, August 21, 1951.

90. 10 Rep. American Bar Association (1887) 441.

91. Wickser, loc. cit. 417.

In 1887, 9 county associations and the Bar Association of the City of Boston, are listed.[92]   In 1900, 15 were reported, in 1911, 17, and in 1929, 20.[93]

Michigan.   Detroit Bar Association, claiming from 1835. This has been spoken of above. In 1942 it received an Award of Merit from the American Bar Association.

Gogebic Ontonagon Bar Association (Ironwood), exact date not stated. The purposes stated as promotion of better legal and social relations among the members. There have been the usual quiescent periods found in associations of 20 members or less. Occasional putting on of a better than average program, and problems of the moment that are out of the ordinary, stimulate interest.[94]

Houghton County Bar Association, exact date of founding not given. Purposes stated to be for the mutual benefit of the lawyers of the county.[95]

Kalamazoo County Bar Association. About 1900 a bar association existed in Kalamazoo of a very informal sort. It met once a year for a formal banquet and on

92. 10 Rep. American Bar Association (1887) 441–442.
93. Wickser, loc. cit. 417.
94. Answers to questionnaire.
95. Answers to questionnaire.

death of members for resolutions. About 1908 a selective organization known as the Barristers was formed and soon grew to include a majority of the younger members of the bar. In about 1915, the Kalamazoo County Bar Association and the Barristers were merged to form the present Kalamazoo County Bar Association with meetings held eight times a year at which meetings subjects of a legal nature were discussed or lectures heard. The organization was formed to sponsor a feeling of comradeship among the attorneys to advance the interests of the bar. Since the merger there has never been a period of quiescence and so far as the "old-timers" can recall meetings have been held eight times yearly since that date.[96]

Muskegon County Bar Association, founded approximately 1918. The purposes are stated to be to promote the congenial association of attorneys, to elevate the legal profession in the eyes of the public, and for study of and action on legal problems of the Court and in the community. It has had no period of quiescence although the files and records indicate an impetus in activity commencing in 1942, the early part of World War II.[97]

Grand Rapids Bar Association, organized February 8, 1902. The purposes as stated in the Articles of Incor-

96. Answers to questionnaire.
97. Answers to questionnaire, Arthur M. Rude, Esq., Secretary.

poration are: "To maintain the honor and dignity of the profession of law, to increase its activities in promoting due administration of justice and to cultivate social intercourse among its members. . . . Although there are and probably always have been those individuals who feel that the Bar Association is in a perpetual state of quiescence, nevertheless the minutes and records of the Grand Rapids Bar Association indicate that it has remained relatively active throughout the course of its existence." [98]

Cheboygan County Bar Association, formed about 1932, "to promote interest in increasing the salaries of Michigan Supreme Court Justices, or Circuit Court Judges in smaller Circuits; to establish local minimum attorney fees, to investigate and, when necessary, to prosecute those accused of unauthorized law practice, to restrain unethical advertising, to foster sociability." The Association never has been quiescent. [99]

Hillsdale Bar Association, incorporated in 1938. The purposes stated as professional and social benefits to its members. No periods of quiescence. [100]

---

98. Answers to questionnaire.

99. Answers to questionnaire.

100. Answers to questionnaire.

Shiawassee Bar Association, organization date not known; no information as to purposes.[101]

Livingston County Bar Association, organized January 10, 1923. Purposes: To promote uniformity of opinion concerning problems confronting practicing attorneys, to promote understanding between members of the bar of Livingston County, etc. Inactive for several years, 1935 to 1945.[102]

Huron County Bar Association, claims existence since 1920. Objects said to be harmony, policy, and professional interests. Continually active during those years. Probably been most active in past five years. Meets twice a year for social-business meetings, and subject to call of President.[103]

Menominee County Bar Association, date of formation unknown. Objects, for professional advancement and social contacts. Have been periods of quiescence. The younger lawyers aroused the association and it is more active now than before.[104]

Twenty-Fifth Judicial Circuit Bar Association, formed 1950. Has taken active part in curbing illegal

101. Answers to questionnaire.
102. Answers to questionnaire.
103. Answers to questionnaire.
104. Answers to questionnaire.

practice of law, in legislative matters, professional ethics, bar activities, admission to practice, schedules of minimum fees, etc.[105]

Mecosta County Bar Association, formed approximately 1912—records not available. Objects, discussion of mutual problems; to assist the Circuit Court in arranging calendar in local circuits; to arrive at minimum bar rates; discuss questions of ethics, etc. Is failing to hold regular meetings, because no problems requiring attention on local level, and death of officers without meetings to appoint new ones. The activity of the Tri-County Bar Association also relieved some of the burdens of the local bar.[106]

Branch County Bar Association, formed February 2, 1903. Objects, "To cultivate and aid in the improvement of the Law, to promote the administration of justice, uphold the honor of the profession of the Law, and encourage cordial intercourse among members of the Association." It has been active since its organization without any periods of quiescence.[107]

Suburban Bar Association of Wayne County, formed in October 1934. Objects, "To cultivate and promote

105. Letter of Michael J. Anuta, President, July 19, 1951.
106. Answers to questionnaire.
107. Answers to questionnaire.

friendship and mutual helpfulness among its members, as well as to further the administration of justice, maintain and support the honor and dignity of the Legal Profession by strict compliance with the Canons of Professional Ethics as promulgated by the American Bar Association, and promote the general welfare; entirely without profit." No periods of quiescence.[108]

Barry County Bar Association (Hastings), formed in 1946. Objects, "To establish uniformity of minimum fees; provide a means of holding discussion sessions of matters of common interest." Organization existed many years ago, but during the war years was inactive; was reconstituted because of great deal of unauthorized practice. However, very little success has been achieved in this direction, although the association was active in getting an attorney appointed to fill a vacancy in the Probate Judgeship.[109]

Twentieth Judicial Circuit Bar Association, formed late in 1948. Objects: "The attorneys of the Circuit (20th Judicial) decided that it might be more helpful if there were an association for the circuit, rather than one for each county (Allegan County and Ottawa County), Allegan county being inactive, some of its members faith-

108. Answers to questionnaire.

109. Answers to questionnaire.

fully attending the Ottawa County Bar Association sessions, it being an active organization for many years.
. . . Efforts of some of the members from Allegan for
either an Association of their own or a circuit association,
with some suggestions on the part of the circuit judge and
Ottawa members, brought about the new organization and
the Ottawa Bar closed its organization." [110]

Twenty-Sixth Judicial Circuit Bar Association,
formed January 1943. Formed to succeed the former Al-
pena Bar Association and to include Presque Isle and
Montmorency Counties which did not have sufficient lawyers to support individual county bar associations. "Our
bar association meets at the beginning of each term of
Court. Like other bar associations in the northern part
of the lower peninsula we miss out on the State Bar Regional meetings as most of the members feel it is too far
to travel to the Northern Peninsula to attend these meetings. A regrouping of the bar associations in this respect,
I believe, would be helpful in creating a more active interest on the part of our members." [111]

Dickinson County Bar Association, formed around
1920. Objects, to provide a meeting place for lawyers
for discussion of their mutual problems, and also to pro-

110. Answers to questionnaire.
111. Letter of William F. Knapp, Esq., Secretary.

vide for social relationships between the attorneys. No period of quiescence.[112]

Marquette County Bar Association, formed "about 1890 or before." Objects, thought to be "to promote the professional interests of lawyers plus special aspects." "The Association lapsed into planning an annual banquet—older lawyers, in office, not interested in professional activities of association or more frequent meetings. Election of younger lawyers to offices brought about more frequent planned meetings, with educational programs." [113]

Genesee County Bar Association, formed "about 1898." Objects, to promote a more harmonious Bar, and to raise the standards of practice. There has never been a period of quiescence.[114]

Saginaw County Bar Association, formed May 10, 1851. Reorganized on January 11, 1892, with election of officers on May 9, 1892; incorporated as a non-profit corporation on May 13, 1924; re-incorporated as a non-profit corporation on May 7, 1946. The Articles of Association of January 11, 1892, state it was formed "for the purpose of promoting social intercourse among its members and

112. Answers to questionnaire.

113. Answers to questionnaire by W. A. McCrea, Esq., Secretary.

114. This information was obtained from George Cook, Esq., who was Secretary of the Bar Association when it was first formed.

increasing its usefulness in the administration of justice."
The Articles of Association of May 13, 1924 and May 7,
1946, state the purpose of the Association is: "To maintain the honor and dignity of the profession of the law, to
increase its usefulness in promoting the due administration of justice, to cultivate social intercourse among its
members and to acquire and maintain a law library." No
periods of quiescence.[115]

Grand Traverse, Leelanau, and Antrim County Bar
Association. Exact date of organization unknown. Objects not stated. No fixed dates for meetings.[116]

Women Lawyers Association of Michigan, formed in
Detroit in 1919. "The Association was originally formed
to advance the interest of women members of the legal
profession, women about to enter the profession, and to
strengthen professional ties. Women lawyers were few
in number and lacked a clearing house for their problems. As an Associated Group it was felt they could exchange ideas and give each other the benefit of individual
experience, with the goal of attaining a high standard of
legal practice and earning the respect of the bench
and bar." No quiescent period.[117]

---

115. Answers to questionnaire by Albert A. Smith, Esq., Secretary.

116. Answers to questionnaire by J. M. Fitzpatrick, Esq., Secretary.

117. Answers to questionnaire, Charlotte Sutton, President, Vera B. Clou-
tier, Corresponding Secretary.

Dearborn Bar Association, formed October 1, 1931. "To promote friendship and social fraternization, instill mutual good will and advance the general welfare and good standing of licensed attorneys. To promote and maintain ethical practice by licensed members of the legal profession. To protect and improve the judicial system and all legislation affecting either the judicial system or the administration of justice generally. To educate the public in the functions of a lawyer and services to his client and the community. To promote and protect the public in all its relations with the legal profession and the administration of justice." No noticeable periods of quiescence.[118]

Iona and Montcalm Bar Association, believed to have been formed during the year 1923, and to have been in continuous existence since formation. Object, "The Association encompassed both counties as it was felt that one association was preferable because of the congenial atmosphere that existed among its lawyers." [119]

St. Joseph County Bar Association, formed 1910. Object, for closer association between lawyers on an informal and social basis, also to organize for better local

118. Answers to questionnaire.
119. Letter of Edwin C. Boos, Esq., Secretary.

administration of justice. No period of quiescence since formation.[120]

Calhoun County Bar Association, formed 1911. "To facilitate the inter-exchange of opinions and discussions of questions concerning the law and its practice among the resident county attorneys and to promote the acquaintance of them." No period of quiescence.[121]

Isabella County Bar Association, formed 1940. "To foster a better spirit among members, promote the ethics of our profession, to present and attempt to solve mutual problems, and establish uniform minimum fees." "It has never been very active because there were only three members during the war. Now—six. The organization is too small to operate effectively." [122]

Cass County Bar Association, formed 1942. Objects, social reasons, to improve the local bar and the profession.[123]

Thirty-fourth Judicial Circuit Bar Association, formed January 20, 1948. "1. To promote good relations among the attorneys in the six counties in this circuit. 2. To promote to and keep at a high level, the

120. Answers to questionnaire.
121. Answers to questionnaire.
122. Answers to questionnaire.
123. Answers to questionnaire.

standards of the attorneys. 3. To promote a more uniform set of procedures among the attorneys as to litigation. 4. To promote a more concerted effort in reforms in the practice of the law, and 5. To promote such beneficial projects as the establishment of the friend of the court." No periods of quiescence.[124]

I am indebted to Russell E. Bowers, Esq., for gathering the foregoing information. He states that the completed questionnaires represent 45 per cent. of the local associations.

In 1887, 5 local associations are listed, only one of them (the Detroit Bar Association) apparently at all active.[125] In 1900, 6 local associations are listed in 1911, 36, in 1929, 27.[126]

Minnesota. Hennepin County Bar Association (Minneapolis), formed 1919, and in continuous existence since. In answer to the questionnaire it is said that information as to the original purpose of the organization has been lost.

In 1887, the Minneapolis Bar Association (evidently the same as the one last mentioned) and the St. Paul Bar

124. Answers to questionnaire by James V. Rutledge, Esq.

125. 10 Rep. American Bar Association (1887) 442.

126. Wickser, loc. cit. 417.

Association are listed.[127] In 1900, 8 are listed, 9 in 1911, and 25 in 1929.[128]

Missouri. Clay County Bar Association (Liberty), formed in 1915 for social purposes. It has been in continuous existence since its organization.

Newton County Bar Association, formed in 1917, has been on the whole in continuous existence, but there have been some lapses of more or less inactivity. The occasion of the organization was that President Wilson desired bar cooperation with the war effort. The organization has since gone on chiefly for social purposes.

Tenth Judicial District Bar Association (Counties of Marion, Ralls, and Monroe), organized September 18, 1918, and in continuous existence since. The principal function of the Association is said to have been to promote good fellowship among members of the bar.

The Lawyers Association of Kansas City, organized September 18, 1935, and in continuous existence since. The object is stated to have been to promote the interests of lawyers and their relations with the public regardless of political influence.

Carthage Lawyers Association (Carthage, Jasper County), founded March 30, 1939, in continuous exist-

127. 10 Rep. American Bar Association (1887) 442.
128. Wickser, loc. cit. 417.

ence since. The object is stated to have been to bring the members of the profession closer together; to conduct institutes and hold discussions as to developments of the law and to promote the good name of the bar. In returning the questionnaire it was said that in that county there was also a Jasper County Bar Association, and a Joplin Bar Association. Further inquiry, however, failed to elicit information as to those associations.[129]

In 1887, 2 local bar associations, the Kansas City Bar Association, and the St. Louis Bar Association are listed.[130] In 1900, 2 local associations are listed, in 1911, 3, and in 1929, 45.[131] In 1941 the St. Louis Bar Association was given an Award of Merit by the American Bar Association.

Nebraska. Omaha Bar Association, organized 1879 by a group of the leading members of the Omaha Bar at that time, among them James M. Woolworth, Esq., afterwards President of the American Bar Association. The object was said to be to bring the members of the bar together for exchange of views and the general welfare of the bar.[132]

129. Answers to questionnaire.

130. 10 Rep. American Bar Association (1887) 441.

131. Wickser, loc. cit.

132. Letter of Byron G. Burbank, Esq., in active practice in Omaha since 1885.

[315]

In 1887, this association was the only local association listed. In 1900, 3 were listed, 3 also in 1911, and 15 in 1929.[133]

From personal knowledge, I doubt, however, except for the Omaha Association, whether there was any active local bar association in Nebraska until after 1907.

New Hampshire. The Grafton and Coos Bar Association has been spoken of heretofore. It is the only one listed in 1887.[134] Four are listed in 1900, 4 in 1911, and 9 in 1929.[135]

New Jersey. Union County Bar Association (Union), incorporated January 23, 1902. The objects stated are: To maintain the honor and dignity of the profession of the law; to cultivate social relations among the members thereof; to investigate all complaints affecting the professional conduct of lawyers practicing in Union County, and the adoption of such action in relation thereto as shall seem just and expedient; to guard against the admission to the Bar of immoral or incompetent persons; and in general to advance the honor, welfare and efficiency of the members of the Bar, and to aid in the administration of justice. There has been no period of quiescence. There

133. Wickser, loc. cit.

134. 10 Rep. American Bar Association (1887) 443.

135. Wickser, loc. cit.

is a complete set of minute books from the date of incorporation.

Irvington Bar Association, formed about 1930, the exact date unknown. It became inactive after a short period but was reorganized on June 23, 1948, and has since continued to function actively. The object stated is promotion of social intercourse and good fellowship, discussion of legal questions of general practical importance, investigation of complaints affecting the professional conduct of lawyers practicing in Irvington, and in general the advancement of the honor, welfare, efficiency and enjoyment of the members of the Bar.[136]

Clifton City Bar Association. Date of first organization unknown but dormant during 1940–1941, and replaced in 1951 by the Clifton Lawyers Club, a social organization. The members are members of the Passaic County Bar Association, and the monthly luncheons are followed by discussions or addresses.[137]

Burlington County Bar Association, organized September 8, 1932. It has been active continuously since organization. Its membership includes 100 per cent. of the active practitioners in the County.

136. Letter of Frederic C. Stoddard, Esq., Secretary.
137. Letter of Joseph B. Stadtmauer, Esq.

[317]

Camden County Bar Association (Camden), incorporated April 23, 1881. It has been active from the beginning, among other things making a proposal for an improved judicial system at the outset of its existence, making another proposal on the same subject in 1885, and in 1896 renewing the agitation.

Bergen Bar Association (Hackensack), formed in 1899 for the purpose of creating better relationships between members of the Bar and between members of the Bar and the general public. It has been active without interruption. It was given an Award of Merit by the American Bar Association in 1943.

Gloucester County Bar Association (Woodbury), incorporated February 15, 1901, to maintain and uphold the honor and dignity of the profession of the law, to aid in the due administration of justice and to cultivate social relations among its members. The minutes prior to 1936 have been lost, but it is said there has been no time when the Association has ceased to function.

Hudson County Bar Association (Jersey City), formed March 1, 1877, to maintain the honor and dignity of the profession of the law, to cultivate social relations among its members and to promote the due administration of justice. It is said there has never been any period of quiescence.

Association of the Montclair Bar, formed in 1946 and uniformly active since that time holding five meetings annually. Among other things, it sponsors public lectures in cooperation with local institutions.

West Hudson Bar Association, organized November 7, 1925, incorporated December 27, 1926. The objects are stated very fully substantially as in the present day type of association.

Warren County Bar Association (Phillipsburg), organized October, 1927. The Association holds three business meetings and a dinner meeting each year but has not been notably active.

Bar Association of South Orange and Maplewood, formed March 1, 1949. The purposes are said to be to serve the public as an organized association, to act upon common problems facing lawyers practicing in the two suburban communities as distinguished from problems facing attorneys practicing in Newark. The Association is said to have been very active. It has organized the Lawyers Referral Service, and conducted a public relations program.

Essex County Bar Association (Newark). The Association was organized in 1879 and incorporated June 21 of that year. It was organized to promote social intercourse and good fellowship, to maintain a law library, to

[319]

investigate complaints affecting the professional conduct of lawyers practicing in Essex County and in general to advance the honor, welfare, efficiency and enjoyment of the members of the bar. It has had no periods of quiescence. It publishes "Library News" in connection with its library activities.

Middlesex County Bar Association (New Brunswick), organized March 12, 1947, to promote the dignity of the profession as well as fellowship. It usually had only an annual meeting but in recent years has met at least six times a year at dinner meetings. It is claimed that the organization was to some extent a continuation of one organized in 1914, which it is claimed succeeded an older one going back to perhaps 1900. But no records are vouched.

Somerset County Bar Association, formed 1900 to promote understanding between members of the bar. It is said to have functioned continuously since its organization.

Dover Lawyers Association, formed November 13, 1946, for the purpose of integrating the practitioners in the area and interesting them in promoting their mutual interests, abilities and knowledge. In continuous existence since organization.

[320]

The foregoing information was procured for the Survey by Merritt Lane, Jr., Esq., Chairman of the New Jersey State Bar Association.

In 1887, 5 local bar associations were listed, 2 of them not answering the Survey questionnaire in 1950.[138] In 1900 there are said to have been 9 local associations, in 1911, 15, in 1929, 17.[139] The Hudson County Association is in the 1922 list of the American Bar Association.

New York. The Association of the Bar of the City of New York has been spoken of above, and also the Queens County Association. Others which responded to the questionnaire or to Mr. Porter's article are:

Bar Association of Erie County, organized at Idlewood (Erie County) in September 1886, and reorganized at Buffalo June 25, 1887. It has been in continuous existence since organization. The purposes are not stated.

Brooklyn Bar Association, organized July 2, 1889, also in continuous existence since organization. It appears that in 1889 the press reported the activities of a lawyer in a widely publicized divorce action and accused him of concealing facts. The article set forth that Kings County (Brooklyn) was without any active bar association or if one was in existence nothing of it was known

---

138. 10 Rep. American Bar Association (1887) 443.

139. Wickser, loc. cit.

by leading members of the bar. One of the Justices of the Supreme Court asserted that there had been an association at one time but that it was never active. The Association referred to was "The Bar Association of Brooklyn" an unincorporated association formed in 1872. It is said that in 1896 the members of that organization which had practically gone out of existence joined the Brooklyn Bar Association. The need for an organized bar arising from the publicity given to the conduct of a member of the bar above referred to was the occasion of the present organization.

Westchester County Bar Association, organized February 11, 1896, and continuously existing since. The purposes stated in the articles of incorporation are, cultivation of the science of jurisprudence, promoting reforms in the law, facilitating the administration of justice, elevating the standards of integrity, honor and courtesy in the legal profession and cherishing the spirit of brotherhood among the members.

Bronx County Bar Association, formed in 1902 and in continuous existence since. The purpose was stated to be to improve the judicial service to the community by obtaining the construction of a court house in The Bronx after which the Association continued for general bar association activities.

New York County Lawyers' Association. This organization, formed in April, 1908, and in continuous existence since, has been termed justly the giant of bar associations. The 133 who were the first committee on organization in June, 1908, included 75 members of the Association of the Bar of the City of New York. The general principle of selective membership, a basic tenet of the Association of the Bar of the City of New York, was the main reason for the formation of the Lawyers' Association. The founders were convinced that admission to the bar should be the only requirement for active membership. Any member of the bar who had met the rigid standards now set up by law for admission to the bar should by virtue of that circumstance be eligible to any Bar Association. The Association has had an enormous growth and development. Within a year of its organization it had become the largest Bar Association in the country. By 1928 the membership exceeded 5,000 and in 1950, 7,166. It has had much to do in assisting in law reform, in connection with unlawful practice of the law, in maintaining discipline, in obtaining the construction of better court house facilities, and more recently in legal referral. Also it maintains a placement bureau which has proved to be of great service in affording those seeking employment the best opportunity of finding positions for which they are qualified. It publishes "The Bar Bulletin." It now

[323]

has a magnificent building in the City Hall area. A full account may be found in Blaustein, New York County Lawyers' Association—Giant Bar Association, published for the Survey.

Genesee County Bar Association, formed December 10, 1910, but largely inactive until 1925. On November 1, 1925, the Association began to hold regular meetings each month except July, August, and September, and has been continuously active since that time.

Yonkers Lawyers' Association, formed in 1915 and in continuous existence since that time. Its purpose is stated to be to cultivate the science of jurisprudence, to elevate the standards of integrity, honor and courtesy in the legal profession.

In 1887, only one local association, namely, the Association of the Bar of the City of New York was listed.[140] In 1900, 10 were listed, in 1911, 49, and in 1929, 60.[141]

North Carolina.[141a] Mecklenburg Bar Association (Charlotte), organized February 28, 1912, and in continuous existence since. The original minute book has been

---

140. 10 Rep. American Bar Association (1887) 443.

141. Wickser, loc. cit.

141a. See Bryson, The Organized Bar in North Carolina, 30 North Carolina Law Rev. 335 (1952).

destroyed or lost so that the further information requested in the questionnaire could not be furnished.[142]

Greensboro Bar Association, organized 1919 and in continuous existence since. No information was furnished as to the objects of the Association.[143]

In 1887, no associations in North Carolina were listed, none were listed in 1900, or in 1911, but 38 in 1929.[144] In 1945 the Cumberland County Bar Association received an Award of Merit from the American Bar Association.

North Dakota. Barnes County Bar Association (Valley City), formed in 1910 to promote better understanding and closer relations between members of the bar. The Association has only one meeting a year, or at most, semi-annual meetings.

Cass County Bar Association (Fargo), has records dating back only to February 1, 1930. The early minutes have been lost and the exact date of its founding and the original purpose are not known. The Association is now active and has been such continuously since 1930.

Ramsey County Bar Association (Devils Lake), was organized in 1926, but became quiescent and completely

142. Answers to questionnaire.
143. Answers to questionnaire.
144. Wickser, loc. cit.

inactive in 1935. In 1938 the Devils Lake Bar Association was formed and that Association is still operating. Devils Lake is the only city of any size in Ramsey County.

District Bar Association of Southwestern North Dakota, was apparently a get-together association of lawyers in Dickinson, which has had no definite program of meetings, but has been meeting once or twice a year for discussion of problems of mutual interest.

Burleigh County Bar Association (Bismarck), has been a very active bar association for many years. The exact date of its formation is not known.

Grand Forks County Bar Association, organized in January, 1937, has been continuously active.

The foregoing information was supplied by Thomas P. McElroy, Jr., Esq., of Grand Forks, North Dakota.

In 1887, the Grand Forks County Bar Association is the only association listed for Dakota Territory. In 1900, there was one local association, 14 were listed in 1911, and 11 in 1929.[145]

Ohio. Columbus Bar Association has been spoken of above. It is an example of an association formed originally for social purposes which became a bar association of the modern type exactly as some of the older library as-

---

145. Wickser, loc. cit.

sociations did. It has become a very active and important association and was given an Award of Merit by the American Bar Association in 1948, and again in 1949.

Huron County Bar Association (Norwalk), claiming to have been organized before 1893. On February 8, 1893, the Huron County Law Library Association was incorporated but is distinct from the Huron County Bar Association having separate officers. Both are still active.[146]

Columbiana County Bar Association (Lisbon). The records of its organization are no longer available but it is supposed to date from 1896 and has been in continuous existence since that date. There is no available record as to the purpose for which it was organized.[147]

Fairfield County Bar Association (Lancaster), organized in 1933 and continuously in existence since that date. No purposes of the organization are stated.[148]

Springfield Bar and Library Association, organized in 1892, largely for the purpose of establishing a law library. The Association now has a good working law library but apparently does not function actively as a bar association.[149]

---

146. Answers to questionnaire.
147. Answers to questionnaire.
148. Answers to questionnaire.
149. Answers to questionnaire.

Trumbull County Bar Association, organized August 2, 1879, in continuous existence since that date. The objects are said to be maintaining the honor and dignity of the profession of the law, cultivating social intercourse and acquaintance among the members of the bar, increasing their usefulness in aiding the administration of justice and in promoting legal and judicial reform.[150]

The answers received from Ohio do not include some of the most important local associations. In 1887, Cuyahoga Bar Association, now called the Cleveland Bar Association, the Hamilton County Bar Association, now known as the Cincinnati Bar Association, the Franklin County Bar Association now known as the Columbus Bar Association, which are spoken of fully above, and the Dayton Bar Association, are named. In 1900, 27 local associations are listed, in 1911, 31, and in 1929, 87. Unhappily it was impossible to obtain definite information about most of these including some very important associations. For example, the Toledo Bar Association was given an Award of Merit by the American Bar Association in 1950. The same Award was made to the Lake County Bar Association in 1946.

Oklahoma. Cleveland County Bar Association (Norman), organized prior to 1900 and in continuous existence since that time. Its chief purpose originally

150. Answers to questionnaire.

was to examine candidates for admission to the bar of the Territory of Oklahoma.[151]

Grady County Bar Association (Chickasha), formerly called Chickasha Bar Association, but name changed in 1907 when counties were formed. This Association was organized in 1902 for the purpose of aiding in securing a suitable body of law for Indian Territory in cooperation with other local bar associations in the Territory.[152]

Atoka County Bar Association, formed in 1902 to discourage unethical practice of law in the Indian Territory in which "there were many fly by night lawyers who dropped into the court town and did a questionable practice for a few months and passed on." [153]

Texas County Bar Association (Guymon), formed January 1, 1908, and in continuous existence since. Its primary purpose was to set up a standard of fees.[154]

Canadian County Bar Association (El Reno), formed about 1920, in recognition by members of the local bar of the advantage of organization for the protection of the lawyers and the public.[155]

---

151. Letter of Earl Sneed, Jr., Esq., President of the Association, June 7, 1950.

152. Answers to questionnaire.

153. Letter of J. L. Cook, Esq., President.

154. Answers to questionnaire.

155. Letter of H. L. Fogg, Esq., President of the Association, May 13, 1950.

Garfield County Bar Association (Enid). The date of the original organization is not exactly known but is supposed to be about 1925. It has been in continuous existence since that time but the original purpose is not now known.[156]

Woods County Bar Association (Alvah), supposed to have been organized in 1924, but reorganized in 1940, for the promotion of mutual interests of members of the bar, and as a clearing house for different matters as they arose. It has had a continuous existence since 1940.[157]

Oregon. Multnomah Bar Association, formed February 3, 1906, to encourage good will within the profession. It has been in continuous existence since 1906. 42 of the original 157 members were surviving at the date of the letter.[158] It is in the American Bar Association list of 1922.[159]

Klamath County Bar Association, formed May 28, 1925, in continuous existence since that date. The purpose of the organization was to advance good fellowship

156. Letter of Hugh Conway, Esq., President of the Association, June 9, 1950.

157. Answers to questionnaire.

158. Letter of Seva M. Elliott, Esq., Portland, Oregon, May 29, 1950.

159. 47 Rep. American Bar Association (1922) 440.

among the members of the legal profession, locally and state wide.[160]

No associations in Oregon were listed in 1887, 2 local associations were listed in 1900, 6 in 1911, and 25 in 1929.[161]

Pennsylvania. The Philadelphia Bar Association has already been spoken of fully.[161a]

Dauphin County Bar Association (Harrisburg), chartered June 17, 1898, in continuous existence since that time. The purpose is stated to be: "To promote the administration of justice; to encourage a thorough legal education; to uphold the honor and dignity of the bar; to cultivate cordial intercourse among the members of this association; and to perpetuate the history of the profession and the memory of its members, and kindred purposes." [162]

Westmoreland Law Association (Greensburg), formed July 12, 1886, continuously in existence since that date. There are no particulars as to its purposes.[163]

---

160. Answers to questionnaire.

161. Wickser, loc. cit.

161a. See Hanna, The Organized Bar in Philadelphia, 25 Temple Law Quarterly 301 (1952).

162. Answers to questionnaire.

163. Ibid.

Lawrence County Bar Association (Newcastle), formed April 18, 1887, in continuous existence since that date. There are complete minutes of the Association from its organization. The purpose was apparently to draw men with exceptional ability at the bar into closer association.[164]

Bar Association of Mercer County, formed December 9, 1895, and in continuous existence since that date. The chief purpose was to promote the dignity and honor of the legal profession, to increase its usefulness, and to maintain a law library.[165]

Franklin County Bar Association, organized 1899, in continuous existence since that date. The membership of the Association constituted practically the entire bar of Franklin County, and the Association was formed for the general welfare of the bar, the furtherance of high professional standards and social intercourse of its members.[166]

The Bar Association of Lehigh County (Allentown), organized February 10, 1905, and in continuous existence since that date. The objects in addition to maintaining a library are stated to have been to encourage a thorough

164. Ibid.

165. Ibid.

166. Letter of Edwin D. Strite, Esq., President of the Association, May 17, 1950.

legal education, to uphold the honor and dignity of the bar, to cultivate social and professional intercourse among its members, and to perpetuate the history of the profession and the memory of its members within this judicial district.[167]

The Allegheny County Bar Association at Pittsburgh has been spoken of above.

In 1887, 34 local associations are listed.[168] In 1900, 42 are listed, in 1911, 68, and in 1929, 66.[169] It will have been observed that a great many of these associations were originally library associations which grew into bar associations as we understand them today.[170]

South Carolina. Spartanburg County Bar Association, active since 1882, but the exact date of organization unknown. The principal purpose was to meet before each term of the civil court for the purpose of setting a roster of the cases to be tried. On a few occasions the Association took action to discipline violators of the code of ethics. It has now become very active, interesting itself in all legislation affecting the courts and practice.[171]

167. Answers to questionnaire.
168. 10 Rep. American Bar Association (1887) 444–445.
169. Wickser, loc. cit.
170. Wickser, loc. cit.
171. Answers to questionnaire.

Horry County Bar Association, organized January 1, 1915, in continuous existence since that date. No objects are specified.[172]

No local associations were listed in 1887, in 1900, or in 1911. Twenty-seven are listed in 1929,[173] of which, however, only one responded to the questionnaire.

South Dakota. Theodore M. Bailey, Jr., of Sioux Falls, South Dakota, writes as follows: "The problem of running down all of the local bar associations in our state is just about like cleaning out the Augean stables. Our strongest organization, as I understand it, is the integrated State Bar. Because of the small number of lawyers in this State, and because of the wide areas without anything but grass and Indians, the local Bar Associations are more or less loose organizations. With the exception of the very thinly populated areas each county has some type of a local Bar group, but to my knowledge there is no official list of these organizations or their officers. I don't know any one who is qualified even in my own county to give the information that is desired. It appears the old records have been lost and I hazard a guess that our county would probably have kept better records than any of the others." [174]

172. Letter of H. H. Woodward, Esq.
173. Wickser, loc. cit.
174. Letter of T. M. Bailey, Jr., Esq., Sioux Falls, S. D., July 30, 1951.

There was but one bar association in Dakota Territory in 1887 and that at Grand Forks now in North Dakota. In South Dakota, 7 local associations are listed in 1900, 3 in 1911, and 7 in 1929.[175]

In view of Mr. Bailey's letter it is a legitimate question whether any were actually functioning between 1900 and 1929.

Tennessee. Chattanooga Bar Association, founded April 15, 1897, and in continuous existence since that time. In 1897, the principal office building in Chattanooga was destroyed by fire so that the local lawyers set about it to provide for a common law library. The Association celebrated its golden anniversary in 1947, following receipt of the American Bar Association Award of Merit during that year. Five of the charter members were still surviving. Among the charter members were Alex W. Chambliss, afterward Chief Justice of the Supreme Court of Tennessee, and William L. Frierson, Solicitor General of the United States during President Wilson's administration.[176]

Memphis and Shelby County Bar Association, formed May 23, 1922, in continuous existence since that time.

---

175. Wickser, loc. cit.

176. Letter of Clarence Kolwyck, Esq., President of the Association in 1947.

The purpose is said to have been promotion of the administration of justice.[177]

In 1887, there were said to be two local associations, one at Nashville, the other at Memphis.[178] The Association at Memphis, however, did not appear to be very active. In 1900, 6 local associations are said to have been in existence, 4 in 1911, and 7 in 1929.[179]

Utah. Box Elder County Bar Association, formed in 1912, in continuous existence since that time. The purpose was to take action against people who were practicing law without license.[180]

In 1887, the Bar Association of Salt Lake City is listed.[181] None are listed for 1900, or 1911, but 6 for 1929.[182]

Texas. Very little information could be obtained from Texas. The South Central Texas Bar Association, formed June 1, 1941, ceased to function during the war. It was never very active after that and has now gone out

---

177. Answers to questionnaire.

178. 10 Rep. American Bar Association (1887) 446.

179. Wickser, loc. cit.

180. Answers to questionnaire.

181. 10 Rep. American Bar Association (1887) 447.

182. Wickser, loc. cit.

of existence. Unhappily, no other organization responded to inquiries.

No local bar associations were listed in 1887.[183] Two
are listed in 1900, 2 in 1911, and 39 in 1929.[184] But three
local associations which did not respond to the questionnaire have been doing notable work. The Dallas Bar Association in 1939, The Nueces County Bar Association at
Corpus Christi in 1941, and the Wichita County Bar Association in 1951 received Awards of Merit from the
American Bar Association.[185]

Vermont. The Rutland County Bar Association,
organized on November 12, 1907, has been in existence
continuously since that date.[186]

A letter of Paul N. Olson, Esq., of the Junior Bar
Conference, State Chairman, of date 27 July 1951 says:
"The Vermont Bar Association . . . is the only real
active Bar organization in this state. A good many, or
perhaps all, of the counties have county organizations but
so far as I am able to learn these county organizations do
not carry on active bar work and their sole activity ordinarily is holding one or two dinner meetings each year at
which officers are elected."

183. 10 Rep. American Bar Association (1887) 446.

184. Wickser, loc. cit.

185. 76 Rep. American Bar Association (1951) 683.

186. Answers to questionnaire.

In 1887 no local associations were listed.[187] None were listed in 1900 or 1911, but one in 1929.[188]

Virginia. Bar Association of the City of Richmond, organized 1885, in continuous existence since that date. Original purposes not stated.[189] It is in the 1887 and 1922 lists of the American Bar Association.[190]

The Norfolk and Portsmouth Bar Association, organized November 23, 1898, and in continuous existence since that time. There was, however, a law library organization beginning in 1877. This is another example of a law library association growing into a bar association.[191]

Charlottesville and Albemarle County Bar Association, formed in 1916, in continuous existence since that time. The chief object originally was simply to bring the lawyers together.[192]

In 1887, two associations were listed by the American Bar Association, the Richmond Association and the Louisa Bar Association of Louisa Court House.[193] In 1900, 3

187. 10 Rep. American Bar Association (1887) 446.
188. Wickser, loc. cit.
189. Answers to questionnaire.
190. 10 Rep. American Bar Association (1887) 446; 47 id. 440.
191. Answers to questionnaire.
192. Answers to questionnaire.
193. 10 Rep. American Bar Association (1887) 446.

local bar associations were listed, in 1911, 20, and in 1929, 31.[194]

West Virginia. Monongalia County Bar Association, formed November 24, 1897, and in continuous existence since that time. The purposes were stated to be, promoting reform in the law, upholding the integrity, honor, and courtesy of the legal profession in Monongalia County, for establishing a local law library, for cultivating cordial intercourse and friendly relations among the members of the Association. The law order books of Monongalia County show that the local attorneys met as a group as far back as 1869 but without any formal organization.[195]

Lewis County Bar Association, organized about 1900 and claiming continuous existence since that date. But it seems never to have had more than a nominal existence with infrequent meetings. In 1951 a movement was going on to reorganize the Association.[196]

Harrison County Bar Association, organized June 2, 1932, succeeding the Clarksburg Bar Association, organized July 24, 1902. There has been no break in the succession since 1905. John W. Davis, Esq., father of the Hon. John W. Davis, was the chief promoter of the

194. Wickser, loc. cit.

195. Answers to questionnaire.

196. Letter of John Sterrett Holy, Esq., Weston, W. Va., August 14, 1951.

Clarksburg Bar Association. The purpose was stated to be to increase the usefulness of the profession of the law in promoting the due administration of justice and to establish and maintain a law library.[197]

Ohio County Bar Association, said to have been organized about 1880, and in continuous existence since that time. Its purpose is stated to be to promote the interests of the legal profession. This is the only local bar association in West Virginia listed in 1887.[198]

Brooke County Bar Association said to have been organized about 1900 to promote the interests of the legal profession. It is claimed to have been in continuous existence since its organization.[199]

Hancock County Bar Association, claims to have been organized in 1900 and to have been in continuous existence since that time. It was formed originally for members of the bar to spend occasional evenings together, and now has a dinner at least once each term of court. It is purely a social organization.[200]

McDowell County Bar Association, formed about 1900 to create higher standards of the legal profession,

197. Answers to questionnaire.

198. 10 Rep. American Bar Association (1887) 446.

199. Letter of C. J. Jacob, Esq., the oldest member of the Brooke County Bar.

200. Answers to questionnaire.

and claims to have been in continuous existence since that time.[201] It seems to have been chiefly a social organization.

Mingo County Bar Association. The original records have been lost but it is claimed to have been in continuous existence since some time shortly after 1895. It seems to have been chiefly a social organization.[202]

Wood County Bar Association, formed about 1904, but not in continuous existence. It seems to have been originally chiefly a law library association.[203]

Regional Bar Association of the Fourth Judicial Circuit, formed in 1930, in continuous existence since that time. The reason of its organization is said to have been that the small county bar associations were then not large enough to be useful and it was felt important to make uniform rules of practice.[204]

Logan County Bar Association, organized prior to 1906, but there are no records of the exact date. It has had continuous existence except for certain periods during

201. Letter of D. J. F. Strother, Esq., the oldest member of the McDowell County Bar.

202. Information furnished by Randolph Bias, Esq., the oldest living member of Mingo County Bar.

203. Letter of Walter T. Crofton, Jr., Esq., Parkersburg, W.Va., August 20, 1951.

204. Information procured from James E. Watson, 3d, Esq., Secretary of the Junior Bar Section of the West Virginia State Bar.

the first and second world wars when no meetings were held and the officers continued in office until enough members were present to reform the group. The present organization was revived in 1946 after a war time lapse. The chief interest has been to inform and familiarize the members of the latest developments in different fields of the law.[205]

Boone County Bar Association, organized about 1925, but with some lapses of activity. In 1946 it became an active organization with a purpose of improving the ethics of the profession and preventing encroachments upon the work of lawyers.[206]

Jefferson County Bar Association, claiming to have been organized in 1924, but with no continuous existence there having been organization again in 1932, again in 1941, and again in 1947. It is no longer in existence. It is said that the purpose of the organization was "because every one else did." [207]

South Branch Valley Bar Association (Pendleton, Grant, Hardy, and Hampshire Counties), formed about

205. Information procured from James E. Watson, 3d, Esq., Secretary of the Junior Section of the West Virginia State Bar.

206. Information procured from James E. Watson, 3d, Esq., Secretary of the Junior Section of the West Virginia State Bar.

207. Information furnished by James E. Watson, 3d, Esq.

1927 but seems to have met only intermittently and to have been a purely social organization.[208]

Bar Association of the Twenty-first Judicial Circuit, organized in 1945 because of bad feeling between different attorneys and poor cooperation between them. A local active bar association is reported to have done much good in all respects. There had been a local association as far back as 1922, but it had only intermittent meetings.[209]

In 1887, only the Ohio County Bar Association was listed.[210] In 1900, 3 were listed, in 1911, 20, in 1929, 31.[211]

Wisconsin. Milwaukee Bar Association, organized originally under the name Milwaukee Law Institute in May, 1858, changed later to Association of the Bar of Milwaukee, and later to its present name. About 100 Milwaukee County attorneys, a majority of the practicing lawyers in Milwaukee County in 1858 organized the Law Institute to "establish and maintain a higher standard of professional acquirement and deportment, and to promote

208. Letter of Hon. H. M. Calhoun, Jr., Moorfield, W. Va.

209. Letter of Hon. Ernest A. See, Judge of the Circuit Court, Keyser, W. Va., September 8, 1951.

210. 10 Rep. American Bar Association (1887) 446.

211. Wickser, loc. cit. For information as to the local bar associations of West Virginia I am specially indebted to Frederick O. Bryer, Esq., Charles Town, Jefferson County, W. Va.

a proper degree of harmony among ourselves." It was apparently chiefly a social organization at first but claims continuous existence from 1858.[212]

Winnebago County Bar Association (Oshkosh) organized March 22, 1879, and claims continuous existence since that date. It seems to have been organized for social purposes.[213]

Dodge County Bar Association (Beaver Dam), claims organization from about 1880. It has held annual dinners and there seems to have been no formal organization until recent years. For a long time Bar dinners were held once a year. Also memorials of deceased members were prepared. Apparently until recently it was purely a social organization. At present the Association has become active.[214]

Rock County Bar Association (Janesville). The records begin in 1882, and there has been a continuous existence since that time. It seems to have been at first a social organization.[215]

---

212. Answers to questionnaire. It was not in the American Bar Association list of 1922, and not in Mr. Hill's list of 1887, but is in the American Bar Association list of 1887.

213. Letter of David Pinkerton, Esq., Oshkosh, Wis.

214. Letter of George B. Swan, Esq., President of the Dodge County Bar Association, Beaver Dam, Wis., June 9, 1950.

215. Answers to questionnaire.

Calumet County Bar Association (Chilton), organized June 19, 1917, with a continuous existence since that time. Its object is stated as cooperation among members of the bar and better service to clients.[216]

Inter-County Bar Association, organized in 1925, with purpose not stated but apparently a typical local association of the present generation.[217]

Marshfield Bar Association (Marshfield), formed in 1946 with a continuous existence. Organized to promote a better relation among attorneys.[218]

Wood County Bar Association. The date of its organization is uncertain and its existence is said to have been "more or less" continuous. It is evidently a chiefly if not wholly social organization.[219]

In 1887 only the Milwaukee Bar Association is listed.[220] In 1900, 7 are listed, in 1911, 6, in 1929, 45.[221] Except for the Milwaukee Association the older ones seem to have been mostly of the old purely social type.

---

216. Letter of George W. Goggins, Esq., President of the Association, May 6, 1950.

217. Letter of C. J. Strang, Esq., of Grantsburg, Wis.

218. Answers to questionnaire.

219. Answers to questionnaire.

220. 10 Rep. American Bar Association (1887) 446.

221. Wickser, loc. cit.

Wyoming. Laramie County Bar Association, organized in 1909. Said to have been in fairly continuous existence since that time. It was somewhat loosely organized for a number of years but for the last twenty-five years, with the exception of the war years, has been holding fairly regular meetings. It seems to have been largely an organization for social purposes.

No local associations in Wyoming were listed until 1929 when the number is put at 6.[222]

Unhappily no answers to questionnaires and no response to Mr. Porter's request published in the American Bar Association Journal came from local Bar Associations in nine states, in two of which, at least, there is the best evidence of outstanding local activity. The states are:[223]

Arkansas, none in 1887, none in 1900, 3 in 1911, 15 in 1929.

Colorado, none in 1887, 9 in 1911, 12 in 1929. The Denver Bar Association is in the American Bar Association list of 1923.

Connecticut. The New Haven Junior Bar Association is in the American Bar Association list of 1887. Two are given in 1900, 4 in 1911, and 11 in 1929.

---

222. Wickser, loc. cit.

223. The figures as taken from Wickser, loc. cit.

Delaware. One in 1887, also in Hill's list, 1 in 1900, 3 in 1911, and 3 in 1929.

Louisiana. The New Orleans Law Association in 1887 (American Bar Association list), 1 in 1900, none in 1911, and 17 in 1929. The Baton Rouge Bar Association received an Award of Merit from the American Bar Association in 1950.

Montana. One in 1887, The Helena Bar Association, in the American Bar Association list, 3 in 1900, 7 in 1911, and 12 in 1929.

New Mexico. One in 1911 is alone listed.

Rhode Island. One in 1887, 1900, and 1911, 2 in 1929. The Providence Bar Club is in the American Bar Association list of 1923.

Washington. None in 1887, 7 in 1900, 27 in 1911, 32 in 1929. The Seattle Bar Association is in the American Bar Association list of 1923, and received an Award of Merit from the American Bar Association in 1944.

Since 1939, the American Bar Association has made Awards of Merit to local Bar Associations for the most outstanding and constructive activity during the year. Since 1944, two Awards have been made annually, one to a larger and one to a smaller Association.

[347]

There is more than one reason why the attempt to get a full statement as to existing local Bar Associations fell so far short of what could be wished. For one thing, the effect of the integrated State Bar, including every lawyer in its organization, has in some states taken over what had to be done, if at all, by local organizations. In California, however, because of the great geographical extent of the state and the diversity of conditions in different parts of the state, there has been a noteworthy group of strong local associations, two of which have been given Awards of Merit by the American Bar Association. Also, particularly in New York and California, there has been a development of regional associations, a type which had existed in New Hampshire in the two regional associations which in 1899 united to form the State Bar Association. Again, in some states of less geographical extent, the growth of a strong State Bar Association has largely done away with the need of local bar associations for other than social purposes. Moreover, in many localities the older purely social type of Bar Association is dying out. Associations which exist only for an annual dinner are not likely to pay much attention to questionnaires. And in any case the officers of a local association are likely to be busy lawyers with no time for the flood of questionnaires which descends upon everyone today. That so much information was nevertheless gathered is due chiefly to the efforts of

[348]

Charles O. Porter, Esq., of the Oregon Bar, and of Charles
H. Burton, Esq., of Washington, D. C., in 1951 Chairman
of the Junior Bar Conference of the American Bar Association.

Perhaps there is enough to give a good general picture
of the situation in the country as a whole as it is today.

In England, the Law Society, and its predecessor the
Incorporated Law Society, have undone the mischief
wrought by exclusion of attorneys from the Inns. Complete, responsible organization of the solicitors has done
away with Caleb Quirk, Esq., of Alibi House and Dodson
and Fogg, and Mr. Vholes, and Sampson Brass. The Universities are training both solicitors and barristers and the
Law Society, as well as the Inns of Court, provides for
legal education. In the United States the development of
a representative association for the whole country, with
strong, well organized State Associations or State Bars
behind it, making for an organized profession, conscious
of its professional character and responsibilities, both in
each state and in the nation, is undoing the mischief done
in America when we sought to reduce the practice of law
to the level of individual business. Thus we are not merely preparing for, we have taken a long step toward, the
last stage in reprofessionalizing the Bar—the integrated
Bar in all the states.

*

X.

Epilogue

*

X.

Epilogue

I have spoken of the rise of Bar Associations in the last three decades of the nineteenth century, and the growth of Bar organization in the present century as a progress in undoing the mischief wrought in the deprofessionalizing of the practice of law in America before and after the Civil War. This undoing is a real achievement. But what has been achieved is more than an undoing. We are restoring the practice of law as a profession. But it must be made a profession adapted to and so capable of maintaining itself in the society of today and of tomorrow.

As Wigmore has happily put it, "The most important thing about the practice of law is that it is, and in the inherent nature of things demands always that it shall be, a profession." That is, from the very nature of the work of the agent for litigation, and even more from the nature of the work of the advocate, each involving, on the one hand, a relation of the highest trust and confidence to the client, and, on the other hand, an equally high relation of trust and confidence as an officer of the court both to the court and to the public, and, as assisting in the administration of justice, high duties toward the law, the practice of law should be carried on by an organized body of men pursuing a common calling as a learned art in the spirit of a public service.

There are today undoubted and serious threats to the idea of a profession. One threat may be seen in the general and increasing bigness of things in which individual responsibility as a member of a profession is diminished or even lost, and economic pressure upon the lawyer may make the money-making aspect of the calling the primary or even the sole interest. To the young lawyer at the outset there is a threat in the conditions which seem often to make him an employee in a body of workers for a small salary and so to bring him within the field of the movement to organize "white-collar workers" in trade unions. A third threat goes along with the rise of the service state which aspires to take over service rendered by the professions and replace it by service rendered by administrative bureaus of the state. Finally, the endeavor of many callings to become professions, although not professing a learned art and while primarily money-making in purpose and spirit, must be reckoned with also. Undoubtedly the movement to elevate the standards of business and of all callings is worthy of praise. But in elevating these, vigilance is needed that the purpose is not achieved by pulling down the standards of the old recognized professions to a common level with the newer ones.

[354]

Lawyers must be put on guard by the movement, as it is put, to socialize medicine. Effective service to the public, such as is assured by the tradition of duty of the physician to the patient, to the medical profession, and to the public, and the tradition of the duty of the lawyer to the client, to the profession, to the court, and to the public, authoritatively declared in codes of professional ethics, taught by precept and example, and made effective by the discipline of an organized profession, cannot be had from unorganized individual practitioners, responsible to no one, not bred to a professional tradition and motivated, as in a trade, solely by quest of pecuniary gain. Even less can the professional tradition be replaced by a political tradition of office holders owing primary allegiance to political parties and depending for advancement on the favor of political leaders. Professional organization and professional tradition are also to the general public interest because of their effect on the learned arts which the professions follow as callings.

Progress in civilization, in the raising of human powers to their highest unfolding, so far as achieved through advance in science, in arts, and in learning, results from experimentation, that is, from trial and error. If we look at it from the standpoint of the medical profession, every physician, every hospital, is impelled to research and experiment and invention. Moreover, the professional spirit

[355]

of public service brings about promulgation of the results of research and investigation and putting the results at the service of the profession and so of the public. They are not individual trade secrets. They are not patented. They do not need to be argued to bureaus, and those who would use them do not have to await their official adoption. We cannot find effective substitutes for the medical or the legal profession in huge bureaus of graduates of medical schools or of law schools brought up to seek public office and organized in the civil service as employees of the state. The difference between a public service performed by a profession and a public function performed by a bureau is crucial.

If the idea of professions is given up and all callings have the making of a livelihood for their primary purpose, and especially in an economic order in which the great majority of the community are on the payroll of the government or of some corporation, public, public service, charitable, or private, individuals will think of themselves as employees and so become liable to be caught up in a regime of employees' organizations, collective bargainings over wages, and strikes. Instead of organization of physicians for the advancement of medicine, organization of lawyers for the advancement of justice according to law, and organization of teachers for the advancement of teaching, we shall have organization of employees of every

[356]

grade, and of every kind of employer, for the advancement of wages and dictation of the conditions of employment. There is already a movement by the two major labor organizations to unionize the "white collar workers" in business and industry. The younger members of the bar in the legal departments of public service companies or big industries or great insurance companies may well, but from their inclusion in a professional organization, feel themselves in the number of employees to be organized as such. Already the American Federation of Labor has organized Municipal employees, and in one of our great cities, the Probation Officers, of whom we had been thinking as members of a rising profession of social workers, are members of a Probation Officers' Union, a branch of a Municipal Employees' Union, affiliated with a national organization. May we expect to see the young lawyers in the office of the City Attorney, along with the clerks and stenographers, the Municipal Probation Officers, the clerks, secretaries and typists in the various city departments, the firemen and the policemen, in a Union of Municipal Employees, and from time to time striking for higher pay when collective bargain contracts expire or when one of their number is removed or discharged? This supposition is by no means chimerical. The National Labor Relations Board has held, and was upheld by the Supreme

Court of the United States in holding, that plant guards during the last World War at first enlisted in the army and later made part of a city police force, could be organized in unions by the Congress of Industrial Organizations. Then why may not county employees be taken into unions so that the clerical force in the Court House may go on a strike and tie up the administration of justice? Why not, then, should the Assistant District Attorneys be in the County Employees' Union also? Next there would be unions of state employees so that the secretaries of the judges of the Supreme Court would have vested rights in their jobs and have a legal privilege of striking *en masse*. Already there are unions of federal employees and these may seek to include the young men, members of the bar, who are secretaries to the judges of the Courts of Appeals and of judges of the highest court of the land. Every department and major administrative agency of the government has many lawyers on its roster. Unions of federal employees may claim them as "white collar workers." The Service State, in its zeal to serve the employed by wholesale promoting of unions and collective bargaining may threaten not merely the professions but the security of the political organization of society itself by stimulating and allowing an extreme development.

Teachers in the public schools have been unionized in more localities than one and members of University facul-

[358]

ties are now active in a Teacher's Union in some of our old historic institutions. Shall we, then, see closed shops of higher learning, with union faculties bargained with collectively, check off for union dues and all the concomitants of organized pursuit of higher wages in what had been thought a learned profession? Here again zeal for service to the employed generally not only threatens to destroy a profession but in so doing threatens also effective performance by the state of the function of public education which it had been performing well almost from the beginning of our polity.

When such things are in the air an integrated state bar rather than a selective or non-selective but voluntary Bar Association is strongly indicated.

In an era of bigness on every side, of large scale organization of all activities, and of strenuous acquisitive competitive self assertion, the professional idea must encounter the rise to power of organizers of an expanding class of employees. As individuals in the professions have come to be retained regularly or employed permanently by great corporations or appointed to substantially permanent positions under the federal government or state or municipal governments or administrative agencies, a constantly larger number of practitioners, in their capacity of employees, are tempted to forget their membership in a profession and to become enlisted in organizations with the trade spirit of emphasis on wages rather than the professional one of emphasis on pursuit of a calling in the spirit of public service. This prevailing of the trade idea may make straight the path of absorption of the professions in the Service State. It is not difficult to see what may prove to be the course of that path. Three possible stages suggest themselves by what has gone on already. First will be unionizing of all callings which may be taken to involve employment, at least so far as some in the calling are not more conveniently, for the purposes of the organizers and leaders, capable of classification as employers. Next, getting control of professional education by government subsidies and thus subjecting the professions to bureaucratic management. Then finally, by seeking to bring cheap professional assistance to every one's back door by government taking over of the callings pursuing learned arts to complete the process of substituting bureaus for professions.

Such a consummation may be presented as an alluring picture of a carrying out of the idea of the Service or Welfare State to its full logical development. It began by performing a few major services. In time it has undertaken more and more until it has become jealous of performance of public service of any kind by any other agency. The advocates of the omnicompetent state will say that in primitive or pioneer society certain public services are rendered by any one who seeks to try his hand on the basis of such qualifications as he assumes to have. Later, as society advances, such services are rendered by well qualified practitioners organized in professions, the qualifications, however, as those professions develop, being prescribed or ascertained by governmental authority. Ultimately, then, it will be said, as political organization of society reaches maturity, all public services of every sort will be exclusively governmental functions to be exercised by government bureaus.

Very likely not all of those who are teaching or preaching the doctrine of the Super-Service State will, at the moment, admit the conclusion. But before we go far with them on the path in which they have been going, lawyers should pause to see whither it leads.

It cannot be insisted too strongly that the idea of a profession is inconsistent with performance of its function, exercise of its art, by or under the supervision of a government bureau. A profession presupposes individuals free to pursue a learned art so as to make for the highest development of human powers. The individual servant of a government exercising under supervision of his official superiors a calling managed by a government bureau can be no substitute for the scientist, the philosopher, the teacher, each freely applying his chosen field of learning and exercising his inventive faculties and trained imagination in his own way, not as a subordinate in an administrative hierarchy, not as a hired seeker for what he is told to find by his superiors, but as a free seeker for the truth for its own sake, impelled by the spirit of public service inculcated in his profession.

Integration of the Bar has, therefore, a mission of the first importance. By keeping the followers of the different specialties of practice, the different groups into which the lawyers in the large cities of today tend to re-group themselves, conscious of a higher organization of which they are members and to which, as the profession itself, they are responsible, it can stand fast against the disintegrating tendencies which, threatening professions, threaten ultimately the law. It is the culmination of what was well begun at the end of the colonial era and went on once more in the revival after 1870.

It has often been remarked in many connections that we seem in many ways to be turning back to some of the universal ideas of what we once mistakenly called the Dark Ages. In the great creative era of the later Middle Ages men had ideas of doing things for the glory of God and the advancement of justice and not solely toward competitive individual acquisition. We are learning to invoke some of these ideas once more. Not the least of them is the idea of a profession.

TABLE OF PUBLICATIONS AND ARTICLES QUOTED OR CITED

[366]

WARREN—History of the American Bar—Continued
    Page 214–215, 218 ----------------------------------- 233
        214–217 -------------------------------------- 180
        220 -- 234
        242 -- 198
        243 -- 199
        244 -- 198
        307–308 -------------------------------------- 199

WASHBURN—Judicial History of Massachusetts
    Page 53 --- 142
        148 -- 142
        151 -- 144
        189 -- 148
        200–201 -------------------------------------- 149
        201 -- 174
        211–212 -------------------------------------- 160
        224 -- 165
        226–227, 231–239, 312–313 ------------------- 173
        255 -- 132
        308–311 -------------------------------------- 160
        12 --- 132

WENGER—Institutes of the Roman Law of Civil Procedure,
    translated by Fisk (1940) ------------------------- 41

WHITEHEAD
    Judicial and Civil History of New Jersey (1897) ---------- 155
    Supreme Court of New Jersey, 3 Green Bag, 401, 402, 404,
    405 -- 179

WICKSER—Bar Associations, 15 Cornell Law Quarterly (1930)
    Page 390 -------------------------141, 169, 208, 231, 232, 255
        393 --231, 232
        394 -- 169
        394 note 7 ---------------------------------- 208
        396 -- 255
        417 ----283, 284, 288, 291, 293, 296–298, 301, 302, 313–316,
                321, 324–326, 331, 333–339, 343, 345, 346

WIGMORE—Journal, American Judicature Society, vol. 20, p.
    176 (1937) --------------------------------------- 248

*

INDEX

Massachusetts—Continued,
   Hampden County Bar Association, continuous existence since
      1864, 244.
   Law library associations, organization under Act of 1842, 245.
   Local bar associations, 301.
   Plymouth County Bar Association, continuous existence since
      1867, 244.
   Rules of court at time of Revolution providing for grades in
      bar, 198.
   State bar association, organization, 275.
   Suffolk County bar meetings, period from Revolution to Civil
      War, 210 et seq.
   Town meetings during depression following Revolution call-
      ing for abolition of "order of lawyers", 233.
Master, origin of degree, 64.
Mecklenburg Bar Association, North Carolina, organization, 324.
Mecosta County Bar Association, Michigan, organization, 306.
Medieval England, organization of lawyers, 77–93.
Memphis and Shelby County Bar Association, Tennessee, forma-
   tion, 335.
Mendocino County Bar Association, California, organization, 285.
Menominee County Bar Association, Michigan, organization, 305.
Mercer County Bar Association, Pennsylvania, formation, 332.
Michigan,
   Constitution permitting practice of law to persons over 21
      and of good moral character, 225.
   Local bar associations, 302–313.
   State bar association, integration, 274.
Middlesex County Bar Association, New Jersey, organization, 320.
Milwaukee Bar Association,
   Beginnings, 246.
   Organization, 343.
Mingo County Bar Association, West Virginia, organization, 341.
Minneapolis Bar Association, formation, 313.
Minnesota,
   Local bar associations, 313.
   State bar association, reorganization, 274.
Mississippi,
   Holmes County Bar Association, organization, 265.

[398]

т.
.